This guide was originally researched and written by **HENRY STEDMAN** (above). He's been writing guidebooks for more than 25 years and is the author or co-author of over a dozen Trailblazer titles including *Kilimanjaro, Inca Trail, Coast to Coast Path, Hadrian's Wall Path, London LOOP* and all three books in the *South-West Coast Path* series. On most walks he's accompanied by Daisy: two parts trouble to one part Parson's Jack Russell. When not travelling, Henry lives in Battle, East Sussex, editing and arranging climbs on Africa's highest mountain through his company, Kilimanjaro Experts.

Hardened hiker and prolific traveller, **DANIEL McCROHAN** (left), researched and updated this second edition. A guidebook writer for almost 15 years, he specialises in China, where he lived for more than a decade but he relishes any chance he gets to explore his British homeland, particularly if it means another excuse to go camping!

Daniel has now worked as a writer on eight books in Trailblazer's British Walking Guides series, and as an editor on numerous other titles. He's also the co-author of the most recent edition of Trailblazer's *Trans-Siberian Handbook*. For Lonely Planet he has written or co-written more than 40 guidebooks and was a co-host on their television series, *Best in China*. He is now training to become a Mandarin-Chinese teacher.

When he's not travelling or memorising Chinese characters, Daniel can usually be found running or cycling in the Surrey Hills with his two equally energetic children, or slowly sipping his way through his prized collection of loose-leaf teas. To follow his adventures around the globe visit 🖥 danielmccrohan.com, or track him down on twitter (@danielmccrohan).

Authors

**Dales Way**
First edition: **2016**; this second edition **2022**

**Publisher** Trailblazer Publications
The Old Manse, Tower Rd, Hindhead, Surrey, GU26 6SU, UK
🖳 trailblazer-guides.com

**British Library Cataloguing in Publication Data**
A catalogue record for this book is available from the British Library

**ISBN 978-1-912716-30-2**

© **Trailblazer** 2016, 2022: Text and maps

**Editor and layout**: Anna Jacomb-Hood
**Cartography**: Nick Hill   **Proof-reading**: Henry Stedman
**Illustrations**: © Nick Hill (p66-7)   **Index**: Anna Jacomb-Hood
**Photographs (flora)**: C1 top right © Henry Stedman; all other flora © Bryn Thomas
**All other photographs**: © Daniel McCrohan unless otherwise indicated

The maps in this guide were prepared from out-of-Crown-
copyright Ordnance Survey maps amended and updated by Trailblazer.

### Acknowledgements

**FROM DANIEL MCCROHAN**: Apologies this time to Taotao, Simon and Yoyo for not being
able to bring you with me on this latest hiking adventure. You can console yourselves with
the fact that you stayed warm and dry at home while Dad was struggling up hills with a sod-
den tent! A heartfelt thank you, meanwhile, to the kind people along the route who found
places for me to stay when it was simply too wet to camp, particularly the staff at The
George and Dragon in Dent, and the lovely Hazel who let me stay in her holiday home in
Grassington when all the B&Bs were full. It's that kind of hospitality that makes walking
the Dales Way such a joy. I'd also like to thank the readers who wrote in or whom I met on
the trail, in particular Iain Combe, Nicola Copeman and Tara at Mickledore Travel. At
Trailblazer, big thanks to Anna Jacomb-Hood for editing, to Nick Hill for maps, to Henry
Stedman for proofreading, and of course to Bryn Thomas for trusting me with yet another
of Trailblazer's unrivalled guidebooks.

### A request

The author and publisher have tried to ensure that this guide is as accurate and up to date
as possible. Nevertheless, things change. If you notice any changes or omissions, please
write to Trailblazer (address above) or email us at 🖳 info@trailblazer-guides.com. A free
copy of the next edition will be sent to persons making a significant contribution.

### Warning: hill walking can be dangerous

Please read the notes on when to go (pp13-15) and safety (pp54-7). Every effort has been
made by the author and publisher to ensure that the information contained herein is as accurate and up to date as possible. However, they are unable to accept responsibility for any
inconvenience, loss or injury sustained by anyone as a result of the advice and information
given in this guide.

**PHOTOS – Front cover** and **this page**: The 17th-century Lincoln's Inn Bridge across
the River Lune (Map 27).  **Previous page**: The bench (**top**) that acts as the finishing line
at Bowness and (**bottom**) Lune Viaduct.  **Overleaf**: Coming down from Cam Fell to
Ribblesdale and its impressive viaduct in the distance.

**Updated information** will be available on: 🖳 **www.trailblazer-guides.com**

Printed in China; print production by D'Print (☎ +65-6581 3832), Singapore

# Dales Way

38 large-scale maps (1:20,000) & guides to
23 towns and villages

**PLANNING – PLACES TO STAY – PLACES TO EAT**
**ILKLEY TO BOWNESS-ON-WINDERMERE**

HENRY STEDMAN &
DANIEL McCROHAN

TRAILBLAZER PUBLICATIONS

# INTRODUCTION

# PART 1: PLANNING YOUR WALK

# PART 2: MINIMUM IMPACT & OUTDOOR SAFETY

# PART 3: THE ENVIRONMENT & NATURE

Contents

Contents

**Above**: The Dales Way passes through the arches of the 19th century Lune Viaduct (Map 27).

## ABOUT THIS BOOK

This guidebook contains all the information you need. The hard work has been done for you so you can plan your trip without having to consult numerous websites and other books and maps. When you're packed and ready to go, there's comprehensive public transport information to get you to and from the trail and detailed maps (1:20,000) to help you find your way along it. It includes:

● All standards of accommodation with reviews of campsites, bunkhouses, hostels, B&Bs, guesthouses and hotels
● Walking companies if you want an organised or self-guided tour and baggage-transfer services if you just want your luggage carried
● Itineraries for all levels of walkers
● Answers to all your questions: when to go, degree of difficulty, what to pack, and the approximate cost of the whole walking holiday
● Walking times in both directions and GPS waypoints
● Cafés, pubs, tearooms, takeaways, restaurants and food shops
● Rail, bus & taxi information for all villages and towns on the path
● Street plans of the main towns and villages both on and off the path
● Historical, cultural and geographical background information

---

### ❏ THIS GUIDE AND COVID

This edition was researched when England was emerging from some pretty tight restrictions. As a result, many of the hotels, cafes, pubs, restaurants, offices and tourist attractions were operating at reduced hours and were uncertain if and when they would get back to a pre-Covid level. As restrictions continue to ease, it's reasonable to assume that places will open on additional days and hours and, what's more, other businesses will reopen though sadly it is possible some will have closed.

In this book we have noted the opening times as they were at the time of research, or as the owners of the various establishments predicted they would be by the time this was published. It will be more essential than usual for walkers to check opening days and hours. For this reason we have noted businesses that have a Facebook page as, other than calling, that and Google are the best places to check up-to-date operating days/hours.

# INTRODUCTION

The Dales Way stretches for approximately 81 miles (130km) between the towns of Ilkley, at the southern end of Yorkshire Dales National Park, and Bowness-on-Windermere, the most popular tourist destination in the Lake District National Park.

The walk is often described as one of the easiest of the long-distance paths in Britain and it's true

**The Dales Way is often described as one of the easiest of the long-distance paths in Britain ... but it's not entirely without gradients**

that most of the first half of the trail is largely level as it follows the meandering River Wharfe. The Dales Way is not entirely without gradients, of course, and there are steep sections, particularly as the path approaches the source of the Wharfe and the watershed, and again on the approach to the Lakes. It's likely that you'll also have to complete a couple of long days on the trail, too, as the path passes through countryside where facilities and accommodation are scarce. Nevertheless, the fact remains that the Dales Way is one of the UK's shortest and most straightforward long-distance trails. Finding and sticking to the trail is also particularly easy, thanks to the wealth of signposts along the way and the superb maintenance of the trail itself.

**Above**: Sweeping views beyond Conistone Pie (Map 10).

INTRODUCTION

The old bridge at Ilkley marks the beginning of the Dales Way.

No surprise, then, that this is considered to be a path that can be tackled by almost anyone, regardless of their age: You'll see babies conveyed along the trail in prams and on the backs of their parents, while the most fashionable hair colour on the Dales Way amongst both sexes is what can most kindly be described as a distinguished silvery-grey. And it is a great trail for those who've never attempted a long-distance path before and want to dip their toes in the water and see whether hiking is for them, before moving on to tackle some of the more challenging long-distance trails such as the Coast to Coast Path, or the Pennine Way.

But the delights of this trail aren't confined to novices. For though it may be only just over 80 miles in length, the Dales Way manages to pack an awful lot of interest into its relatively short span. The charming, lively Victorian spa town of Ilkley; the old cotton mill centre of Addingham and the mining town of Kettlewell; the majestic ruins of Bolton Abbey and the busy tourist hub at Grassington; and the picture-perfect settlements at Appletreewick, Burnsall, Kettlewell, Starbotton, Hebden and Buckden – all are encountered on or just off the trail, and all before you've even completed the first half of the walk!

**Though it's only just over 80 miles in length, the Dales Way manages to pack an awful lot of interest into its relatively short span**

The Wharfe itself is splendid too. Where it is placid and becalmed, anglers wade in to fish for trout and weary hikers sit, paddle in the shallows and cool

There are **link routes** to Ilkley so you can join the Dales Way from Harrogate, Bradford or Leeds – see pp69-74. The Harrogate link route takes you past Swinsty Reservoir (above).

their overheated feet, while kingfishers and dippers flit across the surface. But in certain places the Wharfe is frothing and furious, most famously at the raging Strid, the final resting place of more than one foolhardy traveller down the centuries.

Nor does the scenery lose any of its grandeur as you wave farewell to the Wharfe in favour of neighbouring Dentdale. Here the delights of the natural landscape are supplemented by several magnificent viaducts and bridges, built during the railway

## ❏ JUST HOW LONG IS THE DALES WAY?

One would have thought, for such an easy-to-follow and well signposted trail, that there wouldn't be much dispute about the total length of the trail. But you'd be wrong because, for some reason, none of the authorities seems to be able to agree on the exact distance the Dales Way walker covers. The sign at the start says 82 miles, though the official website states that the distance from Ilkley to Bowness-on-Windermere is *about* 80 miles. Another guidebook records the distance as 78 miles, as does The Long Distance Walkers Association. The two baggage-transfer companies operating on the Dales Way, Sherpa Van and Brigantes, state that it's 82 miles and 'about 80 miles' respectively, while Wikipedia says it's 84 miles.

The author of this guidebook, Henry Stedman, measured the Dales Way using his own GPS unit and found it to be 81 miles, or 81¾ miles if taking the Alternative (High Level) Route (see pp125-30), which is neatly exactly halfway between the two most extreme estimates given above. But while that figure may indeed be a decent estimate of the length of the trail itself, it is not, of course, the total number of miles you will cover on your trip, for it does not account for all that walking to the pub or B&Bs off the track, going the wrong way and even, as some Pythagorians like to consider, the fact that walking up and down hills technically covers more ground than if the terrain was flat!

boom of the 19th century, which you pass by, alongside and under on your way to the smooth-topped Howgills, a delightfully hilly corner of the Yorkshire Dales. And then at the end of the trail (and having passed under a couple more breathtaking viaducts), you are rewarded for all your efforts over the previous days with magnificent views of some of England's mightiest peaks as you move into the Lake District – and your second national park on the trail.

Pages and pages could be spent eulogising about the beauty and diversity of this path. But as anyone who's walked a long-distance trail before knows, the things you see on the way are only part of the enjoyment. For walking is just as much about the people you meet and the food you eat, the things you stop to do and the things that happen to you along the way. It is of such things that memories are made.

# History

Managing to construct such a lovely and relatively level trail through some of England's bumpiest landscapes takes a certain sort of genius and the person in possession of that genius was **Colin Speakman**, who together with his friend Tom Wilcock and Colin's wife Fleur developed the trail, beginning back in the late '60s. The actual trail has been changed and improved several times down the years as access to new land and routes has become available; though these days the alterations are far less frequent and far less dramatic too as the path becomes more established and recognised.

INTRODUCTION

## ❏ YORKSHIRE DALES NATIONAL PARK AND NIDDERDALE AONB

The term 'Dale' is an old Norse word meaning 'valley'. The Dales are a series of valleys in Northern England, predominantly within the county of Yorkshire, that have been enlarged and shaped by glaciers, mainly in the most recent Ice Age around 100,000 years ago. **Yorkshire Dales National Park** encompasses most of the major dales – Swaledale, Wensleydale, Wharfedale and others – with umpteen other smaller dales, including Dentdale and Lunedale that feature on the Dales Way, that run like filigree between them. Established in 1954 to protect the Dales' unique landscape and environment, the park covers a total area of 841 square miles (2178 sq km). It lies on both sides of the Pennines and spills over the Cumbrian border to encompass the Howgills, the little-known region of smooth-topped hills on the western side of the Dales.

The original boundaries of the park pretty much described the limits of the **Askrigg Block**, an enormous slab of granite deep underground. Down the millennia on top of this slab of granite has been laid carboniferous limestone which gives rise to the unique topography, the terraces and pavements, that are such a distinctive characteristic of the area. On the Dales Way you actually walk over the **Dent Fault System** (see box p138), which in essence means you are stepping off the Askrigg Block; in doing so you then enter the Howgills, now also part of the national park, whose geology is defined by the Ordovician and Silurian slates and gritstones, which were laid down about 100 million years before the Dales' limestone.

But the national park is not just about the geology and nature, as splendid as it is. Farmers have worked and shaped this terrain for many, many centuries and the landscape is now predominantly a man-made one. The Yorkshire Dales are also home to the **Victoria Caves** where evidence has been found of the hippo, rhino, hyena and mammoth which would have lived here around 130,000 years ago. More recently, following the last Ice Age the cave was used for hibernating by brown bear and amongst the bones was an 11,000-year-old harpoon point – the first evidence of human habitation in the Dales.

On the eastern side of the Dales the park boundary abuts **Nidderdale AONB** (Area of Outstanding Natural Beauty), which is often included as part of the actual national park but it is in fact separate to it. Subtract Nidderdale from your map of Dales National Park and you'll see that the Dales Way bisects the park from south-east to north-west. Thus, apart from Swaledale, the most northerly dale, the Dales Way does a very good job of providing walkers with the opportunity of seeing as much of the park as possible. And if you take Harrogate Link Route, described on pp72-3, you cross right through Nidderdale, too.

Most of the Dales area is given over to fields of livestock and pasture, each separated from the next by **dry-stone walls**. There are estimated to be 12,000-15,000 miles of walls in Yorkshire Dales National Park alone, with every metre of wall built from about one metric tonne of stone.

(**Opposite**): The lethal Strid (see p90) – narrow enough to tempt the foolhardy to attempt to leap across; though slip and you'll be dragged under the water by the deadly currents. Better to stick to the riverbank and admire from a safe(-ish!) distance. (© Henry Stedman)

Though Tom is sadly no longer with us, Colin Speakman continues to play an active part in the life of the trail and is the chair of the **Dales Way Association** (🖥 dalesway.org, see p42) which was founded in 1991 to help support, maintain and promote the Dales Way.

## How difficult is the Dales Way?

In all honesty, it's not. Sure, there are a few steepish ascents that will have you blowing hard, and your knees might complain during some of the longer descents too. But overall the Dales

**Overall the Dales Way is short, fairly level and well signposted**

Way is short, fairly level, well signposted, and with plenty of towns and villages en route should you need to buy provisions or seek help. With civilisation never far away your chances of losing your way, or suffering from hypothermia or heatstroke are slender; indeed, the biggest danger along the whole path is being squashed by a car on the busy road before Bolton Abbey. Nevertheless, it would be foolish to take the Dales Way too lightly. Like any long-distance trail, it deserves respect. Most importantly, perhaps, you should read up about each stage of the trail beforehand and prepare properly for it, for there are a couple of stages where shops, cafés and accommodation are pretty much non-existent, so you need to plan your day sensibly, maybe by preparing a packed lunch before you set off and taking plenty of water. (You should also read the section on trail safety, pp54-7).

Time for tea at Burnsall, a perfect stop on a sunny day. There's no shortage of pubs and tea rooms along the Way.

## How long do you need?

Most people take about a week to complete the Dales Way. It can be done much more quickly and if you feel the need, by all means do it in four days or fewer. If, on the other hand, you prefer to take 6-8 days or more on the trail, taking the

**Most people take about a week to complete the Dales Way**

time to drink in the magnificent scenery, while pausing here and there to smell the flowers or gaze at otters frolicking in a stream, then you are probably walking the Dales Way as it is meant to be walked.

# When to go

## SEASONS

Britain is a notoriously wet country and the Yorkshire Dales and Lake District are two of the wettest parts of it. With the Dales Way taking less than a week, it is possible to walk the entire route without experiencing even a drop of rain. But you'd be lucky. That said, with 150 wet days per annum in the Yorkshire Dales, you'd be even unluckier to have wet weather every day of your trek.

The main walking season in the Dales runs from Easter to when the clocks change at the end of October. You can walk outside this season, of course, but the shorter days, the lack of fellow walkers and inclement weather mean that it's a trickier undertaking – and if there's snow about it's also considerably more dangerous. Furthermore, you may also find that many of the B&Bs and other amenities are closed for the season, particularly in rural areas.

Grand views across Outershaw Beck from the camping field at Swarthghyll Farm (Map 17).

## Spring

A beautiful spring day is one of the true, unfettered joys of living in Britain. With birds singing, flowers budding and lambs gambolling, it's just wonderful. However, spring also happens to be one of the wettest times of year, so be prepared for the worst and bring your rain gear; this will improve your chances of not being rained upon no end. Aside from Easter, you should find the trail to be very quiet – allowing you to enjoy the delights of the season undisturbed.

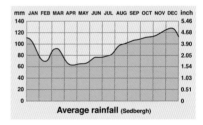

Average rainfall (Sedbergh)

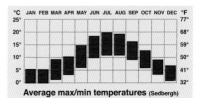

Average max/min temperatures (Sedbergh)

## Summer
The main disadvantage with summer is that it can get a little too busy in the Dales and the Lake District (though arrive outside the main school summer holidays and it shouldn't be too bad). Accommodation prices are also at their

### ❏ FESTIVALS AND ANNUAL EVENTS
Note that most festivals were cancelled during the Covid pandemic. The ones listed here all intended to start up again in 2022, but do double check that they are still running before you make your own plans.

#### April to June
● **Dentdale Music & Beer Festival** (🖳 dentmusicandbeer.com)  A 3-day free festival held in mid to late June – one of the most picturesque places to get hammered to the strains of street musicians. Originally founded in response to the foot-and-mouth crisis in the early 2000s, all profits are still ploughed back into community projects, such as the primary school or the restoration of Dent's church bells.
● **Sedbergh Music Festival** (🖳 sedbergh.org.uk/festivals/sedbergh-music-festival)  A biennial music festival, due to be held next over a fortnight in June 2022.
● **Grassington Festival** (🖳 grassington-festival.org.uk; **fb**)  Started in 1981 and taking place almost every year over 15 days in late June and early July, Grassington plays host to some fine live music, dance, theatre, comedy, film, visual art displays, masterclasses, workshops – and much, much more. One of the founders was Colin Speakman (see p9).
● **Ilkley Food & Drink Festival** (🖳 ilkleyfoodfestival.com)  Held on East Holmes Fields (see Map 1) beside the River Wharfe over a weekend in June, this family-friendly festival is a chance to sample local drinks and delicacies, international street food, live music and children's entertainment.

#### July to September
● **Bowness-on-Windermere Summer of Fun** (🖳 facebook.com/Windermerefestival) takes place over August weekends at The Glebe. A child-oriented festival, events vary from year to year but can include mini-Olympics and a Teddy's Got Talent Show.
● **Sedbergh Sheep Fest** (🖳 facebook.com/sedberghsheepfest) occurs over nine days in September every year, with most shop windows adorned with a sheep (not a real one) in fancy dress. Parades, street entertainers, concerts, photo competitions and other fun events abound.

#### October to December
● **Ilkley Literature Festival** (🖳 ilkleyliteraturefestival.org.uk)  Annual festival of literature and the arts usually taking place over around 17 days in early October.
● **Kendal Mountain Festival** (🖳 kendalmountainfestival.com) takes place over a weekend in November – a rather odd time, seeing as it bills itself as the UK's foremost festival for 'outdoor enthusiasts'. A very social gathering, the festival includes a film competition and plenty of guest speakers.
● **Grassington Dickensian Festival** (🖳 facebook.com/grassingtondickensian; **fb**)  The town may have little to do with the revered Victorian novelist – there's no evidence that he ever visited – but that doesn't stop the locals dressing up in their finest 19th-century dress to parade around town for three days in December. Given how pretty the town is at any time of year, it does make for a very photogenic festival. Musicians, dancers and street entertainers all add to the jollity.

highest at this time of year. Other than this, there are no negatives to walking in summer. The weather is usually better (though bring your waterproofs nevertheless – remember, it does rain for 150 days a year in the Dales, and some of those have to be in summer!), the days are at their longest and all the campsites, cafés and other facilities will be open. Furthermore, if you're in need of company you won't be short of walking companions on the Dales Way – which could be useful if

Be prepared at times for a waterlogged Way, as seen here just south of Appletreewick. A brolly and decent boots may well prove indispensable.

you're far from civilisation and need help. Remember to book your accommodation in advance if walking in this season, particularly if staying in B&Bs.

## Autumn

September and early October are lovely times to walk. The relative 'chaos' of the summer months have abated to be replaced by a more tranquil, sedate scene. The shops, B&Bs and pubs should all still be open, as should the campsites, and you'll often find that their owners are more relaxed and friendly, presumably because they've survived and thrived in the main walking season, and thus can afford to take their foot off the gas and relax a little. The weather is usually pretty settled at this time, though do follow the forecasts closely as there are occasional storms. By the time mid October rolls around the days are getting rather short and the weather may well be getting wilder – time for most walkers to hang up their boots for another year.

## Winter

Happen upon one of those clear, crisp winter days when the wind is becalmed and the sun is shining and you're in for a treat – and if there's snow on the ground it can feel as if you're walking in the middle of a Christmas card. That said, those days can be few and far between. What's more, most of the accommodation outside the larger towns will be closed and many of the pubs, shops and cafés operate reduced opening days and hours. It is also, of course, more dangerous to be out on the fells at this time – and given the record of flooding in the region over the past few years, it's not particularly sensible to be walking by the riverside all day – which pretty much rules out all of the Dales Way.

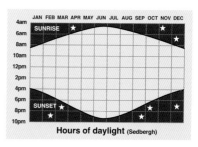

**Hours of daylight** (Sedbergh)

**Above**: The path winds past the ruins of Bolton Abbey (see p87) and the Priory Church (© Henry Stedman). **Below**: Walkers pass a farm near Appletreewick (Map 6).

**Left top**: Crook of the Lune Bridge (Map 28) dates back to the 16th century.
**Bottom left**: Hubberholme Church (Map 14), described by JB Priestley as 'one of the smallest and most pleasant places in the world'. **Bottom centre**: The cobbled village of Dent (Map 23).

**Above**: The Way passes under lofty Lowgill Viaduct (Map 29), built in 1859. **Left**: An idyllic camping spot at friendly Grayrigg Foot Farm (see p150). **Below**: Rowing boats bask in a glorious sunset over Bowness Bay on Lake Windermere (Map 36).

## Practical information for the walker

### ROUTE FINDING

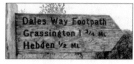

The presence of signposts and way-marking is good along the Dales Way and finding the correct trail shouldn't be a problem. Even in the remotest sections, such as the crossing from Cam Houses into Dentdale (see pp120-30), where landmarks are few and the mist often rolls in, there seems to be little problem in staying on the correct trail, with the path fairly clearly scored into the ground and signposts frequent. Sure, there may be occasions on the trail when you have to pause, scratch your head and study the maps in this book closely – you may even initially choose the wrong path – but it usually becomes obvious pretty quickly that you've made a mistake and need to head back to rejoin the correct trail.

As well as looking out for signposts, do try to keep at least one eye on the maps in the Route guide section of this book to make sure you're not unwittingly straying too far off course – though don't spend all your time with your head buried in this book, or you'll be losing sight of why you came here in the first place.

### GPS

GPS technology is an inexpensive, well-established if non-essential, navigational aid. Within a minute of being turned on and with a clear view of the sky, **GPS receivers** will establish your position and elevation anywhere on earth to an accuracy of within a few metres. Most **smartphones** also have a GPS receiver built in and mapping software available to run on it (see box p39).

Don't treat a GPS as a replacement for maps, a compass and common sense. Every electronic device is susceptible to battery failure or some electronic malfunction that might leave you in the dark. GPS should be used merely as a backup to more traditional route-finding techniques and is best used in conjunction with a paper map.

---

**(Opposite)**: Great views (and good grazing) on the gentle slopes leading down to Bowness-on-Windermere (Map 35).

## Using GPS with this book – waypoints

Though a GPS system is not essential on the Dales Way, for those who have one this book provides GPS waypoints for the route. **Waypoints** are single points like cairns. This book identifies key waypoints on the route maps. These waypoints correlate to the list on p169 which gives the grid reference and a description. You can download the complete list as a GPS-readable .gpx file of grid references (but with no descriptions) from ⌨ trailblazer-guides.com. It's anticipated that you won't tramp along day after day, ticking off the book's waypoints, transfixed by the screen on your GPS or smartphone; the route description and maps should be more than adequate most of the time.

It's worth repeating that most people who've ever walked the Dales Way did so without using GPS so there's no need to rush out and buy a GPS unit – or a new GPS-enabled smartphone for that matter. Your spending priorities ought to be on good waterproofs and footwear. However, correctly using this book's GPS data could get you back on track and dozing in front of the pub fireplace all the sooner.

## ACCOMMODATION

The route guide (Part 5) lists a fairly comprehensive selection of places to stay along the trail. The two main options are: camping (and perhaps staying in the odd hostel/bunkhouse too), or using B&Bs/pubs/hotels. Few people stick to just one of these the whole way, preferring, for example, to camp most of the time, stay in a hostel where possible but splash out on a B&B or hotel every once in a while.

The table on p32 provides a snapshot of what type of accommodation and services are available in each of the towns and villages, while the tables in the box on p31 provide some suggested itineraries. The following is a brief introduction as to what to expect from each type of accommodation.

## Camping

Campers are fairly well served on the Dales Way and it's possible to devise an itinerary that allows you to camp every night you're on the trail. There are a couple of big advantages with camping: it's more economical, with most campsites charging somewhere between £7 and £12pp. Secondly, and best of all, there's **rarely any need to book**, except possibly in the very high season, and even then you'd be highly unlucky not to find somewhere. This, of course, gives you greater flexibility, allowing you to alter your itinerary at the last moment – something that's far more complicated, if not impossible, to do if you're staying in B&Bs.

The campsites vary and you get what you pay for: some are just a farmer's spare field with a toilet and a tap; others are full-blown caravan sites with sparkling ablutions blocks, laundry facilities, wi-fi, shops, coffee shops and fire pit hire. Showers are usually available, occasionally for a fee, though more often than not included in the rate. Some places also offer **glamping** (timber lodges, yurts, safari tents and shepherd's huts) but they will cost more.

Note that some of the bigger towns along the way – including Ilkley and Sedbergh – do not have recognised campsites within two miles of them. Note,

PLANNING YOUR WALK

too, that there are a couple of big sections, from Buckden to Dent and Sedbergh to Burneside, where there are no shops, so if you're planning on cooking your own food while camping you'll need to plan accordingly and carry your food with you.

**Wild camping** (ie camping not in a regular campsite; see p53) is also possible along the route but please don't put up your tent without first getting permission from the landowner since – unlike in Scotland – it is illegal to do so.

Remember that camping, be it wild or 'tame', is not an easy option, especially for a solo walker. Walked continuously, the route is wearying enough without carrying the means to sleep and cook with you. Should you decide to camp at campsites, you could consider employing one of the baggage-transfer companies mentioned on p27, though this does mean the loss of spontaneity which is the whole point of camping – and, of course, they can't deliver to any wild camping locations!

### Bunkhouses/bunk barns

Bunkhouses/bunk barns are agreeable places with fluffed-up bedding, bathrooms you'd be happy to show to your parents and even kitchen and lounge areas. The description 'bunkhouse' is often used in place of 'small hostel' or 'independent hostel' to distinguish a private enterprise from lodgings under the YHA banner (see below) which can sometimes be huge properties with scores of beds, hyperactive school groups and, depending on your age, unhappy memories of a long-gone institutional past.

Along the Dales Way those who want to stay in bunkhouses/bunk barns are poorly served. It's not that there aren't many, it's just that most of them accept group bookings only and individuals aren't allowed to stay unless they book the entire place for themselves (which costs several hundred pounds a night). If they're not busy they may allow individual walkers to stay, but it does mean that you can't book your spot more than a day or two in advance and many bunkhouses wouldn't even contemplate this arrangement, wanting group bookings only.

### Hostels

There are three hostels on (or just off) the Dales Way. Two are independent but the one at Kettlewell is affiliated with the **Youth Hostels Association of England and Wales** (YHA). Despite the name, anyone of any age can join the YHA. You don't have to be a member to stay at one of their hostels, but it is cheaper if you are: at Kettlewell Hostel there is a discount of up to 15% for current members. However, it wouldn't be worth joining just for this walk. For details about membership contact the YHA (☎ 01629 592700 or Live chat through the website, 🖳 yha.org.uk).

The hostels along the Dales Way come equipped with a whole range of facilities including a laundry service and drying rooms, lounges with television, free wi-fi, and fully equipped kitchens. Breakfast and/or dinner (of varying quality) are offered, as is a packed lunch. They are also great places to meet fellow walkers, swap stories and compare blisters. Weighed against these advantages is the fact that you may have to share your night with a heavy snorer sleeping in the same dorm. Some rooms now have en suite facilities but in others you have to share a shower room, though there are usually enough showers so that the waiting time is minimal.

If you're travelling out of the main season (particularly between November and February) you may find some hostels are shut to walkers during the week, or completely. Even in high season some are not staffed during the day and walkers may have to wait until 5pm before checking in, though you may be able to access the kitchen and leave luggage in a secure room before 5pm. And finally, the cost of staying in a hostel, once breakfast has been added on, is in some instances not that much cheaper than staying in a B&B, especially if you're walking with someone with whom you could share the cost of a B&B room.

## Bed and breakfasts

Bed and breakfasts (B&Bs) are a great British institution and many of those along the Dales Way are absolutely charming, with buildings often three or four hundred years old. Older owners often treat you as surrogates for their long-departed offspring and enjoy nothing more than looking after you.

As the name suggests, they provide you with a bed in a private room and breakfast – a hearty, British-style cooked one unless you specify otherwise beforehand – though they range in style enormously. Most B&Bs on the route have **en suite rooms** – which means a room with bath or shower facilities is attached to the bedroom. Where a room is advertised as having **private facilities**, it means that the bathroom is not directly connected to the room though

---

### ❏ AIRBNB

The rise and rise of Airbnb (🖳 airbnb.co.uk) has seen private homes opened up to overnight travellers on an informal basis. While accommodation is primarily based in cities, the concept is spreading to more rural areas, but do check thoroughly what you are getting and the precise location. At its best, this is a great way to meet local people in a relatively unstructured environment, but be aware that these places are not registered B&Bs, so standards may vary, yet prices may not necessarily be any lower than for a normal B&B.

As for the Dales Way, a quick look at the site will show you some places advertised in Ilkley, although when you look more closely you'll see that only two or three are centrally located; still, given the paucity of 'regular' B&B accommodation in some towns along the route, this could prove a lifesaver. There are further options all the way along the path. Note, however, that in this book we haven't listed specific properties that can be found on the Airbnb website as they tend to change quite frequently. Don't forget that you'll still need to sort out where you're going to eat, so while that cottage in the middle of nowhere may look perfect, you'll need to have somewhere nearby that serves food or else bring some supplies along (and make sure the place you're staying has cooking facilities!).

❏ **SHOULD YOU BOOK YOUR ACCOMMODATION IN ADVANCE?**

Accommodation along certain sections of the Dales Way is patchy at best, particularly the 22-mile stretch between Buckden and Dent and the 16-mile haul from Sedbergh to Burneside (two sections which together total about half the walk!). In the high season of **June to August**, therefore, unless camping, it's essential you have your night's accommodation secured. How soon you start booking is up to you but doing so the night before is no longer dependable. If you start booking **up to six months** in advance you'll have a good chance of getting precisely the accommodation you want. Booking so early does leave you vulnerable to changing circumstances of course, but with enough notice it's likely your deposit will be returned as they can easily fill your bed; ask on booking. Outside the high season and away from weekends, as long as you're **flexible**, you might get away with booking just a couple of weeks, days or even just hours in advance. Having said that, some establishments find that May and September are in fact their busiest months. However, **weekends** are busy everywhere, especially in **the Lakes**.

If you've left it too late and can only get accommodation for parts of the walk but are set on a certain period, **consider camping** to fill in the gaps. If using a baggage-transfer service, they can cart the gear from door to door at no extra effort to yourself. Campers, whatever time of year, should always be able to find somewhere to pitch their tent, though ringing in advance will at least confirm that the campsite is still open. There are also a few **hostels** and a **bunkhouse** if you're willing to 'slum it' for a night. Do be careful when travelling out of high season, however, as many hostels close during the week and shut altogether in winter. Once again, it's worth booking in advance.

there is a bathroom elsewhere that is reserved solely for the use of the room's occupants. Finally, **shared facilities** mean that you share a bathroom with the occupants of at least one other room. With private/shared facilities there may be a bath, which is what most walkers prefer at the end of a long day, and the bathroom is seldom more than a few feet away from your room.

Rooms usually contain either a double bed (known as a double room), or two single beds (known as a twin room). Some places have rooms which sleep up to three/four people (see p76). Solo trekkers should take note: single rooms are not so easy to find so you'll often end up occupying a double/twin room, for which you'll have to pay a single occupancy supplement (see p30).

Some B&Bs provide an evening meal (almost always you need to book this in advance); if not, there's often a pub or sometimes a restaurant nearby or, if it's far, the owner may give you a lift to and from the nearest place with food. Packed lunches (where available) should also be requested in advance. For details of likely costs see p30.

**Booking** Most B&Bs have their own website and may offer online/email booking but for some you will need to phone. Most places ask for a **deposit** (about 50%) which is generally non-refundable if you cancel at short notice. Some places may charge 100% if the booking is for one night only. Always let the owner know as soon as possible if you have to cancel your booking so they can offer the bed to someone else. Larger places take credit or debit cards. Most smaller B&Bs prefer payments by bank transfer for the deposit; the balance can be settled with another bank transfer or cash, though some places may be happy to have a cheque (if it is easy for them to pay it in to a bank).

## Guesthouses, hotels, pubs/inns
A guesthouse offers bed and breakfast but should have a better class of décor and more facilities, such as a lounge for guests; they are also likely to offer an evening meal. All of which makes guesthouses sound very much like hotels except, unlike a hotel, they are unlikely to offer room service.

**Pubs/inns** may also offer B&B accommodation and tariffs are no more than in a regular B&B. However, you need to be prepared for a noisier environment, especially if your room is above the bar.

**Hotels** do usually cost more, however, and some might be a little displeased by a bunch of muddy trekkers turning up. That said, most places on the walk, particularly in the quieter towns and villages, are used to seeing trekkers, make a good living from them and welcome them warmly.

As with B&Bs (see p21), you may have to pay a deposit when booking. See also Budgeting, p30.

## FOOD AND DRINK

### Breakfast
Stay in a B&B/guesthouse/hotel and you'll be filled to the gills each morning with a cooked English breakfast. This generally consists of a bowl of cereal followed by a plateful of eggs, bacon, sausages, mushrooms, tomatoes, and possibly baked beans or black pudding, with toast and butter, and all washed down with coffee, tea and/or fruit juice. Enormously satisfying the first time you try it, by the fourth or fifth morning you may start to prefer the lighter continental breakfast or porridge, which most establishments now also offer.

Alternatively, and especially if you're planning an early start, you might like to request a packed lunch instead of this filling breakfast and just have a cup of coffee before you leave.

### Lunch
Your B&B host, or hostel, can usually provide a packed lunch at an additional cost and if requested in advance, though there's nothing to stop you preparing your own. There are some fantastic locally made cheeses and pickles that can be picked up along the way, as well as some wonderful bakers still making bread in the traditional manner. Alternatively, stop in a pub or café.

Remember, too, to plan ahead: at least four of the stages in this book are devoid of eateries or shops so read ahead about the next day's walk to make sure you never go hungry.

### Elevenses/afternoon teas
Never miss a chance to avail yourself of the treats on offer in the tearooms and cafés of Cumbria and Yorkshire. Nothing relaxes and revives like a decent pot of tea and the opportunity to accompany it with a scone served with jam and cream, or a cake or two, is one that should not be passed up.

## Evening meals

**Pubs** are as much a feature of this walk as the viaducts and vistas that you enjoy along the way, and in one or two cases (the Craven Arms at Appletreewick springs to mind, and the busy Red Lion at Burnsall) the pub is as much a tourist attraction as the finest ruined abbey. Most of them have become highly attuned to the needs of walkers and offer both lunch and evening meals (with often a few regional dishes and usually a couple of vegetarian/vegan options), some locally brewed beers, a garden to relax in on hot days and a roaring fire to huddle around on cold ones. The standard of the food varies widely, though portions are usually large, which is often just about all walkers care about at the end of a long day.

In bigger towns that other great British culinary tradition, the **fish 'n' chip shop**, can usually be found (Grassington, Sedbergh, Burneside, Kendal, Staveley and Bowness all have one); most of these towns have some sort of

---

### ❑ LOCAL FOOD AND DRINK

Yorkshire isn't renowned for the subtlety of its local delicacies but the **food** does tend to be hearty and tasty – which is all most trekkers care about. The most famous local delicacy is Yorkshire pudding, a side dish usually accompanying a roast dinner (especially roast beef) and made of eggs, flour and milk or water. In some instances, it actually acts as the dish itself, with the rest of the main course – the meat, veg and gravy – placed inside one giant Yorkshire pudding!

Another curious local custom is the habit of putting hot food, such as roast beef, inside a baguette and then serving it with gravy. The unitiated can never quite work out the best way of tackling this, and whether cutlery should be involved, but to be fair these strange hot baguettes are quite more-ish.

As for the local **drinks**, well it won't surprise you to find that beer production is thriving in the Dales. At Ilkley there's **Wharfedale Brewery** (🖳 wharfedalebrewery .com), which is based at the back of the Flying Duck near the town centre and is where the Dales Way Association often meets, and **Ilkley Brewery** (🖳 ilkleybrewery .co.uk). **Goose Eye Brewery** (🖳 goose-eye-brewery.co.uk) is based in Keighley, as is **Copper Dragon** (🖳 copperdragon.co.uk); in nearby Skipton there's **Dark Horse** (🖳 darkhorsebrewery.co.uk).

The largest brewery on the trail, however, is at the other end of the walk at Staveley where the shiny glass and metallic **Hawkshead Brewery & Beer Hall** (🖳 hawksheadbrewery.co.uk), also a restaurant, is not what one imagines a traditional brewery to look like, though you can't fault the beers they produce. As befits its location, the brewery's beers come with names like Lakeland Gold (4.4%) and Windermere Pale (3.5%). But away from the population centres you'll still find creditable breweries such as **Dent Brewery** (🖳 dentbrewery.co.uk) which supplies several pubs including The George and Dragon in Dent itself. If you like a dark beer, Dent Porter (3.8%) is one of the nicest around.

There are several superb pubs where you can sample some of the finest local beers including Blue Bell Inn at Kettlewell, The Buck Inn at Buckden, The Red Lion at Burnsall and both Craven Arms and The New Inn at Appletreewick.

© HENRY STEDMAN

Italian, Chinese and/or Indian **takeaway too**. These provide a welcome change from too much pub food and are usually the only places serving food late in the evenings, staying open until at least 11pm.

## Catering for yourself

There are several stores along the path and as long as you plan ahead and aren't too fussy you should be able to find something to cook for yourself. Once again, the sections from Buckden to Dent and Sedbergh to Burneside provide the self-catering trekker with the most problems, as there are no shops anywhere on

---

### ❏ INFORMATION FOR FOREIGN VISITORS

● **Currency**  The British pound (£) comes in notes of £50, £20, £10 and £5, and coins of £2 and £1. The pound is divided into 100 pence (usually referred to as 'p', pronounced 'pee') which come in 'silver' coins of 50p, 20p, 10p and 5p, and 'copper' coins of 2p and 1p. Up-to-date currency **exchange rates** can be found on 🖥 xe.com/currencyconverter, at some post offices, and at most banks and travel agents.

● **Business hours**  Most **village shops** are open Monday to Friday 9am-5pm and Saturday 9am-12.30pm. Many choose longer hours and some open on Sundays as well. Occasionally you'll come across a local shop that closes at lunchtime on one day during the week, usually a Wednesday or Thursday; this is a throwback to the days when all towns and villages had an 'early closing day'. **Supermarkets** are open Monday to Saturday 8am-8pm (sometimes up to 15 hours a day) and on Sunday from about 9am to 5 or 6pm, though main branches of supermarkets generally open 10am-4pm or 11am-5pm.

Main **post offices** generally open Monday to Friday 9am-5pm and Saturday 9am-12.30pm; **banks** typically open at 9.30/10am Monday to Friday and close at 3.30/4pm, though in some places both post offices and banks may open only two or three days a week and/or in the morning, or limited hours, only. **ATMs (cash machines)** located outside a bank, shop, post office or petrol station are open all the time, but any that are inside will be accessible only when that place is open.

**Pub hours** are less predictable; although many open daily 11am-11pm, opening hours in rural areas and during quieter periods (early weekdays, or in the winter months) are often more limited: typically Monday to Saturday 11am-3pm & 5 or 6-11pm, and Sunday 11am/noon-3pm & 7-10.30pm. The last entry time to most **museums and galleries** is usually half an hour, or an hour, before the official closing time.

● **Public (bank) holidays**  Most businesses are shut on 1 January, Good Friday (March/April), Easter Monday (March/April), the first and last Monday in May, the last Monday in August, 25 December and 26 December.

● **School holidays**  School holiday periods in England are generally: a one-week break late October, two weeks around Christmas/New Year, a week in mid February, two weeks around Easter, a week in late May/early June (to coincide with the bank holiday on the last Monday in May), and six weeks from late July to early September.

● **Travel/medical insurance**  Until 31st December 2020 the **European Health Insurance Card** (EHIC) entitled EU nationals (on production of an EHIC card) to necessary medical treatment under the UK's National Health Service (NHS) while on a temporary visit here. However, this is not likely to be the case for EU nationals now, especially once their EHIC card has expired, though it would be worth checking on 🖥 nhs.uk/nhs-services (click on: 'Visiting-or-moving-to-England') before you come to the UK. But the EHIC card was never a substitute for proper medical cover on

PLANNING YOUR WALK

these sections. Part 5 goes into greater detail about what can be found where, while for a quick glance at what's available do look at the Town & Village Facilities Table on p32.

## Drinking water

There may be plenty of ways of perishing on the Dales Way but, given the amount of time you spend walking by a river, and the amount it rains in this part of the country, thirst probably won't be one of them. That said, it's not advisable to drink directly from rivers: you won't ever truly know what's recently defecated or died

your travel insurance, for unforeseen bills and for getting you home should that be necessary. Also consider getting cover for loss or theft of personal belongings, especially if you're staying in hostels, as there may be times when you'll have to leave your luggage unattended.

● **Weights and measures**  Milk in Britain is still sometimes sold in pints (1 pint = 568ml), as is beer in pubs, though most other **liquids** including petrol (gasoline) and diesel are sold in litres. Most **food** is sold in metric weights (g and kg) but the imperial weights of pounds (lb: 1lb = 453g) and ounces (oz: 1oz = 28g) are often displayed too.

Road **distances** are given in miles (1 mile = 1.6km) rather than kilometres, and yards (1yd = 0.9m) rather than metres. The population remains divided between those who still use inches (1 inch = 2.5cm) and feet (1ft = 0.3m) and those who are happy with centimetres and millimetres; you'll often be told that 'it's only a hundred yards or so' to somewhere, rather than a hundred metres or so. The **weather** – a frequent topic of conversation – is also an issue: while most forecasts predict temperatures in °C, some people continue to think in terms of °F (see temperature chart on p13 for conversions)

● **Time**  During the winter the whole of Britain is on Greenwich Meantime (GMT). The clocks move one hour forward on the last Sunday in March, remaining on British Summer Time (BST) until the last Sunday in October.

● **Smoking**  Smoking in enclosed public places is banned. The ban relates not only to pubs and restaurants, but also to B&Bs, hostels and hotels. These latter have the right to designate one or more bedrooms where the occupants can smoke, but the ban is in force in all enclosed areas open to the public – even in a private home such as a B&B. Should you be foolhardy enough to light up in a no-smoking area, which includes pretty well any indoor public place, you could be fined £50, but it's the owners of the premises who suffer most if they fail to stop you, with a potential fine of £2500.

● **Telephones**  The international access code for Britain is ☎ 44, followed by the area code minus the first 0, and then the number you require. Within the UK, to call a number with the same code as the landline phone you are calling from, the code can be omitted: dial the number only. It is cheaper to ring at weekends (from midnight on Friday till midnight on Sunday), and after 7pm and before 7am on weekdays. **Mobile phone reception** is not bad though you'll find a big black spot with no reception stretching from Kettlewell to Dent. If you're using a mobile phone that is registered overseas, consider buying a local SIM card to keep costs down; also remember to bring a universal adaptor so you can charge your phone. See also p26 for details about using a public phone.

● **Internet access**  See p26.

● **Emergency services**  For police, ambulance, fire and mountain rescue dial ☎ 999, or the EU standard number ☎ 112.

PLANNING YOUR WALK

in them further upstream, and the run-off from the neighbouring fields could contain pesticides and other nasty chemicals. Instead, always get your water from a tap where you know the water is safe to drink, although also consider carrying some kind of water-purifying treatment (tablets/filter/steripen etc), just in case you run out of drinking water along the trail and need to collect some from nature. In hot weather aim to drink **three or four litres** per day.

## MONEY

You'll find **banks** – or at least **ATMs** (cashpoints) – along the Dales Way, at places such as Ilkley, Addingham, Grassington, Sedbergh, Kendal, and Bowness. The section you need to watch out for is from Grassington to Dent/Sedbergh, where there aren't any. But there are also not many places where you can spend money on this stretch, unless your B&B and pub/restaurant accepts payment in cash only, or if you have any mishap or change your plans – so make sure you have enough cash to cover these outgoings.

However, the village stores at Kettlewell and Dent offer a **cashback** system; if you pay for goods by debit card they will advance cash against the card. You'll usually have to spend a minimum of £5 with them first. Many of the pubs along the way will also be happy to do this, particularly if there's no ATM nearby. However, be aware some have less cash as many people pay by card now.

**Post offices** also provide a very useful service whereby you can get cash (by debit card with a Pin number) for free if you bank with most British banks or building societies.

Though most places now accept **debit/credit cards**, there's sometimes a minimum spend so it's a good idea to carry at least £50-100 with you in cash, just in case.

The almost obsolete **chequebook** could also prove useful as a back-up but you would probably still need a debit card as guarantee.

## INTERNET ACCESS

Most places to stay offer **wi-fi** free to visitors. If you're camping, you may find the pubs are your best bet for a good connection, though note that The Sportsman's Inn at Cowgill has no internet service, The George Inn at Hubberholme only offers it for residents and elsewhere it can be a little slow.

## OTHER SERVICES

Most small villages have a food store that also houses a **post office** (see Money, above). Nearby you'll usually find a **phone box**, though be warned, some no longer contain telephones (due to lack of demand these days) or if they do they may not work, and others only accept cards (to help combat vandalism). Those accepting cards take a £1 connection fee which is charged whether you get an answer or not. Otherwise 60p is the minimum fee to make a cash call; no change is given.

There are **outdoor equipment shops** and **pharmacies** in the larger towns of Ilkley, Grassington, Sedbergh, Kendal and Bowness, and **tourist information centres** at Ilkley, Grassington, Sedbergh and Bowness.

**Toilets** are marked on the maps but a useful, though sometimes dated, resource for toilets in towns, and some villages, is 🖳 toiletmap.org.uk.

## WALKING COMPANIES

It's possible to turn up with your boots and backpack at Ilkley and just start walking without planning much other than your accommodation (about which, see the box on p21). The following companies, however, are in the business of making your holiday as stress-free and enjoyable as possible.

### Baggage transfer and accommodation-booking
At the time of research two baggage-transfer companies serve the Dales Way; With both you can usually book baggage transfer up to around 8pm the previous evening, though it can be cheaper if you book in advance.

● **Brigantes Walking Holidays and Baggage Couriers** (☎ 01756 770402, 🖳 brigantesenglishwalks.com; Nr Skipton, N Yorks) run a family operated baggage-transfer service with locally based drivers covering the whole of the north of England. They operate from 1st April to 1st October and charge from £9 per person per day.

● **Sherpa Van** (☎ 01748 826917, 🖳 sherpavan.com; Richmond, N Yorks) is a national organisation that runs a baggage-delivery service between March and mid October on the Dales Way. Bookings must be a minimum of £25. For details of their **accommodation-booking** service see their website or call them.

### Self-guided holidays
Self-guided means that the company will organise accommodation, baggage transfer (some contract out the work to other companies), transport to and from the walk and various maps and advice, but leave you on your own to actually walk the path and cover the cost of lunch and dinner.

● **Absolute Escapes** (☎ 0131 610 1210, 🖳 absoluteescapes.com; Edinburgh)
● **Brigantes Walking Holidays and Baggage Couriers** (see above)
● **Celtic Trails** (☎ 01291 689774, 🖳 celtictrailswalkingholidays.co.uk; Chepstow)
● **Contours** (☎ 01629 821900, 🖳 contours.co.uk; Matlock)
● **Discovery Travel** (☎ 01983 301 133, 🖳 discoverytravel.co.uk; Isle of Wight)
● **Footpath Holidays** (☎ 01985 840049, 🖳 footpath-holidays.com; Nr Warminster, Wilts)
● **Freedom Walking Holidays** (☎ 07733 885390, 🖳 freedomwalkingholidays.co.uk; Goring-on-Thames)
● **Great British Walks** (formerly The Walking Holiday Company; ☎ 01600 713008, 🖳 great-british-walks.com; Monmouth)
● **Let's Go Walking** (☎ 01837 880075, or ☎ 020 7193 1252, 🖳 letsgowalking.co.uk; Devon)

PLANNING YOUR WALK

- **Macs Adventure** (☎ 0141 530 8886, 🖳 macsadventure.com; Glasgow)
- **Mickledore** (☎ 017687 72335, 🖳 mickledore.co.uk; Keswick, Cumbria)
- **Nearwater Walking Holidays** (☎ 01326 279278, 🖳 nearwaterwalkingholi days.co.uk; Cornwall).
- **NorthWestWalks** (☎ 01257 424889, 🖳 northwestwalks.co.uk; Wigan)
- **Responsible Travel** (☎ 01273 823700, 🖳 responsibletravel.com; Brighton)
- **Shepherds Walks Holidays** (☎ 01669 621044, 🖳 shepherdswalksholidays .co.uk; Northumberland)
- **The Carter Company** (☎ 01296 631671, 🖳 the-carter-company.com; Bucks)
- **Walkers' Britain** (formerly Sherpa Expeditions; ☎ 020 8875 5070, 🖳 walk ersbritain.co.uk; London)
- **Walk The Trail** (☎ 01326 567252, 🖳 walkthetrail.co.uk; Cornwall)
- **Wandering Aengus** (☎ 016974 78443 🖳 watreks.com; Lake District)
- **Where2Walk** (☎ 07824 304060, 🖳 where2walk.co.uk; Yorkshire Dales)

## Group/guided walking tours

If you don't trust your navigational skills or simply prefer the company of other walkers as well as an experienced guide, one of HF Holidays guided walks may be of interest. Packages generally include all meals, accommodation, transport arrangements, minibus back-up and baggage transfer.

- **HF Holidays** (☎ 0345 470 8559, 🖳 hfholidays.co.uk; Herts)  Offer a walk along the entire route based at their country house Newfield Hall, Airton; they also offer guided walks from Sedbergh (their base for those is Thorns Hall)
- **Northern Guiding** (☎ 01132 736417, 🖳 northernguiding.co.uk; Leeds)  Run by a qualified Mountain Leader who offers private guiding either on your own or in groups and can make bespoke walks.

## WALKING WITH A DOG                    [see also pp170-1]

The Dales Way is a dog-friendly path, though it's extremely important that dog owners behave in a responsible manner. Dogs should always be kept on leads while on the footpath to avoid disturbing wildlife, livestock and other walkers. Dog excrement should be cleaned up and not left to decorate the boots of others; take a pooper scooper or plastic bag if you're walking with a dog.

It's particularly important to **keep your dog on a lead** when crossing fields with livestock in them, especially around calving or lambing time which can be as early as February or as late as the end of May. Most farmers would prefer it if you did not bring your dog at all at this time.

## DISABLED ACCESS

Many areas of the trail are inaccessible to the majority of wheelchair users, but access has been provided in a few sections, such as from The Red Lion pub in Burnsall to the suspension bridge at Hebden.

For more on countryside access for the disabled, contact Disabled Ramblers (🖳 disabledramblers.co.uk).

# Budgeting

England is not a cheap place to go travelling and, while the north may be one of the less expensive regions, the towns and villages in the national parks get all the business they can handle and charge accordingly.

There's nothing wrong with planning a budget trek, for example by camping every night and cooking your own food, but don't be too 'fundamentalist' on this matter, for there's no point scrimping and saving if it just means you'll have a miserable time. In particular, if the weather's unceasingly soggy don't persevere with camping night after night; there are few things more depressing on any trek than carrying a heavy, saturated tent, especially if the overnight rain also meant that you got little sleep. So if it looks as if it's going to rain again, and you're already feeling exhausted, bite the bullet and pay the extra to get a proper roof over your head. That way at least you can dry out your luggage (many places have a drying room), get a good night's sleep and recharge your batteries (both literally and metaphorically).

If the only expenses of this walk were accommodation and food, budgeting would be a piece of cake. Unfortunately, in addition to these there are all the little **extras** that push up the cost of your trip: for example beer, cream teas, buses or taxis, baggage-transfer, laundry and souvenirs. It's surprising how much these add up! None of these is absolutely essential to helping you complete the trek, but each could make your trek a lot more straightforward – and a great deal more enjoyable too.

## CAMPING

If you wild camp (with the permission of the landowner – see p53), you can survive on as little as £5-10 per person (pp) per day, but assuming you use campsites, you can still get by on less than £15pp per day so long as you don't visit pubs, avoid museums and other tourist attractions, and cook all your own food on your camping stove.

Even then, unforeseen expenses will probably nudge your daily budget up. Include the occasional pint, and perhaps a pub meal every now and then, and the figure will be nearer £20-30pp per day.

## HOSTELS

The charge for staying in a hostel is around £20-25pp per night. Whack on another £6 for breakfast and £10 for lunch in a café, and £10-15 for an evening meal (though you can use their self-catering facilities for both), and overall, it will cost £30-40 per day, or £50-60 to live in a little more comfort, enjoy the odd beer and go out for the occasional meal. However, there aren't enough hostels to cover the walk so you will have to camp or stay in B&B as well.

## B&Bs, PUBS, GUESTHOUSES AND HOTELS

B&B prices start at around £30pp per night based on two sharing a room, though £40pp is more common. For more luxurious places in a popular tourist haunt such as Grassington expect to pay as much as £75pp. Add on the cost of food for lunch and dinner – a packed lunch from a B&B may be around £6 and an evening meal £15-20 – and you should reckon on about £70pp minimum per day. Staying in a guesthouse or hotel will cost more.

If walking on your own remember that there is almost always a supplement for single occupancy and you may even have to pay the full price of the room.

# Itineraries

Part 5 of this book has been written from east to west (or, more accurately, from south-east to north-west), but there is of course nothing to stop you from tackling it in the opposite direction (see below).

To help plan your walk look at the **planning maps** (see opposite inside back cover) and the **table of town & village facilities** (on p32), which gives a run-down on the essential information you'll need regarding accommodation possibilities and services as at the time of writing.

You could follow one of the **suggested itineraries** (see box opposite) which are based on preferred type of accommodation and walking speed. There's also a list of **day and weekend walks** on pp33-5 which cover the best of the path; most of these are well served by public transport; in addition, see box p34 for an itinerary for doing the walk in day trips. The bus services table is on pp48-9 (see box p45/46 for rail/coach services) and **public transport map** on p47.

Once you have an idea of your approach turn to Part 5 for detailed information on accommodation, places to eat and other services in each village and town on the route. Also in Part 5 you will find summaries of the route to accompany the detailed trail maps.

## WHICH DIRECTION?

To be honest, it doesn't really matter. Most people trek from south-east to north-west. So, if you are walking alone but wouldn't mind some company now and again you'll find that most of the other Dales Way walkers are heading in your direction. There is also something to be said for finishing your walk in the Lake District, from where you can continue your adventure by scaling a few of England's highest peaks.

It could be argued that by heading in the other direction the prevailing (west) winds will, more often than not, be behind you. Having said that, wind is rarely a big issue on this trail, and, if you do walk north-west to south-east you could end up squinting more as the sun will be in your face for much of the day (assuming you see it, of course).

## SUGGESTED ITINERARIES

The suggested itineraries (see box below) are based on two different accommodation types: camping and bunkhouses/hostels; and B&Bs. Each is then divided
into three alternatives depending on your walking speed (relaxed, medium and
fast). They are only suggestions so feel free to adapt them.

Don't forget to **add your travelling time** before and after the walk to get a
better idea of how many days you'll need in total.

### CAMPING (AND HOSTELS)

| | Relaxed pace | | Medium pace | | Fast pace | |
|---|---|---|---|---|---|---|
| **Night** | **Place** | **Approx distance** miles / km | **Place** | **Approx distance** miles / km | **Place** | **Approx distance** miles / km |
| 0 | Ilkley | | Ilkley | | Ilkley | |
| 1 | Appletreewick | 12 / 19.6 | Appletreewick | 12 / 19.6 | Appletreewick | 12 / 19.6 |
| 2 | Kettlewell | 11½ / 18.5 | Buckden | 16¼ / 25.5 | Buckden | 16¼ / 25.5 |
| 3 | Oughtershaw | 11½ / 18.5 | Cowgill | 17¼ / 27.3 | Cowgill | 17¼ / 27.3 |
| 4 | Ribblehead† | 7 / 11.4 | Bramaskew Farm | 15 / 24.3 | Bramaskew Farm | 15 / 24.3 |
| 5 | Dent | 11¾ / 18.7 | Burneside | 11½ / 18.5 | Bowness | 21 / 33.8 |
| 6 | Bramaskew Farm | 9¾ / 15.5 | Bowness | 9½ / 15.4 | | |
| 7 | Burneside | 11½ / 18.5 | | | | |
| 8 | Bowness | 9½ / 15.4 | | | | |

**Notes**: It is possible to camp in all the above places (apart from Ilkley); in addition
there are hostels at Kettlewell and Bowness. The earliest campsite on the trail is near
Bolton Abbey, 6 miles (9.6km) beyond Ilkley.

† Includes 1½-mile walk off path to Station Inn for bunkhouse and wild camping.
Campers may prefer to continue to Cowgill (10 miles from Oughtershaw but then next
day to Dent is 5¼ miles)

### STAYING IN B&B-STYLE ACCOMMODATION

| | Relaxed pace | | Medium pace | | Fast pace | |
|---|---|---|---|---|---|---|
| **Night** | **Place** | **Approx distance** miles / km | **Place** | **Approx distance** miles / km | **Place** | **Approx distance** miles / km |
| 0 | Ilkley | | Ilkley | | Ilkley | |
| 1 | Appletreewick | 12 / 19.6 | Burnsall | 13¼ / 21.5 | Grassington | 16¾ / 27.2 |
| 2 | Kettlewell | 11½ / 18.5 | Buckden | 15 / 23.6 | Swarthghyll | 19¼ / 31 |
| 3 | Swarthghyll | 12½ / 20 | Ribblehead | 14¼ / 22.6 | Dent | 16¼ / 26.2 |
| 4 | Lea Yeat | 10 / 16 | Dent | 11¾ / 18.7 | Burneside | 21¼ / 34 |
| 5 | Dent | 5¾ / 9.2 | Burneside | 21¼ / 34 | Bowness | 9½ / 15.4 |
| 6 | Sedbergh | 5¾ / 9.2 | Bowness | 9½ / 15.4 | | |
| 7 | Patton Bridge | 13¾ / 22 | | | | |
| 8 | Staveley | 8½ / 13.7 | | | | |
| 9 | Bowness | 6¼ / 10 | | | | |

PLANNING YOUR WALK

## TOWN AND VILLAGE FACILITIES

| PLACE* | DISTANCE* MILES / KM | BANK* (ATM) | POST OFFICE | TOURIST INFO* | EATING PLACE* | FOOD SHOP | CAMP-SITE | BUNK/HOSTEL* | B&B* |
|---|---|---|---|---|---|---|---|---|---|
| **Ilkley** | | ✔/ATM | ✔ | TIC | ww | ✔ | | | ww |
| **(Addingham)** 2½ / 4.1 (¼ mile / 400m off path) | | ATM | | | ww | ✔ | | | ✔ |
| **Bolton Abbey** 3½ / 5.7 | | | ✔ | | w | (✔) | ✔ | | |
| **Barden Bridge** 3½ / 5.7 | | | | | (✔) | | | (G) | |
| **Stangs Lane** 1½ / 2.3 | | | | | ✔ | | ✔ | | w |
| **Appletreewick** 1 / 1.6 | | | | | w | | ✔ | | ✔ |
| **Burnsall** 1¼ / 2 | | | | | ww | | | | ww |
| **(Hebden)** 1½ / 2.4 (½ mile / 800m off path) | | | | | w | | | | ww |
| **Grassington** 2 / 3.4 | | ATM | ✔ | NPC/HUB | ww | ✔ | ✔(2 miles) | (G) | ww |
| **Conistone** 2½ / 4.1 | | | | | | | | | |
| **(Kilnsey)** (1mile / 1.6km off path) | | | | | ✔ | | | | |
| **Kettlewell** 4¼ / 6.6 | | # | | | ww | ✔ | ✔ | H | ww |
| **(Starbotton)** 2¼ / 3.5 (200m off path) | | | | | ✔ | | ✔ | | w |
| **(Buckden)** 2¼ / 3.5 (200m off path) | | | | | ✔ | ✔ | ✔ | (G) | w |
| **Hubberholme** 1¼ / 2 | | | | | ✔ | | | (G) | w |
| **Beckermonds** 4 / 6.3 | | | | | | | | | |
| **Oughtershaw** 1¾ / 2.8 | | | | | | | ✔ | | |
| **Swarthghyll** 1 / 1.6 | | | | | | | ✔ | (G) | ✔(sc) |
| **Far Gearstones** 4½ / 7.2 | | | | | | | | (G) | ✔(sc) |
| **(Ribblehead)** 1½ / 2.4 (road walk) | | | | | ✔ | | ✔(wild) | (G) | ✔ |
| **Lea Yeat/ Cowgill** 4½ / 7.2 | | | | | ✔ | | ✔ | | ✔ |
| **(Dent)** 5½ / 8.8 (200m off path) | | # | ✔ | | ww | ✔ | ✔ | | ww |
| **(Sedbergh)** 5 / 8 (½ mile / 800m off path) | | ATM | ✔ | TIC | ww | ✔ | | (G) | ww |
| **Lincoln's Inn Br** 4 / 6.4 | | | | | | ✔ | | | |
| **Bramaskew & Low Branthwaite** ½ / 0.8 | | | | | | ✔ | | | w |
| **Grayrigg** 6¾ / 9.7 | | | | | | ✔ | | | |
| **(Patton Bridge)** 1 / 1.6 (1 mile off path) | | | | | | | (✔ ON TRAIL) | | ✔ |
| **Burneside** 3¾ / 6 | | | | | w | ✔ | ✔ | | ww |
| **(Kendal)** (train) | | ATM | ✔ | | ww | ✔ | ✔ (1½) | H | ww |
| **(Staveley)** 3½ / 5.7 (¼mile / 400m off path) | | | ✔ | | ww | ✔ | | | ww |
| **Bowness** 6 / 9.9 | | ATM | ✔ | TIC | ww | ✔ | ✔ (1/1.6) | H (1/1.6) | ww |

*see opposite for notes

## THE BEST DAY AND WEEKEND WALKS

The following suggested trails are for those who don't want to tackle the entire path in one go, or just want to get a flavour of the challenge before committing themselves. They include arguably the best parts of the Dales Way; they are all described in more detail in Part 5.

Day walks can take you back to your starting point, either along other routes not mapped in this book or in some cases by using public transport; though in most cases services are limited so check the details (see pp48-9 and also that they still operate) before you set off.

### Bolton Abbey to Grassington          10¾ miles/17.3km (pp87-104)

A short walk but one that encompasses an awful lot, beginning with the delights of Bolton Abbey and including lovely Strid Wood, ancient Barden Bridge, a gorgeous stretch of easy wandering to the riparian villages of Appletreewick and Burnsall, and an elegant stroll to finish up at Grassington. All flat, all wonderful and it is also possible to take different paths on the eastern side of the Wharfe that will take you back to the starting point, a grand walk that will be about 22¾ miles in total (36.6km). Alternatively, bus Nos 74, 74A & 874 can convey you between Bolton Abbey and Grassington.

### Grassington to Buckden          11⅜ miles/18.3km (pp104-13)

The first high-level stage of the trail as you leave Wharfedale's main tourist centre to walk through some ancient archaeology on windswept fells. Great views over the valley are a feature of the descent into Kettlewell, whereafter the terrain is flat and easy as you follow the river's course up to Buckden. The 72A, 72B and 874 bus services run between Buckden and Grassington. Can be combined with the route above for a great weekend's walking!

### Far Gearstones to Lea Yeat via the Dales Way, returning via Wold Fell on the Alternative (High Level) Route
### 19¼ miles/31km (pp129-33 & pp126-30)

A huge loop that takes you across the fell and down under Dent viaduct to Dentdale on the long road route, then up via England's highest railway station and along Galloway Gate and the Pennine bridleway to Cam Houses, where you take the official path once more to Cam High Road and the Pennine Way back

PLANNING YOUR WALK

---

### * NOTES FOR TOWN AND VILLAGE FACILITIES TABLE

| | |
|---|---|
| PLACE | Places in brackets (eg Addingham) are a short walk off the route. |
| DISTANCE | Distances (approx) given are between places directly on the Dales Way. Distances in brackets are for places off the route |
| BANK/ATM | # = no ATM but cashback available in shop |
| TOURIST INFO | TIC = Tourist information centre; NPC = national park visitor centre HUB = Community-run organisation providing tourist and local info |
| EATING PLACE | ✔ = one place, ✔✔ = two, ✔✔✔ = three or more, (✔) = snacks |
| HOSTEL/BUNK | H = independent hostel (Kettlewell affiliated to YHA), (G) = groups only |
| B&Bs | ✔ = one place, ✔✔ = two, ✔✔✔ = three or more; (SC) = self-catering |

to Far Gearstones. If the distance is too ambitious, a much simpler alternative is to come off the official path on Dent Rd, walk down to Newby Head and pick up the Alternative (High Level) route via Gavel Gap to Cold Keld Gate – a much more manageable 9-miler.

If you're relying on public transport you'll need to catch a train to Ribblehead – a 1½-mile (2.4km) walk from Far Gearstones – or Dent station, which is on the trail. There are few facilities en route though The Station Inn (Ribblehead) can provide food and accommodation; The Sportsman's Inn at Cowgill can do the same, though the opening times are more limited at the latter.

---

### ❑ DOING THE DALES WAY IN DAY TRIPS

There are some very handy services that enable you to walk for the whole day before catching the bus back again at the day's end, thereby enabling you to complete most of the path in day trips if you so desire. For example, the **74/74A service** (see box pp48-9 for details) runs between Ilkley and Grassington via several places which are on the path. So you can arrive in Ilkley in the morning, set off on the trail, stop when you get tired at any of those villages – and then catch a bus back to Ilkley. Indeed, on Sunday/Bank Holidays the 874 runs all the way to Buckden. **Note that, whatever day you walk, you need to check and double-check the bus times as they are prone to change – and very few services on the Dales Way are daily and frequent; also many operate only in the main season.**

It's not all plain sailing, of course. Buckden to Dentdale is one 'problem' stage where you'll have to travel via Skipton to get between the two (72A bus from Skipton to Buckden, Northern Rail train back from Dent to Skipton) – a massive detour that few will think worth it. And from Dent/Dent railway station onwards, in order to make things easier for yourself, it's worth **walking at a weekend**. The **S1 bus** service operates only on Saturday but travels between Dent station and Kendal.

Here's a suggested itinerary for doing the entire way in day trips. As always, do check online for the latest info before setting off on any of these stages.

**Day 1**: Drive/public transport to Ilkley. Walk Ilkley to Grassington. Take a 74/74A/874 bus (no service on Tue or Thur) back to Ilkley.

**Day 2**: Drive/bus to Grassington. Walk to Buckden. Take bus 72A (Mon-Fri term time only), 72B (Sat), or 874 (Sun/Bank hols only) back to Grassington.

**Day 3**: Drive/public transport to Skipton. Take bus 72 (daily)/72A (Mon-Fri term time only) to Grassington and then 72A/72B, or 875 (summer Sun & Bank hols only) to Buckden. Walk to Dent railway station on the Alternative (High Level) route. Return by train to Skipton.
[NB If you want to take the regular (low level) route you'll have to backtrack to Dent station where the alternative (high level) route joins the regular route; see Map 21, p133 for where to do this.]

**Day 4**: Drive/public transport to Dent/Dent station. Walk to Sedbergh. Take a Western Dales Bus S1 (Sat only) back to Dent station or S3 or S4 on some other days.

**Day 5**: Drive/bus to Sedbergh. Walk Sedbergh to Burneside. Train Burneside to Kendal then, if driving, take a W1 (Mon-Fri) bus back to Sedbergh.

**Day 6**: Drive/public transport to Burneside. Walk Burneside to Bowness. Take one of the many buses from Bowness to Windermere railway station and, if driving, take a train back to Burneside.

**Sedbergh to Lincoln's Inn Bridge circular 6⅝ miles/10.7km (pp140-7)**
A simple stroll that takes you around the Howgills. Follow the Dales Way to
Lune viaduct, where you should divert off to Howgill Lane then take a right on a
public footpath to climb and traverse the lower slopes of Winder's southern face,
the hill overlooking Sedbergh. Drop down to Howgill Lane to re-enter Sedbergh.

**Burneside to Bowness**         **9½ miles/15.4km (pp152-68)**
The last stretch of the trail is simple enough, though interesting too as you enter
Lake District National Park. Staveley provides a convenient place to stop for
elevenses or lunch. There's no real chance to loop back on foot so you'll either
have to retrace your steps or, more sensibly, take the (555, 599 or 755) bus from
Bowness to Windermere railway station then the train back to Burneside.

# What to take

**Taking too much** is a mistake made by first-time travellers of all types, an
understandable response to not knowing what to expect and not wanting to be
caught short. But unless you want to end up feeling like an overloaded mule
with a migraine you need to pack carefully. Experienced independent hill walkers trim their gear down to the essentials because they've learned that an unnec-
essarily heavy pack can exacerbate injuries and put excess strain on their
already hard-pressed feet.

    Note that if you need to buy all the gear listed, keep an eye out for the ever-
more frequent online **sales** at outdoor gear shops; time it right and you could get
it all half price.

## TRAVELLING LIGHT

Organised tours apart, baggage-transfer services tempt walkers partially to miss
the point of long-distance walking: the satisfaction of striding away from one
place knowing that you're carrying everything you need to get to another. But
if you've chosen to carry it all you must be ruthless in your packing choices.

## HOW TO CARRY YOUR LUGGAGE

Today's rucksacks are hi-tech affairs that make load-carrying as tolerable as can
be expected. Don't get hung up on anti-sweat features; unless you use a wheel-
barrow, your back will always sweat a bit. It's better to ensure there is thick
padding and a **good range of adjustment**. In addition to hip belts (allied with
some sort of stiff back frame), use an unelasticated **cross-chest strap** to keep
the pack snug; it makes a real difference.

    If camping you'll need a pack of at least 60 or 70 litres' capacity. Staying in
hostels 40 litres should be ample, and for those eating out and staying in B&Bs
a 20- to 30-litre pack should suffice; you could even get away with a daypack.

Few backpacks these days claim to be waterproof, and even though most packs come with an elasticated backpack cover like a giant shower cap, you still need to use a waterproof **liner** (heavy-duty garden-bin liners are ideal) or put all your belongings into **smaller waterproof bags** to ensure your stuff stays dry in a place as wet as the Dales. It's handy, in any case, to **compartmentalise** the contents of your pack into smaller bags so you know what is where. Take a few (degradable) **plastic bags** for wet things, rubbish etc; they're always useful. Finally, pack intelligently with the most frequently used things readily accessible.

## FOOTWEAR

### Boots

Don't be tempted by the Dales Way's reputation as an easy walk to turn up at Ilkley in a pair of flip-flops; a good pair of trekking boots is vital. (If you've a real intolerance for ankle protection, a good pair of trail shoes may just suffice; see the last paragraph of this section.) Scrimp on other gear if you must – you'll only use waterproofs some days but you'll be walking every mile on every day. Expect to spend up to £150 on quality, three-season footwear which is light, breathable and waterproof, and has ankle support as well as flexible but thick **soles** to insulate your own pulverised soles. Don't buy by looks or price and avoid buying online until you've been to a shop and tried on an identical pair (and even this can backfire on you). Go to a big outdoor shop on a quiet weekday and spend time trying on everything they have in stock that appeals. Then, with boots safely bought, make sure you try them out beforehand, first round the house or office, and then on a full day's walk or two. That way, while your friends are wailing over blister-blighted toes, you'll be skipping through the meadows and rejoicing in your decision to choose your boots with care.

An old and trusted pair of boots can be re-soled and transformed with shock-absorbing after-market **insoles**. Some of these can be thermally moulded to your foot in the shop, but the less expensive examples are also well worth the investment, even if the need for replacement by the end of the walk is likely. Some walkers wisely carry old trusted boots in their luggage in case their new footwear turns on them – though this can be quite a heavy tactic. Blisters are possible even with a much-loved boot if you walk long and hard enough; refer to p56 for blister-avoidance strategies.

Many may consider boots over the top for the Dales Way; much of the walking is on easy paths and some experienced walkers have turned to **trail shoes**. They won't last as long as boots, be as tough or crucially, have the height to keep your socks dry in the bogs and streams; but the rewards of nimbleness and greater comfort can transform your walk, just as bad footwear can cast a shadow over it.

### Socks

As with all outdoor gear, the humble sock has not escaped the technological revolution (with prices to match) so invest in two non-cotton pairs designed for walking. Although cushioning is desirable, avoid anything too thick which will reduce stability. As well as the obvious olfactory benefits, frequent washing will maintain the socks' springiness.

## CLOTHES

### Tops
The proven system of **layering** is a good principle to follow. A quick-drying synthetic (or the less odiferous merino wool) **base layer** transports sweat away from your skin; the mid-layer, typically a **fleece** or woollen jumper, keeps you warm; and when needed, an outer 'shell' or **jacket** protects you from the wind and rain. Maintaining a comfortable temperature in all conditions is the key. This means not **overheating** just as much as it means keeping warm. Both can prematurely tire you and, although tedious, the smart hiker is forever fiddling with zips and managing their layers and headwear to maintain an optimal level of comfort.

Avoid cotton; as well as being slow to dry, when soaked it saps away body heat but not the moisture – and you'll often be wet from sweat if not rain. Take a change of **base layers** (including underwear), a **fleece** suited to the season, and the best **breathable waterproof** you can afford. **Soft shells** are an alternative to walking in rustling nylon waterproofs when it's windy but not raining.

It's useful to have a **spare set of clothing** so you're able to get changed should you arrive chilled at your destination, but choose **quick-drying clothes**. Once indoors your body heat will quickly dry out a synthetic fleece and nylon leggings. However, always make sure you have a **dry base layer** in case you go down with hypothermia, or someone you're with does. This is why a quality waterproof jacket is important.

### Leg wear
Your legs are doing all the work and don't generally get cold so your trousers can be light which will also mean quick-drying. Although they lack useful pockets, many walkers find leg-hugging cycling polyester **leggings** very comfortable (eg Ron Hill Tracksters). Poly-cotton or microfibre trousers are excellent. Denim jeans are cotton and a disaster when wet.

If the weather's good, **shorts** are very agreeable to walk in, leaving a light pair of trousers clean for the evenings. It also means your lower legs get muddy and not the trousers. On the other hand **waterproof trousers** would suit people who really feel the cold; others may find them unnecessary and awkward to put on and wear, preferring quick drying or minimal legwear.

For muddy sections **gaiters** are a great idea; they also stop irritating pebbles dropping into your footwear. You don't have to wear them all the time, though.

### Headwear and other clothing
Your head is both exposed to the sun and loses most of your body heat so, for warmth, carry a woolly beany that won't blow away and for UV protection a peaked cap; a bandana or microfibre 'buff' makes a good back-up or a sweat band. Between them they'll either conserve body heat or reduce the chances of dehydration. **Gloves** are good in wintry conditions (carry a spare pair in winter).

PLANNING YOUR WALK

## TOILETRIES

Besides **toothpaste/brush** bring **liquid soap** which can also be used for shaving and washing clothes, though **detergent** is better if you're doing a lot of clothes washing. Carry **toilet paper** and a lightweight **trowel** to bury the results out on the fells (see pp52-3). Other items include **ear plugs**, **sun screen**, **moisturiser**, **insect repellent** if camping, and possibly a means of **water purification**.

## FIRST-AID KIT

Apart from aching limbs your most likely ailments will be blisters so a first-aid kit can be minimal. **Paracetamol** helps numb pain – although rest, of course, is the only real cure. '**Compeed**' or '**Second Skin**' treat blisters (see also p56). An **elastic knee support** is a good precaution for a weak knee. A tube of **Nuun tablets** can flavour water and restore lost minerals on the march, and a few sachets of **Dioralyte** or **Rehydrat** powders will quickly remedy more serious dehydration. Other items worth considering are: **plasters** for minor cuts; a small selection of different-sized **sterile dressings** for wounds; **porous adhesive tape**; **antiseptic wipes**; **antiseptic cream**; **safety pins**; **tweezers**; and **scissors**.

## GENERAL ITEMS

### Essential

Carry a **compass**, **whistle**, **mobile phone** (and the charging device for it) as well as at least a one-litre **water bottle** or bag; an LED **headtorch**; **emergency snacks**, a **penknife** and a **watch**.

### Useful

If you're not carrying a proper bivvy bag or tent, a compact foil **space blanket** is a good idea in the cooler seasons. Many people take a **camera**, **batteries** and **sunglasses**. A **book** is a good way to pass the evenings, especially in mid-summer wild camps. A **vacuum flask**, for hot drinks or soup, is recommended if walking in a cooler season. Studies have shown that nothing improves a hilltop view on a chilly day like a hot cup of tea or soup. **Walking poles** are useful if you have weak knees.

If committed to the exposure of wild camping you'll need a **tent** you can rely on; light but able to withstand the rain and wind. In campsites you may just get away with a cheap tent. Otherwise, a good one-man tent suited to the wilds can cost under £120 and weigh just 1.5kg, with a sub-2kg two-man example costing around £250. An inflatable **sleeping mat** is worth many times its weight.

As for **cooking**, you'll need a camping stove, a lighter and a box of matches, a set of camping pots, cutlery, bowls, cups and a cleaning scourer. With all of these, the lighter and smaller the better. It's worth noting that there are plenty of eateries along the Way, so even if you are planning to camp every night, you could get away without cooking your own food. Doing so, though, does save a lot of money, as well as ensuring you'll always be eating with a view!

## MONEY

Most places accept **debit** or **credit cards** as payment these days, but you may find that you have to use **cash** at some B&Bs and campsites, and even at some smaller cafés and shops in more remote areas. You should always carry some cash with you, just to be on the safe side. Remember, **ATMs** (cashpoints) are few and far between on this trail, so it is wise to load up on cash at the start of your walk. See also p26 and the town and village facilities table on p32.

## MAPS

The hand-drawn maps in this book cover the trail at a scale of just under 1:20,000: $3^1/8$ inches = one mile (5cm = 1km). At this generous scale, combined with the notes and tips written on the maps, and the waypoints – not to mention the fact that the Dales Way is so well signposted – it's quite difficult to get lost. That said, a supplementary map of the region – ie one with contours – can prove invaluable should you need to abandon the path and find the quickest route off high ground in bad weather. They also help you to identify local features and landmarks and devise possible side trips.

The most popular map for the Dales Way is **Harvey Maps** (🖳 harvey maps.co.uk) *Long Distance Route – Dales Way* (£14.50). Their website makes a lot of the fact that it's durable, waterproof, weighs only 60g and can also be downloaded digitally for your iPhone, iPad or Android device. All of which is

### ❑ DIGITAL MAPPING

Most smartphones have a GPS chip so you can see your position overlaid onto a digital map on your phone. There are numerous software packages that provide Ordnance Survey (OS) maps for a smartphone, tablet, PC or GPS unit. Maps are downloaded over the internet, then loaded into an app, also available by download, from where you can view them, print them and create routes on them.

Digital maps are normally purchased for an area such as a National Park, but the Dales Way walk is available as a distinct product from some vendors. When compared to the five OS Explorer maps that cover the walk, they are very competitively priced.

It is important to ensure any digital mapping software on your smartphone uses pre-downloaded maps stored on your device, and doesn't need to download them on-the-fly, as this may be expensive and will be impossible without a signal. Note that battery life will be significantly reduced, compared to normal usage, when you are using the built-in GPS and running the screen for long periods.

Many websites have **free routes** you can download for the more popular digital mapping products; anything from day walks to complete Long Distance Paths.

**Memory Map** (🖳 memory-map.co.uk) currently sell OS 1:25,000 mapping covering the whole of the UK for £166. They also have annual subscriptions from £25.

For a subscription of £2.99 for one month, or £23.99 for a year (on their current offer) **Ordnance Survey** (see p40) will let you download and then use their UK maps (1:25,000 scale) on a mobile or tablet without a data connection for a subscription of £2.99 for one month or £23.99 for a year.

great, but undoubtedly the main reason for its popularity is the fact that it's the only one to cover the whole route in one sheet.

The alternative is to get the complete set of **Ordnance Survey Explorer maps** (🖥 shop.ordnancesurvey.co.uk). But to cover the whole route you'd have to purchase five maps and spend about £45. (For those whose trip is being subsidised in some way and thus want to take this route, the relevant maps are: **OL297** Map of Lower Wharfedale & Washburn Valley; **OL2** Map of Yorkshire Dales – Southern & Western Area; **OL30** Map of Yorkshire Dales – Northern & Central Area; **OL19** Map of Howgill Fells and Upper Eden Valley; and **OL7** Map of The Lake District: South-Eastern area.) You can now get custom-made maps that centre on exactly the area you want – though at £16.99, you don't save any money by going down this route.

While it may be extravagant to buy all these maps, members of Ramblers (see box p42) can borrow up to 10 for free from their library, paying only for return postage. Members of a UK library may also be able to borrow the relevant maps from their local library.

## RECOMMENDED READING, LISTENING AND VIEWING

The books listed below may be found in the tourist information centres; the centres at Grassington and Sedbergh have a particularly good supply of books about the path and the places en route. As well as stocking many of the titles listed below, the tourist offices also have a number of books about the towns and villages en route, usually printed by small, local publishers.

If you're a seasoned long-distance walker, or even new to the game and like what you see, check out the other titles in the Trailblazer series; see p175.

### Books

James Herriot (actual name James Wight) wrote eight books about his life as a vet in the Yorkshire Dales in the 1930s-50s. The first was *If Only They Could Talk*; that and his second book were published in the USA as *All Creatures Great & Small*. They were made into a successful TV series (see opposite).

Collins *Bird Guide* with its beautiful illustrations of British and European birds continues to be the favourite field guide of both ornithologists and laymen alike. For a guide to the flora you'll encounter on the Dales Way, *The Wild Flower Key* (Warne) by Francis Rose and Clare O'Reilly, is arranged to make it easy to identify unfamiliar flowers. Another in the Collins Gem series, *Wild Flowers*, is more pocket sized and thus more suitable for walkers.

There are also several field guide **apps** for smart phones and tablets, including those that can aid in identifying birds (🖥 merlin.allaboutbirds.org) by their song as well as by their appearance.

### DVDs and iplayer/podcast downloads

Clare Balding dedicated a whole series (Series 28) of her Radio 4 *Ramblings* show to the Dales Way, and each week she was joined by a guest including, for one episode, Mr Dales Way himself, Colin Speakman. It's an interesting show though in it she manages to find some kind of magic portal, invisible to the rest of us, that means that she can finish one programme at Beckermonds and then start the next at Dent. Similarly, Episode Five finds her pulling into Sedbergh, while Episode Six has her starting at Staveley, a suspiciously convenient five miles only from the very end of the Bowness. Of course, her job is more about entertaining the listening public, which she does admirably, and less about completing the entire walk, which is your job! The series is still available to listen to on BBC Sounds.

**Films** about the Dales Way itself are rather thin on the ground but the region itself is no stranger to the camera. *Calendar Girls*, based on the true story of a local Women's Institute that decided to produce a charity calendar of themselves naked (though with cakes, garden implements, musical instruments etc placed strategically to protect their modesty), was filmed, before the action moved to LA, around the Dales Way village of Kettlewell; though the ladies on whom the film was based were actually from the Rylstone Women's Institute, about 6km south-west of Grassington. Helen Mirren and Julie Walters were the stars.

Also filmed at least in part in the Dales, the Hollywood blockbuster *Robin Hood, Prince of Thieves* starred Kevin Costner in the eponymous role. In one memorable scene, filmed at Aysgarth Falls, Robin Hood strips naked to bathe under the powerful Hardraw Force, a waterfall in the heart of Dales National Park, while Maid Marian spies on him from a nearby rock. Robin Hood bathes alone in the scene, with none of the other Merry Men present, though Maid Marian swears that she saw his Little John.

For many people, their first 'experience' of the Yorkshire Dales was via one of the long-running British **TV series** that seemed to dominate our televisions in the '70s and '80s. However, in 2020 to celebrate the 50th anniversary of the programme a new series of *All Creatures Great & Small* was made by Playground Entertainment for Channel 5 in the UK and PBS for the USA. It was partly filmed in Grassington (see p100) and overall was such a success that a second series was made and shown in 2021. The original version ran for six series and was based on the entertaining books by local vet, James Herriot.

Perhaps the most famous TV series set in Yorkshire, however, and which seems to have its heart in the Dales (though it was actually filmed around Holmfirth, to the south), is *Last of the Summer Wine*. Hilarious to anyone over a certain age (that age being about 75), for the rest of society the merits of this comedy about a group of elderly friends behaving, essentially, like children are simply unfathomable. But this lack of 'youth appeal' didn't stop it from dominating BBC1's Sunday night schedules for almost four decades, from 1973 to 2010, making it Britain's longest-running TV comedy. There's no box set that includes all the shows – presumably they couldn't find a box big enough – but you can find various series on DVD as well as on the smaller TV networks such as Gold, Yesterday and Pick.

The comedian, actor and writer Adrian Edmondson (of *The Young Ones* fame) produced a 12-part series in 2012, *The Dales* (ITV Studios Home Entertainment), that looks at the lifestyle and characters of those who live and work in the region. The documentary both complements and supplements a previous DVD, *James Herriot's Yorkshire* (Guerrilla Films, 2007), that looks at the scenery of the county in general that featured in the aforementioned TV series based on Herriot's books.

## ❑ SOURCES OF FURTHER INFORMATION

### Online trail information

🖥 **dalesway.org** The official site of the Dales Way Association and the first place to visit for updates, route changes and other Dales-based news.

🖥 **thedalesway.co.uk** Run by the baggage carriers and accommodation bookers Sherpa Van; they have some useful info on the B&Bs along the way.

🖥 **ramblingman.org.uk/walks/dalesway** One of the better blogs, written by prolific promenader Andrew Bowden. Lots of useful advice and information though as it's a one-man band the info can be a little dated.

🖥 **wharfedale-nats.org.uk** Website of Wharfedale Naturalists Society, including updates and any unusual sightings of some of the UK's rarer creatures.

### Tourist information organisations

● **Tourist information centres (TICs)** TICs are based in most cities and major towns throughout Britain and provide all manner of locally specific information; some also offer an accommodation-booking service. There are TICs at **Ilkley**, **Sedbergh** and **Bowness-on-Windermere**.

In addition to the above there's a Heritage Centre at **Dent** and a National Park Centre at **Grassington** as well as The Hub, a community-run organisation there which provides information for locals and visitors.

● **Yorkshire Tourist Board** (🖥 yorkshire.com) The tourist board oversees all the tourist information centres in the county. It's a good place to find general information about the county as well as on outdoor activities and local events. They can also help with arranging holidays and accommodation.

● **Cumbria Tourist Board** (🖥 golakes.co.uk) Performing much the same role as Yorkshire Tourist Board but, of course, for the county encompassing the Lake District – and thus just the last stage or so of the Way.

### Organisations for walkers

● **Backpackers' Club** (🖥 backpackersclub.co.uk) A club aimed, according to the website, at those who 'propel themselves across the countryside whether by walking cycling, canoe or even cross country skiing!' They produce a quarterly magazine, provide members with a comprehensive advisory and information service on all aspects of backpacking, organise weekend trips and also publish a farm-pitch directory. Membership costs £20/30 per year for an individual/family.

● **The Long Distance Walkers' Association** (🖥 ldwa.org.uk) Membership includes a journal (*Strider*) three times per year with details of challenge events and local group walks as well as articles on the subject. Membership for UK residents is £18/25.50 individual/family (less if you pay by direct debit). For overseas residents it's £15/26 without/with the *Strider* journal.

● **Ramblers** (🖥 ramblers.org.uk) Looks after the interests of walkers. Members receive their quarterly *Walk* magazine, have access to both the Ramblers Routes online library (short routes only for non-members) and an app as well as group walks. Members also receive discounts at various stores. Individual/joint membership costs £36.60/49.

Finally, there are a couple of **DVDs** about walking in the Dales – and one specifically about the trail itself. *The Dales Way with Mark Richards* (Quantum Leap Group, 2010) is one of a series of Great Northern walks; this one presented by a man who used to be a companion of Alfred Wainwright on some of his Lakeland wanderings. It's on YouTube, too, and linked to on the blogs section of the Dales Way website (🖳 dalesway.org). The same studio also produced the short but spellbinding 52-minute *Yorkshire Dales – A Landscape Of Longing* (Quantum Leap Group, 2005).

The second DVD for those interested in hiking in the Dales is *Great Walks – Yorkshire Dales* (Striding Edge, 2006; 85 mins), part of a three-DVD series that concentrates on popular walking destinations. Included is an 11-mile circular walk in Wharfedale centred around Grassington. Another in the series looks at the *Great Walks – The Howgills* (Striding Edge, 2006; 52 mins).

# Getting to and from the Dales Way

You shouldn't have any trouble getting to the start of the Dales Way, no matter where you're coming from, with Leeds – and, to a lesser extent, Bradford and Harrogate – well served by trains and buses and equally well connected by road. From any of these three places, Ilkley is an easy bus or train journey away – or a day's walk on one of the three link routes (see pp69-74).

Getting away from the Way at Bowness-on-Windermere is only slightly trickier. Windermere railway station is a two-mile walk or bus journey from Bowness. From the station you can catch the branch line to Oxenholme Lake District, which is on the main London to Glasgow West Coast line. Or you can catch a bus from the centre of Windermere to most of the main destinations in the lakes or even a ferry across to the western side of the 'mere', for those who want to continue with their lakeland explorations.

## NATIONAL TRANSPORT

All train **timetable and fare information** can be found at National Rail Enquiries (☎ 08457 484950, 24hrs; 🖳 nationalrail.co.uk); from the website you can be redirected to the websites of the train providers in question in order to make a booking. Alternatively, you can contact the train companies direct (for details see box p45); most operators also now have apps. Timetables and tickets are also available on 🖳 thetrainline.com and 🖳 qjump.co.uk. You are advised to book in advance – it may well save you a small fortune.

If your journey involves changes, it's worth checking which train company operates each leg of the journey. You may find you can save substantial amounts of money by buying separate tickets for each leg of your journey.

**Avanti West Coast** provides services between London Euston and Glasgow/Edinburgh via Oxenholme Lake District and the lakes (the so-called

'West Coast' line), and LNER operates those running between London and Leeds (part of the so-called 'East Coast' line); **Cross Country** provides services to Leeds from a number of towns and cities around Britain but not from London; **Northern Rail** is the main operator for both the Leeds to Ilkley service and the Oxenholme Lake District to Windermere branch line; and **Trans-Pennine Express**, which operates services from Manchester to Glasgow/Edinburgh via Oxenholme Lake District.

Coach (long-distance bus) travel is generally cheaper (though with the excellent advance-purchase train fares that is not always true) but takes longer. The principal coach operator in Britain is **National Express** (☎ 0871 781 8181,

## ❏ GETTING TO BRITAIN

● **By air**  Leeds Bradford Airport (🖥 www.leedsbradfordairport.co.uk) is convenient for the start of the trail and has flights from many European destinations. **Manchester Airport** (🖥 manchesterairport.co.uk) remains the nearest *major* international airport to the Dales Way. Trans-Pennine Express operates services from Manchester Airport to Leeds, and Metro/Northern operates from there to Ilkley, so less than two hours after catching the train at the airport you should be in Ilkley; see box opposite for details of the services. Both Trans-Pennine Express and Northern Rail operate services between Oxenholme Lake District and Manchester Airport which would be convenient at the end of your walk. Nevertheless, though the number of services to and from these airports increases year on year, for most foreign visitors a London airport – particularly **Heathrow** (🖥 heathrow.com) and **Gatwick** (🖥 gatwickairport.com), but also **Stansted** (🖥 stanstedairport.com) or **Luton** (🖥 london-luton.co.uk) – remains the most likely entry point to the country.

Several **budget airlines** (easyJet 🖥 easyjet.com; jet2 🖥 jet2.com; and Ryanair 🖥 ryanair.com) fly from many of Europe's major cities to Manchester and the London terminals (Stansted, Luton, Gatwick and Heathrow).

● **From Europe by train**  Eurostar (🖥 eurostar.com) operates a high-speed passenger service via the Channel Tunnel between Paris, Brussels, Amsterdam (and some other cities) and London St Pancras International. This is convenient for both the LNER line from Kings Cross to Leeds and for Avanti West Coast services between Euston and Oxenholme Lake District (for the branch line to Windermere); for details see box opposite.

● **From Europe by coach**  Eurolines (🖥 eurolines.com) have a huge network of long-distance coach services connecting over 600 cities in 35 European countries (plus Morocco) to London. It's cheap, but once such expenses as food for the journey are taken into consideration, it may not be that much cheaper than taking a flight, particularly when compared to the prices of some of the budget airlines.

● **From Europe by ferry** (with or without a car)  Numerous ferry companies operate routes between the major North Sea and Channel ports of mainland Europe and the ports on Britain's eastern and southern coasts as well as from Ireland to ports in both Wales and England. For further information see websites such as Direct Ferries (🖥 directferries.com).

● **From Europe by car**  Eurotunnel (🖥 eurotunnel.com) operates the shuttle train service for vehicles via the Channel Tunnel between Calais and Folkestone taking one hour between the motorway in France and the motorway in Britain.

24 hrs, 🖳 nationalexpress.com); see box p46 for service details. **Megabus** (🖳 uk.megabus.com) has a more limited service, but stops include Leeds, Birmingham and Manchester and it may be cheaper.

---

**❏ RAIL SERVICES AND OPERATORS**
Note that not all stations are listed.

**Cross Country** (🖳 crosscountrytrains.co.uk; Live Chat available)
● Birmingham New St to Newcastle via Sheffield, Leeds, York & Durham, daily 1/hr
● Birmingham New Street to Newcastle via Sheffield, Leeds, York & Durham, daily 1/hr (some services start in Exeter St Davids or Bristol Temple Meads and some continue to Edinburgh & Glasgow)
● Birmingham New Street to Manchester Piccadilly, daily 1/hr

**(First) TransPennine Express** (☎ 0345 600 1671, 🖳 tpexpress.co.uk
● Liverpool Lime Street to Newcastle via Manchester Victoria, Leeds & York, daily 1/hr
● Manchester Airport/Manchester to Redcar Central via Leeds & York, daily 1/hr
● Manchester Airport/Manchester Piccadilly to Edinburgh via Preston, Lancaster, Oxenholme Lake District & Carlisle, daily 5-7/day
● Manchester Airport/Manchester Piccadilly to Glasgow via Preston, Lancaster, Oxenholme Lake District & Carlisle, daily 2/day

**Northern Rail** (🖳 northernrailway.co.uk, Live Chat available; some services are operated by Northern on behalf of Metro 🖳 wymetro.com)
● **Leeds** to Carlisle via Keighley, Skipton, Settle, Horton-in-Ribblesdale, **Ribblehead**, **Dent**, Garsdale & Kirkby Stephen, Mon-Sat 8/day, Sun 6/day but only 5/day to Dent
● Manchester Airport to **Windermere** via Lancaster, Oxenholme Lake District, **Kendal**, **Burneside** & **Staveley** (daily 4/day but additional services from Oxenholme Lake District mean approx 1/hr between Oxenholme and Windermere)
● Manchester Victoria to **Leeds** via Bradford Interchange, Mon-Sat 2/hr, Sun 1/hr
● **Leeds** to **Ilkley** via Guiseley, Mon-Sat 2/hr, Sun 1/hr (Wharfedale Line)
● Bradford Forster Square to **Ilkley** via Guiseley, Mon-Sat 2/hr, Sun 1/hr (Wharfedale Line)
● York to **Leeds** via **Harrogate**, Mon-Sat 2/hr, Sun 1/hr
● Bradford Forster Square to Skipton via Shipley, Saltaire, Bingley & Keighley, daily 1-2/hr (Airedale Line)
● **Leeds** to Skipton via Shipley, Saltaire, Bingley & Keighley, daily 1-2/hr (Airedale Line)
● **Leeds** to Manchester Victoria via Bradford Interchange & Halifax, daily 1-2/hr (Calder Valley Line)

**Avanti West Coast** (🖳 avantiwestcoast.co.uk)
● London Euston to Glasgow Central via Lancaster, Oxenholme Lake District, Penrith North Lakes & Carlisle, Mon-Fri 15/day, Sat 13/day, Sun 11/day
● London Euston to Edinburgh via Birmingham, Crewe, Preston, Lancaster, Oxenholme Lake District & Carlisle, Mon-Fri 6/day, Sat & Sun 3-4/day

**LNER (London North Eastern Railway**; ☎ 0345 722 5333, daily 8am-10pm; 🖳 lner.co.uk)
● London King's Cross to Leeds via Peterborough, Mon-Sat 1-2/hr, Sun 1/hr (5-6/day continue to Harrogate)

PLANNING YOUR WALK

## Getting to Ilkley
● **By train**  Ilkley railway station is at one end of the Wharfedale Line and served by regular trains from both Leeds and Bradford. In all probability, it is Leeds where you will change trains as the station there is the second busiest outside London (Birmingham New Street is busier than Leeds).

Leeds is on several lines so is easy to reach from anywhere in Britain. It is at the end of the Leeds branch of the LNER line from London; it's also on the CrossCountry network between Scotland, the Midlands and South West England; the TransPennine Express with connections to major northern towns and cities; on Northern Railway's network including the starting point for trains on the scenic Settle to Carlisle line; and it lies at the heart of the Metro network connecting Leeds with places in all directions around the city.

● **Coach/bus**  Leeds and Bradford are, once again, the closest places to Ilkley that National Express buses serve. From there walkers heading to Ilkley can take either a train (see box p45) or, from Leeds, a bus (X84; see box pp48-9).

● **Car**  Leeds is on the A1/M1 so the simplest route from most places in the UK is to get onto the M1 and head towards Leeds, leaving it at junction 45 for the A659, then head due west on the A660 and A65 until Ilkley is reached. The various online route finders will, of course, provide you with more specific and detailed routes for wherever you live.

## Getting to/from Bowness-on-Windermere
● **Train/bus**  Trains to Oxenholme Lake District from London/Glasgow (around 2½-3½hrs / 1¾-2hrs) operate on the Avanti West Coast line. Northern services take about 20 minutes to convey you from there to Windermere railway station, from where several buses (Nos 6, 599 and 755) take no more than 10 minutes to Bowness-on-Windermere and the start of the trail (if walking north-west to south-east).

● **Coach/bus**  At the time of research National Express's services to Kendal and Windermere weren't operating but check their website (see p44).

● **Boat/bus**  Windermere Lake Cruises (☎ 015394 43360, 🖳 windermere-lake cruises.co.uk) operates a Cross Lakes Shuttle service (late Mar to late Oct, daily 10/day) across Windermere which connects with Mountain Goat's bus services to Hawkshead (see box pp48-9) and also other destinations on the western side of the lake. See Windermere Lake Cruises' website for details of lake cruises.

---
❑ **COACH SERVICES**
At the time of research National Express (see p44) were offering fewer services due to Covid; check their website for further details.
**Note** not all stops are listed.
● **131, 132, 133, 180 & 183**  Birmingham to Leeds via Sheffield, up to 12/day
● **175**  Liverpool to Leeds via Salford & Manchester, 1/day
● **240**  Heathrow Airport to Luton Airport, Sheffield, Leeds & Bradford, 1/day + 1/day to Leeds
● **320**  Birmingham to Bradford Interchange via Leeds, 2/day
● **561**  London to Bradford via Milton Keynes, Sheffield & Leeds, 4/day

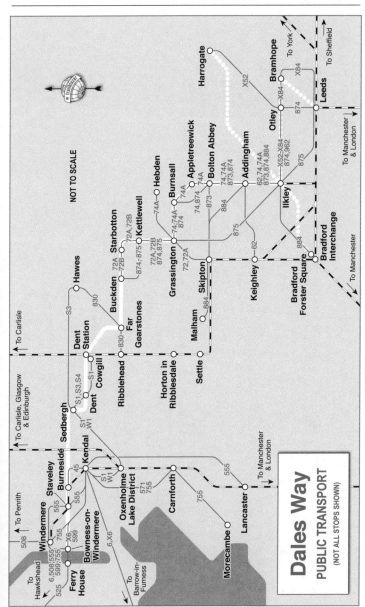

PLANNING YOUR WALK

**Dales Way**
PUBLIC TRANSPORT
(NOT ALL STOPS SHOWN)

PLANNING YOUR WALK

☐ BUS SERVICES & OPERATORS – DALES WAY

See p47 for map

**Notes**

● Service details were as accurate as possible at the time of writing but it is essential to check before travel
● Services on Bank Holiday Mondays are usually the same as Sunday services, not the Monday to Saturday services
● Services generally operate at the same frequency in both directions
● Be aware that where routes are serviced by more than one operator (usually during the peak season), the different operators may not accept each other's tickets
● In rural areas where there are no fixed bus stops it is usually possible to 'hail and ride' a passing bus though it is important to stand where visibility is good and also somewhere it would be safe for the driver to stop
● Some buses are specifically for schoolchildren with a permit and can't be used by fare-paying passengers; however, these are not listed here

| Bus | Route | Frequency | Operator |
|---|---|---|---|
| X52 | Harrogate to Otley & Ilkley | Mon-Sat 9/day | CB |
| X84 | Leeds to Ilkley via Bramhope & Otley | daily 1-2/hr | First Leeds |
| 62 | Keighley to Addingham & Ilkley | Mon-Sat 2/hr, Sun approx 1/hr | Keighley |
| 830 | Ingleton to Ribblehead, Far Gearstones, Hawes & Richmond | summer Sun & bank hols 1/day | DBus |
| 873 | Ilkley to Addingham, Bolton Abbey, Strid Wood & Skipton | Sun & bank hols 3/day | Keighley/DBus |
| 874 | Acomb to Buckden via Leeds, Otley, Ilkley, Addingham, Bolton Abbey, Strid Wood, Burnsall, Grassington, Threshfield, Kilnsey & Kettlewell | summer Sun & bank hols 2/day, winter 1/day plus 1/day Ilkley to Buckden | YP/DBus |
| 875 | Leeds to Ilkley, Grassington, Kilnsey, Kettlewell & Buckden | summer Sun & bank hols 1/day | First Leeds/DBus |
| 884 | Bradford to Malham via Ilkley, Addingham & Skipton | Sun & bank hols 1/day | DBus |
| | Ilkley to Skipton via Addingham & Draughton | winter Sun 2/day | |
| 962 | Otley circular route via Burley, Ben Rhydding station & Ilkley | Mon-Sat 1/hr | Keighley |
| 72 | Skipton to Grassington via Threshfield | daily 7-9/day | Keighley |
| 72A | Skipton to Buckden via Starbotton, Grassington, Threshfield, Kilnsey & Kettlewell | Mon-Fri 1/day term-time only | NYCC |
| 72B | Grassington to Buckden via Starbotton, Kilnsey & Kettlewell | Sat 3-5/day | UWV |
| 74 | Ilkley to Addingham, Bolton Abbey, Strid Wood, Barden, Burnsall & Grassington | summer Sat 4/day | First Leeds |

| | | | |
|---|---|---|---|
| 74A | Ilkley to Grassington/Hebden via Addingham, Bolton Abbey, Barden, Strid Wood, Appletreewick, Burnsall & Threshfield | Mon, Wed & Fri 2/day (1/day continues to **Hebden**) | NYCC |
| S1 | Dent village to **Kendal** via **Sedbergh**, Killington (M6 bridge) & Oxenholme Lake District station | Sat 3/day plus 1/day Kendal via **Cowgill** & 1/day to Sedbergh via **Cowgill** | WDCB |
| S3 | Dent to Hawes via **Sedbergh** & Garsdale (Hawes Hopper) | Wed only 3/day (June to late Oct) | WDCB |
| S4 | Dent to Brough via **Sedbergh** & Kirkby Stephen | Tue & Thur 1/day, Fri 2/day plus 1/day from Sedbergh | WDCB |
| W1 | **Sedbergh** to Kendal via Oxenholme Lake District | Mon–Fri 2/day | WoS |
| 6 | Barrow-in-Furness to **Windermere railway station** via Bowness-on-Windermere (**Bowness Pier**) | Mon–Sat 4/day, Sun 3/day | Stagecoach |
| X6 | Barrow-in-Furness to **Kendal** | Mon–Sat 1/hr, Sun 4/day | Stagecoach |
| 45 | Strickandgate to **Kendal** via Burneside | Mon–Sat 8-9/day | Stagecoach |
| 508 | Penrith to Bowness & Windermere | Easter to Oct daily 6-7/day | Stagecoach |
| 525 | **Ferry House** to Hawkshead (see p46 & p50 for details of Cross Lakes Shuttle from Bowness to Ferry House) | Mar–Oct 8-10/day | Mountain Goat |
| 555 | Lancaster to Keswick via **Kendal, Staveley, Windermere, Bowness Pier** & Grasmere | Mon–Sat 1-2/hr plus three evening services to Grasmere and two to Kendal, Sun Kendal to Keswick 1/hr and Lancaster to Kendal 5/day | Stagecoach |
| 599 | **Bowness Pier** to Grasmere via **Windermere railway station** & Ambleside daily 2-3/hr (in the morning services start at Kendal and in the evening they continue to Kendal, 5-6/day) | | Stagecoach |
| 755 | Morecambe to **Bowness Pier** via Carnforth, **Kendal** & **Windermere railway station** | daily (inc public holidays) 3/day plus 1/day to Kendal | Stagecoach |

**CONTACTS** CB (Connexions Buses; ☎ 01423 339600, ▣ connexionsbuses.com), operated by Harrogate Coach Travel (HCT); **DBus** (Dales Bus; ▣ dalesbus.org); **First Leeds** (▣ firstgroup.com/leeds); **Keighley** (☎ 01535 603284, ▣ transdevbus.co.uk/keighley); **Mountain Goat** (☎ 015394 45161, ▣ mountain-goat.co.uk); **NYCC** (North Yorkshire County Council; ▣ northyorks.gov.uk/public-transport); **Stagecoach** (▣ stagecoachbus.com); **UWV** (Upper Wharfedale Venturer; ▣ vetch.co.uk/uw_bus/index.htm); **WoS** (Woofs of Sedbergh; ☎ 015396 20414, ▣ woofsofsedbergh.co.uk); **WDCB** (Western Dales Community Bus ☎ 015396 20125, ▣ westerndalesbus.co.uk); **YP** (York Pullman (☎ 01904 622992, ▣ yorkpullmanbus.co.uk)

## LOCAL PUBLIC TRANSPORT SERVICES

Public transport is limited along the Dales Way but most villages have some sort of service. The problem is one of frequency – some of the bus services to the smaller villages operate only on certain days and not necessarily year-round. The important thing, therefore, is to plan meticulously; firstly, by using the summary of bus services on pp48-9 and the map on p47; then by checking to make sure the service is still operating. To check the current bus timetables, contact **traveline** (☎ 0871 200 2233, 🖳 traveline.info); this has public transport information for the whole of the UK and is usually easier than contacting the operator directly as many bus services are run by more than one operator.

**Cumbria County Council** website (🖳 cumbria.gov.uk/buses) has timetables of all their bus services for you to download, while for information about services in **North Yorkshire** visit 🖳 dalesbus.org, or 🖳 www.northyorks.gov .uk/public-transport.

PLANNING YOUR WALK

# 2

# MINIMUM IMPACT & OUTDOOR SAFETY

## Minimum impact walking

In this world in which people live their lives at an increasingly fre-
netic pace, many of us living in overcrowded cities and working in
jobs that offer little free time, the great outdoors is becoming an
essential means of escape. Walking in the countryside is a wonderful
means of relaxation and gives people the time to think. However, as
the popularity of the countryside increases so do the problems that
this pressure brings. It is important for visitors to remember that the
countryside is the home and workplace of many others.

By following a few simple guidelines while walking the Dales
Way you can have a positive impact, not just on your own well-being
but also on local communities and the environment, thereby becoming part of the solution.

### ENVIRONMENTAL IMPACT

A walking holiday in itself is an environmentally friendly approach
to tourism. The following are some ideas on how you can go a few
steps further in helping to minimise your impact on the environment
while walking the Dales Way.

#### Use public transport whenever possible
Public transport along the Dales Way is limited in parts and requires
planning. However, it is always preferable to using private cars as it
benefits everyone: visitors, locals and the environment.

#### Never leave litter
'Pack it in, pack it out'. Leaving litter is antisocial so carry a degradable plastic bag for all your rubbish, organic or otherwise, and even
other people's too, and pop it in a bin in the next village. Or better
still, reduce the amount of litter you take with you by getting rid of
packaging in advance.
● **Is it OK if it's biodegradable?**  Not really. Apple cores, banana
skins, orange peel and the like are unsightly, encourage flies, ants
and wasps, and ruin a picnic spot for others; they can also take
months to decompose.

Support local traders!

### Buy local

Look and ask for local produce to buy and eat. Not only does this cut down on the amount of pollution and congestion that the transportation of food creates – so-called 'food miles' – it also ensures that you are supporting local farmers and producers.

### Erosion

● **Stay on the main trail** The effect of your footsteps may seem minuscule but when multiplied by several thousand walkers each year they become rather more significant. Avoid taking shortcuts, widening the trail or taking more than one path, especially across hay meadows and ploughed fields.

● **Consider walking out of season** Maximum disturbance by walkers coincides with the time of year when nature wants to do most of its growth and repair. In high-use areas the trail is often prevented from recovering.

Walking at less busy times eases this pressure while also generating year-round income for the local economy. Not only that, but it may make the walk a more relaxing experience with fewer people on the path and less competition for accommodation.

### Respect all flora and fauna

Care for all wildlife you come across along the path; it has as much right to be there as you. Tempting as it may be to pick wild flowers, leave them so the next people who pass can enjoy them too. Don't break branches off trees.

If you come across wildlife keep your distance and don't watch for too long. Your presence can cause considerable stress, particularly if the adults are with young, or in winter when the weather is harsh and food is scarce. Young animals are rarely abandoned. If you come across young birds keep away so that their mother can return.

### The code of the outdoor loo

For all but a couple of stages, you really shouldn't get caught short and can wait for a toilet until the next town or village. But between Swarthghyll and Dentdale, and from Sedbergh to Burneside facilities are, admittedly, rather scarce (actually, they're non-existent) and for those sections the following advice should be heeded if you need to do something more than just wee. 'Going' in the outdoors is a lost art worth reclaiming, for your sake and everyone else's. As more and more people discover the joys of the outdoors this is becoming an important issue. In some parts of the world where visitor pressure is higher than in Britain, walkers and climbers are required to pack out their excrement. This might one day be necessary here. Human excrement is not only offensive to our senses but, more importantly, can infect water sources.

• **Where to go** If you do have to go outdoors, avoid ruins which can otherwise be welcome shelter for other walkers, as well as sites of historic or archaeological interest, and choose a place that is at least **30 metres away from running water**. Use a stick or trowel to **dig a small hole** about 15cm (6") deep to bury your excrement. It decomposes quicker when in contact with the top layer of soil or leaf mould. Stirring loose soil into your deposit speeds up decomposition. Do not squash it under rocks as this slows down the composting process. If you have to use rocks to cover it make sure they are not in contact with your faeces.

• **Toilet paper and tampons** Toilet paper takes a long time to decompose whether buried or not. It is easily dug up by animals and may then blow into water sources or onto the path.

The best method for dealing with it is to **pack it out**. Put the used paper inside a paper bag which you then place inside a plastic bag. Then simply empty the contents of the paper bag at the next toilet you come across and throw the bag away. Also pack out **tampons** and **sanitary towels**; they take years to decompose and may also be dug up and scattered about by animals.

## Wild camping

Wild camping is not encouraged within the national parks which make up the majority of the walk. This is a shame since wild camping is much more fulfilling than camping on a designated site. Living in the outdoors without any facilities provides a valuable lesson in simple, sustainable living where the results of all your actions, from going to the loo to washing your plates, can be seen.

If you do wild camp always ask the landowner for permission. In most cases this is, of course, completely impractical so don't camp on farmland at all, but out on the uncultivated moors or in forests, and stick by the following:

• **Be discreet** Camp alone or in small groups, spend only one night in each place, pitch your tent late and leave early.

• **Never light a fire** Accidental fire is a great fear for farmers and foresters. Never make a camp fire; take matches and cigarette butts out with you to dispose of safely. The deep burn caused by camp fires, no matter how small, damages turf which can take years to recover. Cook on a camping stove instead.

• **Don't use soap or detergent** There is no need to use soap; even biodegradable soaps and detergents pollute streams. You won't be away from a shower for more than a couple of days. Wash up without detergent; use a plastic or metal scourer, or failing that, a handful of fine pebbles or some bracken or grass.

• **Leave no trace** Endeavour to leave no sign of having been there: no moved boulders, ripped up vegetation or dug drainage ditches. Make a final check of your campsite before departing; pick up any litter leaving the place in the same state you found it in, or better.

## ACCESS

Britain is a crowded island with few places where you can wander as you please. Most of the land is a patchwork of fields and agricultural land and the terrain through which the Dales Way marches is no different. However, there are countless public rights of way, in addition to the official path, that criss-cross the land. This is fine, but what happens if you feel a little more adventurous and want to explore the moorland, woodland and hills that are near the walk?

## Right to roam

The Countryside & Rights of Way Act 2000 (CRoW), or 'Right to Roam' as dubbed by walkers, came into effect in 2005 after a long campaign to allow greater public access to areas of countryside in England and Wales deemed to be uncultivated open country; this essentially means moorland, heathland, downland and upland areas. Some land is covered by restrictions (ie high-impact activities such as driving a vehicle, cycling, horse-riding are not permitted) and some land is excluded (such as gardens, parks and cultivated land). Full details are given on 🖥 gov.uk/government/organisations/natural-england.

With more freedom in the countryside comes a need for more responsibility from the walker. Remember that wild open country is still the workplace of farmers and home to all sorts of wildlife. Have respect for both and avoid disturbing domestic and wild animals.

# Outdoor safety

## AVOIDANCE OF HAZARDS

With good planning and preparation most hazards can be avoided. This information is just as important for those out on a day walk as for those walking the entire Dales Way.

Always make sure you have suitable **clothing** (see p37) to keep warm and dry, whatever the conditions, and a change of inner clothes. Carrying plenty of food and water on those stages where eateries and shops are scarce is vital too. The **emergency signal** is six blasts on the whistle, or six flashes with a torch (flashlight), best done when you think someone might see or hear them.

## Safety on the Dales Way

It may be one of the shortest and easiest of the long-distance paths in Great Britain, but that doesn't mean that it's a completely 'safe path' – for no path can ever be said to be entirely danger-free. The most dangerous section is the stage between Buckden and Dentdale, where the elevation, comparative lack of signage and the sometimes inclement weather all combine to imperil walkers.

**Minimising the risks on the Dales Way** All rescue teams should be treated as very much the last resort and it's vital you take every precaution to ensure your own safety:

● Avoid walking on your own if possible.

● Always carry a torch, compass, map, whistle, mobile phone and wet-weather gear with you.

● Wear sturdy boots or trail shoes.

● Make sure that somebody knows your plans for every day that you're on the trail. This could be a friend or relative whom you have promised to call every night, or the place you plan to stay in at the end of each day's walk. That way, if you fail to turn up or call that evening, they can raise the alarm.

● Before you go, download and get to know the app **What3words** (💻 what3words.com). This app reduces the world to three-metre square areas, each with a unique three-word geocode so it makes it easy to tell people precisely where you are.

● If the weather closes in suddenly and mist descends while you're on the trail, particularly on the moors or fells, and you become uncertain of the correct trail, do not be tempted to continue. Just wait where you are and you'll find that mist often clears, at least for long enough to allow you to get your bearings. If you're

---

❏ **DEALING WITH AN ACCIDENT/EMERGENCY**

If you find yourself in an emergency situation anywhere on the fells, the procedure should be the same: dial ☎ 999, ask for the police and ask them to connect you with Mountain Rescue. For most of the Dales Way, it will be the Upper Wharfedale Fell Rescue Association (UWFRA, 💻 uwfra.org.uk) who will come to your aid. They cover a wide area of the Dales including Nidderdale, Littondale and Mid-Airedale, as well as Wharfedale itself. Based in Grassington, they are called out for a variety of incidents from fell walkers with broken ankles to potholers who have become lost underground.

All the people who work for UWFRA, which operates 24 hours a day, 365 days a year, are volunteers and the association itself is a charitable body relying entirely on donations for their survival.

● Use basic first aid to treat the injury to the best of your ability.

● Work out exactly where you are. If possible leave someone with the casualty while others go to get help. If there are only two people, you have a dilemma. If you decide to get help leave all spare clothing and food with the casualty.

● In an emergency dial ☎ 999 (or the EU standard number ☎ 112). Don't assume your mobile won't work up on the fells. However, before you call try to work out exactly where you are, perhaps using the app What3words (💻 what3words.com – see above) if you have a phone signal.

still uncertain, and the weather does not look like improving, return the way you came to the nearest point of civilisation.
● Fill up with water at every opportunity and carry some high-energy snacks.
● Be extra vigilant if walking with children.

## WEATHER FORECASTS

It's only sensible to try to find out what the weather is going to be like before you set off for the day, especially if heading between Buckden and Dentdale where chances to call for help are limited. Many hostels and tourist information centres will have pinned up somewhere a summary of the weather forecast.

The **Mountain Weather Information Service** (🖥 mwis.org.uk) gives detailed online forecasts for the upland regions of Britain including the Lake District and Yorkshire Dales. Online weather forecasts are also available at 🖥 bbc.co.uk/weather or 🖥 metoffice.gov.uk. Pay close attention to the forecast and consider altering your plans accordingly. That said, even if a fine sunny day is forecast, always assume the worst and pack some wet-weather gear.

## BLISTERS

It's essential to try out new boots before embarking on your long trek. Make sure they're comfortable and once on the move try to avoid getting them wet on the inside and remove small stones or twigs that get in the boot. Air and massage your feet at lunchtime, keep them clean, and change your socks regularly. As soon as you start to feel any hot spots developing, stop and apply a few strips of low-friction zinc oxide tape. Leave it on until your foot is pain free or the tape starts to come off. As you're walking continuously the chances are it won't get better, but it won't get worse so quickly. If you know you have problems apply the tape pre-emptively.

If you've left it too late and a blister has developed you should apply a plaster such as Compeed (or the slightly cheaper clone now made by Boots). Many walkers have Compeed to thank for enabling them to complete their walk; they can last for up to two days even when wet and comprise a gel pad and a slippery outer surface. Popping a blister reduces the pressure but can lead to infection. If the skin is broken keep the area clean with antiseptic and cover with a non-adhesive dressing material held in place with tape.

Blister-avoiding strategies include rubbing the prone area with Vaseline or wearing a thin and a thick sock as well as adjusting the tension of your laces. All are ways of reducing rubbing and foot movement against the inside of your boot.

## HYPOTHERMIA, HYPERTHERMIA & SUNBURN

Also known as exposure, **hypothermia** occurs when the body can't generate enough heat to maintain its normal temperature, usually as a result of being wet, cold, unprotected from the wind, tired and hungry. It's usually more of a problem in upland areas such as in the Lakes and on the fells.

Hypothermia is easily avoided by wearing suitable clothing, carrying and consuming enough food and drink, being aware of the weather conditions and checking the morale of your companions. Early signs to watch for are feeling cold and tired with involuntary shivering. Find some shelter as soon as possible and warm the victim up with a hot drink and some chocolate or other high-energy food. If possible give them another warm layer of clothing and allow them to rest until feeling better. If allowed to worsen, erratic behaviour, slurring of speech and poor co-ordination will become apparent and the victim can very soon progress into unconsciousness, followed by coma and death. Quickly get the victim out of wind and rain, improvising a shelter if necessary.

Rapid restoration of bodily warmth is essential and best achieved by bare-skin contact: someone should get into the same sleeping bag as the patient, both having stripped to the bare essentials, placing any spare clothing under or over them to build up heat. Send or call urgently for help.

Not an ailment that you would normally associate with the north of England, **hyperthermia** (heat exhaustion and heatstroke) is a serious problem nonetheless. Symptoms of **heat exhaustion** include thirst, fatigue, giddiness, a rapid pulse, raised body temperature, low urine output and, if not treated, delirium and finally a coma. The best cure is to drink plenty of water. **Heatstroke** is another matter altogether and even more serious. A high body temperature and an absence of sweating are early indications, followed by symptoms similar to hypothermia (see opposite) such as a lack of co-ordination, convulsions and coma. Death will follow if treatment is not given instantly. Sponge the victim down, wrap them in wet towels, fan them, and get help immediately.

**Sunburn** can happen, even in northern England and even on overcast days. The best way to avoid sunburn – and the extra risk of developing skin cancers that sunburn brings – is to keep your skin covered at all times in light, loose-fitting clothing, and to cover any exposed areas of skin in sunscreen (with a minimum factor of 30). Sunscreen should be applied regularly throughout the day. Don't forget your lips, nose, ears and the back of your neck, and even under your chin to protect you against rays reflected from the ground. Most importantly of all, always wear a hat!

## COLLAPSE OF MORALE

This is not something that can be quickly treated with medication, but is probably the biggest cause of abandoned attempts on the Dales Way. Weather and injury which add up to exhaustion might be presumed to be the most common culprit, but plenty manage the walk in monsoonal conditions and hobble into Bowness-on-Windermere with a great experience behind them. Others though, can suddenly think: 'What's the point, I'm not enjoying this'.

Avoiding a premature end to your trek boils down this: knowing your limitations and addressing your motivation; matching expectations with your companions; avoiding putting yourself under stress and being flexible rather than insisting on hammering out every last mile without repetition, hesitation or deviation. You can add having good equipment to that list too.

# 3

# THE ENVIRONMENT & NATURE

## Conserving the Dales Way

That the Dales Way is such a beautiful walk is not entirely down to luck. Over the past 50 years, while the predations of the modern world continue to gobble up significant swathes of this sceptered isle, various enlightened agencies and organisations have been established to ensure parts of this country, at least, remain as green and pleasant as William Blake promised.

### GOVERNMENT AGENCIES AND SCHEMES

#### Natural England

The main government body charged with preserving the beauty, diversity, flora and fauna of this country is Natural England. It is this body that decides if a location is worthy of protection and what that level of protection should be. For example, it is Natural England who decides whether a long-distance path is worthy of being afforded the status of National Trail (and thus presumably is the body that, surprisingly, considers that the Dales Way *isn't* worthy of National Trail status!). It is also the agency that determines whether an area is worth being considered a National Park, an Area of Outstanding Natural Beauty, a National Nature Reserve, or a Site of Special Scientific Interest.

Which is all well and good – but what exactly do these designations mean? Well, the highest level of landscape protection is the designation of land as a **national park** which recognises the national importance of an area in terms of landscape, biodiversity and as a recreational resource. At the time of writing there were ten national parks in England. Two of these are visited by the Dales Way: the Yorkshire Dales and Lake District national parks. Indeed, most of your time on the Dales Way is spent within these two national parks. This designation does not signify national ownership and these are not uninhabited wildernesses, making conservation a knife-edged balance between protecting the environment and the rights and livelihoods of those living in the parks.

The second level of protection is **area of outstanding natural beauty (AONB)**. The only AONB visited by the Dales Way is Nidderdale AONB, which you enter – briefly – at the very start of the walk between Ilkley and Bolton Abbey. The primary objective for an AONB is conservation of the natural beauty of a landscape. As there is no statutory administrative framework for their management, this is the responsibility of the local authority within whose boundaries they fall.

**National nature reserves (NNRs)** are places where the priority is protection of the wildlife habitats and geological formations. There are currently 224 in England (including Ingleborough, one of Yorkshire Dale National Park's so-called 'Three Peaks') and they are either owned or managed by Natural England or by approved organisations such as wildlife trusts. (**Local nature reserves** are places with wildlife or geological features that are of special interest to local inhabitants; they are designated by local councils and there are nine in Cumbria and 17 in North Yorkshire, though none is on the trail.)

**Sites of Special Scientific Interest (SSSIs)** range in size from little pockets protecting wild flower meadows, nesting sites or special geological features, to vast swathes of upland, moorland and wetland. SSSIs, of which there are currently over 4000 in England, covering about 8% of the country, are a particularly important designation as they have some legal standing. Owners and occupiers of SSSI land must give written notice before initiating any operations likely to damage the site and cannot proceed without consent from Natural England. Many SSSIs are also either a NNR or a LNR.

The region in which you'll be walking is littered with SSSIs though it seems the Dales Way takes a perverse delight in avoiding them wherever possible. That said, several are visited on the way: Strid Wood (renowned for its oaks) on the first stage north of Bolton Abbey; Bastow Wood, north of Grassington (which overlies an old Celtic field system); River Wharfe, and the

❑ **STATUTORY BODIES**
● **Department for Environment, Food and Rural Affairs** (🖳 gov.uk/defra) Government ministry responsible for sustainable development in the countryside.
● **Natural England** (🖳 gov.uk/government/organisations/natural-england) See opposite.
● **Historic England** (🖳 historicengland.org.uk) Created in April 2015 as a result of dividing the work done by English Heritage (see p61). Historic England is the government department responsible for looking after and promoting England's historic environment and is in charge of the listing system, giving grants and dealing with planning matters.
● **Forestry England** (🖳 forestryengland.uk) Custodian of the nation's public forests.
● **National Association of Areas of Outstanding Natural Beauty** (🖳 www.landscapesforlife.org.uk); for further information on North Pennines AONB visit 🖳 northpennines.org.uk.
● **Lake District National Park Authority** (🖳 lakedistrict.gov.uk) and **Yorkshire Dales National Park Authority** (🖳 yorkshiredales.org.uk). The government authorities charged with managing theses parks; they might be worth contacting to find out the latest developments to the path.

adjacent Upper Wharfedale, both north of Kettlewell; Yockenthwaite Meadows, west of Hubberholme; Deepdale Meadows, Langstrothdale; Oughtershaw and Beckermonds, both west of Deepdale Bridge; Upper Dentdale Cave System; River Kent and its tributaries (a good spot for crayfish, apparently); and High Lickbarrow Mires and Pasture, just before Bowness.

Separately, there's the **Special Area of Conservation** (SAC), an international designation which came into being as a result of the 1992 Earth Summit in Rio de Janeiro, Brazil. This European-wide network of sites is designed to promote the conservation of habitats, wild animals and plants, both on land and at sea. Every land SAC is also an SSSI.

## CAMPAIGNING AND CONSERVATION ORGANISATIONS

Voluntary organisations started the conservation movement in the mid 19th century and are still at the forefront of developments. Independent of government but reliant on public support, they can concentrate their resources either on acquiring land which can then be managed purely for conservation purposes, or on influencing political decision-makers by lobbying and campaigning.

Managers and owners of land include well-known bodies such as the following organisations. The **Royal Society for the Protection of Birds** (RSPB; 🖳 rspb.org.uk) has over 150 nature reserves and more than a million members. The **National Trust** (NT; 🖳 nationaltrust.org.uk), a charity with over three million members, aims to protect, through ownership, threatened coastline, countryside, historic houses, castles and gardens, and archaeological remains for

---

❏ **CONSERVATION AREAS**

While the schemes mentioned in this section have all been introduced to preserve the natural glories of the UK, there is also a Conservation Areas programme (🖳 historic england.org.uk/advice/hpg/has/conservation-areas). This scheme was actually introduced way back in 1967 to protect the 'man-made' features of the country. Defined as 'an area of special architectural interest, the character or appearance of which it is desirable to preserve or enhance', there are some 8000 Conservation Areas in England covering everything from registered parks and gardens to scheduled monuments, old wreck sites and listed buildings. There are a total of 37 conservation areas in Yorkshire Dales National Park, and the Dales Way is unusual in that it passes through 11 of them: Bolton Abbey, Appletreewick, Burnsall, Hebden, Grassington, Kettlewell, Starbotton, Buckden, Hubberholme, Dent and Sedbergh. The Settle-Carlisle Railway is also protected under the scheme.

As you pass through these areas you'll struggle to see any significant sign that they are part of any conservation programme, though it's undeniable that they are very pretty. But in these conservation areas the locals are required to seek permission if they want to fell, or even prune, a tree; permission may also be required to modify the exterior appearance of a building, eg by fixing a satellite dish or changing the windows. In spite of these limitations on what a property owner can do, surveys suggest that residents actually enjoy living within a conservation area, and property prices, which are usually higher than similar properties outside these areas, are further evidence of this.

everyone to enjoy. On the Dales Way, the NT's only property is quite an important one: the Upper Wharfe valley, which you'll march through for much of the second and third stages.

Often seeming to overlap the work of the National Trust, **English Heritage** (🖥 english-heritage.org.uk) actually looks after, champions and advises the government on historic buildings and places, whereas the National Trust focuses more on country houses. However, in April 2015 English Heritage was divided into two parts: a new charitable trust that retains the name English Heritage and a non-departmental public body, Historic England (see box p59).

**CPRE The Countryside Charity** (🖥 cpre.org.uk; formerly Campaign for the Protection of Rural England) exists to promote the beauty and diversity of rural England by encouraging the sustainable use of land and other natural resources in both town and country. Their valuable work is supplemented by the **Woodland Trust** (🖥 woodlandtrust.org.uk), which restores woodland throughout Britain for its 'amenity, wildlife and landscape value'.

As for the fauna, the umbrella organisation for the 47 wildlife trusts in the UK is **The Wildlife Trusts** (🖥 wildlifetrusts.org); two relevant to the Dales Way are **Yorkshire Wildlife Trust** (🖥 ywt.org.uk) and **Cumbria Wildlife Trust** (🖥 cumbriawildlifetrust.org.uk).

# Flora and fauna

From woodland and grassland to heathland and bog, the variety of habitats one encounters on the Dales Way is surpassed only by the number of species of flower, tree and animal that each supports.

The following is not in any way a comprehensive guide; if it were, this book would be so big you would not have room for anything else in your rucksack. Instead, it's merely a brief guide to the more commonly seen flora and fauna of the trail, together with some of the rarer and more spectacular species.

## TREES

There's some terrific woodland in Wharfedale. The most memorable that's actually along the path is, of course, Strid Wood, a large area of acidic oak woodland. Elsewhere, the limestone woodlands of Wharfedale, which are characterised by trees such as ash (*Fraxinus excelsior*), downy birch, hazel, hawthorn (*Crategus monogyna*) and rowan (*Sorbus aucuparia*) – several of which have been planted at Little Towne (see p134) – tend to dominate.

The tree most associated with the River Wharfe is the **willow** (*Salix*) and a number of varieties survive along the river's banks including the **weeping willow** (*Salix sepulcralis*), **white willow** (*Salix alba*), which can be easily identified by its long and narrow leaves which taper to curled tips and are hairy underneath, and the **crack willow** (*Salix fragilis*), with its bright green leaves.

## MAMMALS

For much of its length the Dales Way is a riverside walk, whether accompanied by the Wharfe, the Dee, the Lune or one of their minor tributaries. So in addition to the usual wildlife you'll see on most long-distance paths – the rabbits, foxes, badgers, deers and hares – you'll also find some more unusual creatures.

Most prized amongst trekkers would be a sighting of the rarely glimpsed and charismatic **otter** (*Lutra lutra*). This sleek and graceful beast is actually enjoying something of a revival thanks to concerted conservation efforts and, though more common in the south-west, otters are still present in the north of England. In addition to being mesmerising to watch, they are also a good indicator of a healthy unpolluted environment. Don't come to the north expecting otter sightings every day though – indeed, if you see one at all you should consider yourself *extremely* fortunate, for they remain rare and very elusive. There are said to be some by Birks Bridge near Sedbergh but they've also been seen as far downstream as Addingham.

Even rarer than the otter, the **water vole** (*Arvicola amphibius*) is England's fastest disappearing mammal thanks in large part to the predations of the introduced American mink, small enough to squeeze through the entrance of a water vole's burrow. A concerted conservation campaign is underway to improve the vole's chances of survival but they remain rare and unless you're very lucky you'll have to content yourself with views of their burrows on the riverbank.

Away from the river but just as rare, the Yorkshire Dales provide one of the last wild sanctuaries for the **red squirrel** (*Sciurus vulgaris*). While elsewhere in the country these small, tufty-eared natives have been usurped by their larger cousins from North America, the **grey squirrel** (*Sciurus carolinensis*), in the Dales the red squirrel maintains a precarious foothold. Your best bet for seeing one is to visit Kilnsey Trout Farm, near Conistone, over a mile off the path, where a protected population thrives.

One creature that you will see everywhere along the walk is the **rabbit** (*Oryctolagus cuniculus*). Timid by nature, most of the time you'll have to make do with nothing more than a brief and distant glimpse of their white tails as they stampede for the nearest warren at the first sound of your footfall. Because they are so numerous, however, the laws of probability dictate that you will at some stage get close enough to observe them without being spotted; trying to take a decent photo of one, however, is a different matter.

If you're lucky you may also come across **hares**, often mistaken for rabbits but much larger, more elongated and with longer back legs and ears.

---

### ❏ LAMBING

Lambing takes place from mid March to mid May when dogs should not be taken along the path. Even a dog secured on a lead can disturb a pregnant ewe.

If you see a lamb or ewe that appears to be in distress contact the nearest farmer. Also, be aware of cows with calves.

Rabbits and hares used to form one of the main elements in the diet of the **fox** (*Vulpes vulpes*), one of the more adaptable of Britain's native species. Famous as the scourge of chicken coops, their reputation as indiscriminate killers is actually unjustified: though they will if left undisturbed kill all the chickens in a coop in what appears to be a mindless and frenzied attack, foxes will actually eat all their victims, carrying off and storing the carcasses in underground burrows for them and their families to eat at a later date. These days, however, you are far more likely to see foxes in towns, where they survive mostly on the scraps and leftovers of the human population, rather than in the country. While generally considered nocturnal, it's not unusual to encounter a fox during the day too, often lounging in the sun near its den.

One creature that is strictly nocturnal, however, is the **bat**, of which there are 17 species in Britain, all protected by law. Your best chance of spotting one is just after dusk while there's still enough light in the sky to make out their flitting forms as they fly along hedgerows, over rivers and streams and around street lamps in their quest for moths and insects. The most common species in Britain is the pipistrelle (*Pipistrellus pipistrellus*).

The **badger** (*Meles meles*) is relatively common throughout the British Isles. These nocturnal mammals with their distinctive black-and-white-striped muzzles are sociable animals that live in large underground burrows called setts, appearing after sunset to root for worms and slugs.

In addition to the above, keep a look out for other fairly common but little-seen species such as the carnivorous **stoat** (*Mustela erminea*), its smaller cousin the **weasel** (*Mustela nivalis*), the **hedgehog** (*Erinaceus europaeus*) – these days, alas, most commonly seen as roadkill – and a number of species of **voles**, **mice** and **shrews**.

Some walkers are lucky enough to encounter deer. Mostly this will be the **roe deer** (*Capreolus capreolus*), a small native species that likes to inhabit woodland, though some can also be seen grazing in fields. Britain's largest native land mammal, the **red deer** (*Cervus elaphus*), is rarely seen on the walk though it does exist in small pockets around the Lakes. As with most creatures, your best chance of seeing one is very early in the morning or late in the evening.

## PLANTS AND FLOWERS

The river is imperative to the life of the local flora and many plants and wild-flowers abound along the banks and in the meadows which often line the Wharfe.

### By the river
Perhaps the two most striking plant species that you'll come across time and again on your riparian ramble are both non-native. The giant-leaved **gunnera** (*Gunnera manicata*) thrives by rivers and in marshy places where they grow in large colonies, often to the exclusion of other plants. And then there's the incredibly prolific pink-flowered **himalayan balsam** (*Impatiens glandulifera*),

which is actually a member of the busy lizzy family. You may not be particularly enamoured with the way this tall, aggressive foreign invader has monopolised many a prime riverside site at the expense of the less rapacious native wildflowers but you do have to admit it puts on a lovely display.

Even in the relatively few places where balsam hasn't managed to gain a foothold, the riverbanks are still a riot of colour, provided by, amongst others, the **yellow iris** (*Iris pseudacorus*), the pink flowers of the flowering **rush** (*Butomus*), the lilac of **water violet** (*Hottonia palustris*) and an abundance of white-flowered **water crowfoot** (*Ranunculus aquatilis*).

You should also see the reddish stem and fluffy pink flowers of **hemp-agrimony** (*Eupatorium cannabinum*), while below them reside the dark green kidney-shaped leaves of **marsh marigold** (*Caltha palustris*), the blue petals of water **forget-me-nots** (*Myosotis scorpioides*) and the floating oval leaves of yellow water-lilies (*Nymphaea lutea*) – a good sign of nutrient-rich water.

## Meadows, woodland and moorland

Perhaps the most famous and one of the rarest flowers of the Dales – indeed, it's almost become its emblem – is the **bird's-eye primrose** (*Primula farinosa*). Flourishing in June in soggy grassland, this beautiful flower, taller (at 3-20cm in height) than the more common, yellow, ground-hugging primroses, with pinky-lilac petals surrounding a yellow 'eye' – hence the name – is native to the north of England, with its biggest population in the Dales. Occasionally they can still be seen in Wharfedale though they no longer flourish where the ground has been drained or fertiliser has been used.

The **common rock-rose** (*Helianthemum nummularium*) is an evergreen trailing plant with bright yellow flowers which the Northern Brown Argus (see p65) butterfly finds irresistible.

Synonymous with spring and the start of the walking season are **bluebells** (*Hyacinthoides non-scripta*), the bluish-purple bell-shaped flowers of which adorn the woodland and hedgerows. Appearing at a similar time of year are **cowslips** (*Primula veris*), **cuckooflower** (*Cardamine pratensis*), aka Lady's Smock, and meadow **buttercups** (*Ranunculuc acris*). The latter can grow up to one metre in height.

By June the pinkish-lilac petals of the **common valerian** (*Valeriana officinalis*) should be on display in the meadows, as should yellow-centred white petaled **oxeye daisies** (*Leucanthemum vulgare*), the purple florets of **common** (*Centaurea nigra*) and **greater knapweed** (*Centaurea scabiosa*), **bird's foot trefoil** (*Lotus corniculatus*), the tall and fragrant **meadowsweet** (*Filipendula ulmaria*), the golden-yellow **lady's bedstraw** (*Galium verum*), and the highly poisonous bright yellow flowers of the invasive **common ragwort** (*Senecio jacobaea*), which, sensibly avoided by grazing animals, thrives, particularly in pastures.

Britain's rarest native orchid, the **lady's slipper orchid** (*Cypripedium Calceolus*), which was thought extinct until a single plant was discovered in 1930 growing in Yorkshire, has now found a home at Kilnsey Park Estate (see p106), below the path near Conistone. There is rumoured to be one still growing

Foxglove
*Digitalis purpurea*

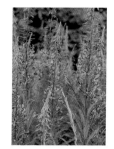

Rosebay Willowherb
*Epilobium angustifolium*

Himalayan Balsam
*Impatiens glandulifera*

Common Vetch
*Vicia sativa*

Harebell
*Campanula rotundifolia*

Red Campion
*Silene dioica*

Lousewort
*Pedicularis sylvatica*

Meadow Cranesbill
*Geranium pratense*

Common Dog Violet
*Viola riviniana*

Wood Sorrel
*Oxalis acetosella*

Heather (Ling)
*Calluna vulgaris*

Bell Heather
*Erica cinerea*

Common Ragwort
*Senecio jacobaea*

Hemp-nettle
*Galeopsis speciosa*

Cowslip
*Primula veris*

Gorse
*Ulex europaeus*

Meadow Buttercup
*Ranunculus acris*

Marsh Marigold (Kingcup)
*Caltha palustris*

Bird's-foot trefoil
*Lotus corniculatus*

St John's Wort
*Hypericum perforatum*

Tormentil
*Potentilla erecta*

Primrose
*Primula vulgaris*

Yellow Rattle
*Rhinanthus minor*

Honeysuckle
*Lonicera periclymemum*

Common Knapweed
*Centaurea nigra*

Yarrow
*Achillea millefolium*

Hogweed
*Heracleum sphondylium*

Rowan (tree)
*Sorbus aucuparia*

Dog Rose
*Rosa canina*

Forget-me-not
*Myosotis arvensis*

Water Avens
*Geum rivale*

Herb-Robert
*Geranium robertianum*

Common Centaury
*Centaurium erythraea*

Ramsons (Wild Garlic)
*Allium ursinum*

Bluebell
*Hyacinthoides non-scripta*

Ox-eye Daisy
*Leucanthemum vulgare*

in the wild; but should you by some miracle stumble upon it, note that it is illegal to even touch this plant, while trying to dig it up and steal it could leave you facing a six-month jail sentence!

Perhaps the most spectacular display by any flower, however, is one that you will usually see from a distance. In August the **heather** (*Calluna vulgaris*) comes into bloom, leaving the top of the fells ablaze with colour. It's a wonderful sight.

## BUTTERFLIES

The meadows and waterside pathways of the Dales Way are rich in many species, even though, for many of the UK's native species, the Yorkshire Dales is pretty much at the northernmost extremity of their distribution.

The only rarity of the UK's 54 or so native species that has found a home in Wharfedale is the **Northern Brown Argus** (*Aricia artaxerxes*) which can be seen mainly in June and particularly in Grassington and Upper Wharfedale where its food-plant, the rock-rose, grows.

That said, many of the species in the Dales are thriving and some previously unseen species are moving into the Dales, such as the speckled wood and ringlet (*Aphantopus hyperantus*), which have become abundant as the climate warms. Walking in September, the most common species you're likely to see are the **small tortoiseshell** (*Aglais urticae*), **large** and **small white** (aka **cabbage white**; *Pieris brassicae/Pieris rapae*) and the **red admiral** (*Vanessa atalanta*). Arrive in early spring and the species you're most likely to see is the aptly named **orange tip** (*Anthocharis cardamines*).

Other common species include the **small copper** (*Lycaena phlaeas*), **comma** (*Polygonia c-album* – look for the obvious white comma shape on the underwing), gorgeous **peacock** (*Aglais io*) and the plain but plentiful **meadow brown** (*Maniola jurtina*).

## INSECTS

Of course, whilst you walk, head deep in England's history or dizzy from another spell of meandering, there is another world in existence all about you: that of the insect.

Whizzing past your ears on the riverbank is the **dragonfly** (*Anisoptera*) and the smaller **damselfly** (*Zygoptera*), amongst them the brilliant-green **banded demoiselle** (*Calopteryx splendens*), and the rare and relatively slow flying **club-tailed dragonfly** (*Gomphus vulgatissimus*). Also airborne are the splendidly named **marmalade hoverfly** (*Episyrphus balteatus*), the amber-winged

**(Opposite)** **Top and bottom**: Much of this walk is through or near farming communities and you'll attract friendly interest from most of the locals, which include Highland cattle and Dalesbred sheep. Keep your dog on a lead near livestock (© Henry Stedman).
**Middle left**: Small Tortoiseshell butterfly (*Aglais urticae*) on a thistle (© Henry Stedman).
**Middle right**: Red Admiral butterfly (*Vanessa atalanta*) on Hemp Agrimony (*Eupatorium cannabinum*; © Jane Thomas).

THE ENVIRONMENT & NATURE

brown hawker (*Aeshna grandis*), **mayfly** (*Ephemeroptera*), and the obligatory bees and wasps.

Meanwhile, on the ground you may come across one of the 70 species of **longhorn beetle** (*Cerambycidae*) native to Britain, the yellow and black **Cinnabar caterpillar** (*Tyria jacobaeae*) and **yellow meadow ants** (*Lasius flavus*).

The singing of grasshoppers and crickets is ubiquitous in summer; those you'll possibly see springing about in the grass include meadow grasshoppers (*Chorthippus parallelus*), **field grasshoppers** (*Chorthippus brunneus*) and **Roesel's Bush crickets** (*Metrioptera roeseli*).

## BIRDS

One of the most exciting sights on the Dales Way is watching a **kingfisher** (*Alcedo atthis*) flit across the water. Usually all you'll get is a brief glimpse of its dazzling iridescent blue and gold plumage as it crosses the Wharfe from one perch to another, but occasionally, particularly in the evenings, one can take a seat on the riverbank and watch as it hunts for fish, plunging under the water to emerge a fraction of a second later with a beak full of fish.

The **dipper** (*Cinclus cinclus*) is the kingfisher's rotund, monochromatic cousin, often swooping above the water in a similar fashion though without some of the agility and with none of the colour of the king.

Another bird you'll see on the Wharfe is the **heron** (*Ardea Cinerea*), an elegant, angular, grey bird with a sinewy neck. Often spied standing motionless in the river's shallows, though sometimes, particularly near the source of the Wharfe by Beckermonds, you'll find them surveying the land from the top of one of the old stone barns, like a feathered weather vane.

Other water birds that occasionally pop up on the trail to say hello are the **goosander** (*Mergus merganser*) which, with their tufted crest and slightly wild, staring eyes, always look slightly unhinged.

More familiar waterfowl that you'll probably encounter along the way include the **swan**, usually the mute version (*Cygnus olor*) – orange beak, prominent black nob on the forehead – though occasionally the odd **whooper swan** (*Cygnus cygnus*) may land (long, wedge-shaped yellow beak, occasionally brown-stained neck); it has perhaps separated from the main flock that usually winters around the Ouse Washes further east.

The only bird that can rival swans for pure whiteness is the **snow goose** (*Anser caerulescens*), sometimes seen downstream of the Crook of Lune Bridge. Ducks include the ubiquitous **mallard** (*Anas platyrhynchos*), **teal** (*Anas crecca*) and its close relative the **garganey** (*Anas querquedula*).

**LAPWING/PEEWIT**
L: 320MM/12.5"

THE ENVIRONMENT & NATURE

**BARN OWL**
L: 355MM/14"

Not strictly a water bird, though one you'll see frequently on the water's edge, is the elegant **wagtail**, both pied (*Motacilla alba yarrellii*) and grey (*Motacilla cinerea*), the latter's rather dull moniker failing to do justice to a beautiful, 'exotic' bird with a lovely yellow chest and a long, almost bird-of-Paradise tail. If you see a bird perched on a rock in the river or on the river's rocky shore with its tail twitching up and down you can be pretty sure it's a wagtail.

Birds of prey near the path include the commonly seen **kestrel** (*Falco tinnunculus*) and **buzzard** (*Buteo buteo*), as well as the much less-spotted, nocturnal **barn owl** (*Tyto alba*), **tawny** (*Strix aluco*) and little **owls** (*Athene noctua*).

One of the most common birds seen on the path, particularly in the latter half of the walk, is the **pheasant** (*Phasianus colchicus*). Ubiquitous on the moors, the male is distinctive thanks to his beautiful long, barred tail feathers, brown body and glossy green-black head with red at the side, while the female is a dull brown. Another way to distinguish them is by the distinctive strangulated hacking sound they make. Rather stupid, ungainly birds, they nevertheless have the capacity to scare the life out of walkers by flying up noisily from the long grass as you approach, their wings slapping together loudly as they fly off.

Another reasonably common sight on the fells of Yorkshire is the **lapwing** (*Vanellus vanellus*), also known as the **peewit**. Black and white with iridescent green upper parts and approximately the size of a pigeon or tern, the lapwing's most distinctive characteristic is the male's tumbling, diving, swooping flight pattern when disturbed, believed to be either a display to attract a female or an attempt to distract predators from its nest, which is built on the ground.

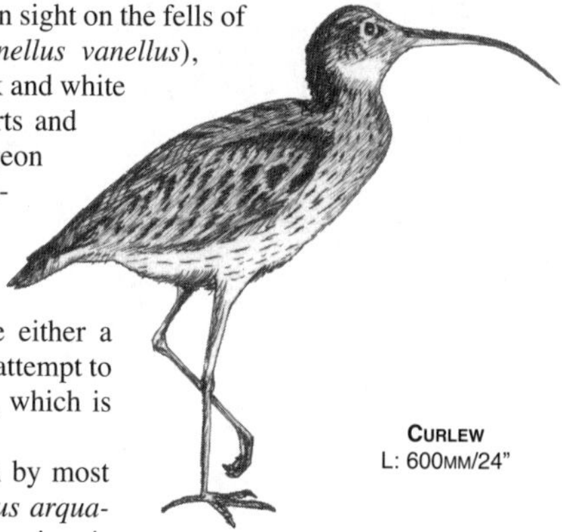

Less common but still seen by most walkers is the **curlew** (*Numenius arquata*), another bird that, like the lapwing, is

**CURLEW**
L: 600MM/24"

associated with coastal and open fields, moors and bogs. With feathers uniformly streaked grey and brown, the easiest way to identify this bird is by its thin elongated, downward curling beak. Both the lapwing and the curlew are actually wading birds that nest on the moors in the spring, but which winter by the coast.

Other birds that make their nest on open moorland and in fields include the **redshank** (*Tringa totanus*), **golden plover** (*Pluvialis apricaria*), **snipe** (*Gallinago gallinago*), **dunlin** (*Calidris alpina*) and **ring ouzel** (*Turdus torquatus*).

In the deciduous woodland areas on the trail, look out for **treecreepers** (*Certhia familiaris*), **tits** (family *Paridae*, including blue, coal, long-tailed and great), **nuthatches** (*Sitta europaea*), **pied flycatchers** (*Ficedula hypoleuca*) and **redstarts** (*Phoenicurus phoenicurus*), while in the conifers watch out for **crossbills** (*Loxia curvirostra*) and **siskins** (*Carduelis spinus*).

---

### ❏ BEWARE OF THE COW!

Most people are aware of the dangers of bulls – indeed, there are restrictions placed upon farmers who mustn't allow adult bulls to graze in fields that are crossed by a public right of way – but few people realise that cows can also be dangerous. Each year there are reports of people who have been attacked, or even trampled to death by cows. Between 2015-16 and 2019-20 the Health & Safety Executive investigated 142 incidents, 22 of which resulted in the death of a person. However, only four of these were walkers or other members of the public, the rest being farm workers.

Cows are particularly protective if there are young calves in the herd, but even without any calves around, a herd of cows can suddenly be spooked, either by a walker or, more likely, by a walker's dog. If you find yourself in a field of worryingly aggressive cattle, move away as carefully and quietly as possible, and if you feel threatened by them let go of your dog's lead and let it run free rather than try to protect it and risk endangering yourself. Your dog will outrun the cows. You might not be able to.

Those without canine companions should follow similar advice; move away calmly, do not panic and make no sudden noises. Chances are the cows will leave you alone once they establish that you pose no threat.

If you come to a field of cows with calves in the herd, think twice about crossing the field; if you can, go another way.

You can report incidents involving dangerous cattle at 🖳 killercows.co.uk.

# THE LINK ROUTES 4

## From Harrogate, Bradford or Leeds

The Dales Way runs for approximately 81 miles (130km) from Ilkley, just outside the southern border of the Yorkshire Dales National Park, to Bowness, just inside the eastern boundary of the Lake District National Park. Walk between those two points on the designated path and nobody can argue that you haven't completed the entire trail – and with a clear conscience you can get an 'I've done the Dales Way' certificate and, if you're feeling so inclined, can even wear a T-shirt emblazoned with a similar sentiment.

However, the Dales Way has also sprouted 'link' routes that head to Ilkley from the three main towns and cities nearest to it, namely Harrogate, Bradford and Leeds.

It's understandable to feel a bit suspicious of 'link routes' on national trails. You don't ask a marathon runner to run an extra couple of miles before they even get to the starting line so why ask someone on a long-distance path to cover even more mileage before hitting the trail proper? And you could argue that these link routes add nothing extra (other than mileage) to the 'proper' path. Scenery-wise, they bear little in common with the dramatic scenery of the trail itself, so on these link routes you could be forgiven for feeling like you're reading the prologue of one book, before putting that tome down and reading a completely separate novel. Furthermore, with Ilkley well supplied with pretty much every facility a trekker could want, and with a perfectly adequate train and bus service running between there and the three towns listed above, it's not as if these feeder routes provide the only link between the trail and 'civilisation'.

Anyway, it matters not, of course, whether anyone likes feeder routes or not; they are part of the Dales Way furniture and, as such, they need to be written about in a guidebook such as this one. And besides, according to the main founder of the Dales Way, Colin Speakman, they have existed for almost as long as the Way itself. In truth these three paths are not without their charms. So, having just spelled out why these routes may not appeal to everyone, in the interest of balance, the following goes some way to telling you what advantages these routes may bestow on those who do attempt them. For one thing, they will push you nearer to the magic 100-mile mark for the entire walk once you've completed the actual Dales Way – and in the case of the Leeds link, 21 miles (34km) long, over it.

*(cont'd on p72)*

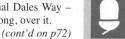

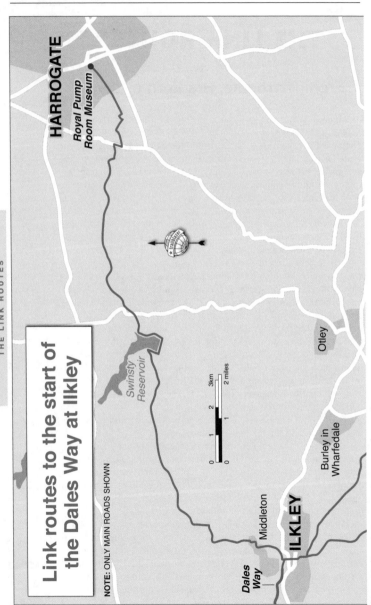

Link routes to the start of
the Dales Way at Ilkley

NOTE: ONLY MAIN ROADS SHOWN

HARROGATE

Royal Pump
Room Museum

Swinsty
Reservoir

Otley

Burley in
Wharfedale

Middleton

ILKLEY

Dales
Way

0    1    2    3km
0         1         2 miles

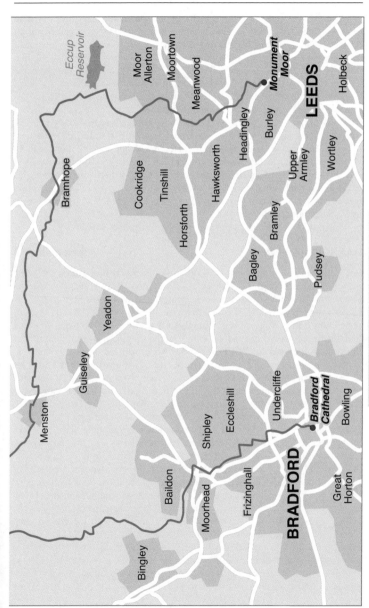

You do also get to see three of the more interesting cities and towns in England: bustling, lively Leeds; cosmopolitan (and surprisingly charming) Bradford; and the tourist magnet of Harrogate, a proud Victorian spa town and, according to more than one poll in the past few years, the 'happiest place to live in the UK'. If the 21-mile Leeds link is biting off more than you can chew, the link from nearby Bradford is much shorter at 12½ miles (20km).

Arguably the most enjoyable, however, is the Harrogate Link at 16½ miles (26.5km). It is the one trail which really stands out as a lovely walk in its own right, taking you as it does from the heart of Harrogate across the Nidderdale AONB – a region that seems so very much part of Yorkshire Dales National Park, and in terms of beauty stands comparison with any valley within the park, yet for some reason lies outside the park's borders. It is this route that is described in greater detail first in the section below, with the other two routes in much less detail afterwards. If you wish to undertake any of these link routes it is strongly advised that you get a copy of the relevant OS maps as indicated in the descriptions below.

See pp45-9 for details of rail and bus services to the various cities.

## HARROGATE LINK                                    [see map p70]

[see map p70]

For a thorough description of this **16½-mile (26.5km) link route**, including some excellent detailed 'Wainwright-style' hand-drawn maps, visit the **Harrogate Ramblers** website (🖳 harrogateramblers.org.uk). Note that this is actually the second link route from Harrogate, the first having been all but abandoned now due to rights of way issues – so if you're using old maps do check that it is the new route you're following. The relevant OS map you'll require for this route is Explorer No 297 (Lower Wharfedale) which covers the entire path.

This link route begins at the northern end of the town's **Valley Gardens**, across from the famous **Pump Rooms**, from where you should make your way towards the floral 'roundabout' at the heart of the park, just past the café. From there, you enter into the woods (with Jesus looking on), following the way-marked trail across the road and on to Crag Lane, with the car park for the Royal Horticultural Society's **Harlow Carr Gardens** on your right. The trail, too, leads right along the road for 100m then left to the Harrogate Arms, now closed. Here the tarmac comes to an end but you should continue into the woods with the fence of Harlow Carr Gardens on your left. It feels as if you are almost looping back on yourself but eventually the trail emerges at Pot Bank Cottage.

Go past the houses rather than taking the detour on your left and you'll soon emerge onto the road with a gate on your right leading steeply down to the bridge over Oak Beck. Cross over the bridge and hurry up the hill avoiding (hopefully!) the fast-moving traffic until you reach the sanctuary of Pot Bridge Farm, at the brow of the hill on your left. Follow this track through the farm to the small plot of trees after scruffy Oatlands Farm; an arrow daubed onto the side of an old water tank points the way. A series of fields follows, passing farmsteads including Central House Farm and, at the end of this stretch, Long

Liberty Farm. The first of the great reservoirs on this trail, **Beaver Dyke Reservoir**, and its adjoining neighbour **John O'Gaunt's Reservoir**, lie close by, reached by turning left on hitting the farm's access road, then right off it past the cow barns and through the gate. This latter reservoir is named after nearby **John of Gaunt's Castle**, a ruin of an old hunting lodge which is visible across the water from the trail (a couple of benches have been conveniently placed to encourage you to stop and savour the views).

At the end of the reservoir you hit a grassy lane, where you should turn left then right (don't drop down to the reservoir itself), to continue onto the old track known as Bank Slack. You are now entering **Nidderdale AONB** and should continue your south-westerly bearing across occasionally boggy fields to Brame Lane (in **Norwood**) and *The Sun Inn* (☎ 01943-880220, 🖥 thesun-inn.com; **fb**; WI-FI; 🐾; food Wed-Fri noon-2.30pm & 6-8pm, Sat noon-8pm, Sun to 5pm); note the pub is closed on Mondays and Tuesdays.

Cross the road to take the track down through fields and forest to **Swinsty Reservoir**. Follow the water's eastern edge, crossing over the dam to the reservoir's western side. The next bit can be slightly tricky to follow: a path at the dam's western end takes you up the bank and right, into the woods. A few hundred metres in take a left (waymarked) and then a couple of hundred metres later turn left again (unmarked) on the main path heading up the hill to the edge of the wood and a gate with a blue 'Yorkshire Water' sign. You'll know you're on the right track if, having gone through the gate, you cross a bridleway to a second gate, then follow a path that leads eventually, after several fields, to lovely **Timble**. Over a mile of road walking follows now, but the roads are quiet; heading over the crossroads onto a road that's forbidden to vehicles, you find yourself – eventually – entering the forest at **Great Timble**.

Keep straight on, ignoring paths that shoot off on both sides, until you finally emerge from the forest and via two gates onto Denton Moor. The obvious path here takes you along Lippersley Ridge to the first stone boundary marker, with a 'D' carved into its southern side. Continuing further along the path you come to a round cairn cum open shelter, which marks the high point of the walk. Retracing your steps for just a couple of metres, a small path leads you past several numbered stone shooting butts. The path seems to be taking you towards a stone lodge but before you reach it a vague path heads off west. Follow this and keep on looking west and in time you should spy **March Ghyll Reservoir**. At a path junction take the left-hand trail that aims right towards the reservoir, the path descending to a gate in a wall and a couple of sheep fields. Descending off the moor to **Hollingley Farm**, keeping the wall to your left all the way, turn right at the farmyard to pretty Fairy Dell, continuing onwards and upwards to East Moor Farm and further on to West Moor Farm.

After passing **Hill Top Farm** you should follow the road that heads south through Middleton and down to Curly Lane. At the lowest point of the lane, just before it starts to rise again, there's a footpath leading you past a swimming pool and on to the river; a right turn takes you to the main, metal bridge leading into Ilkley (see p77).

## BRADFORD LINK                                    [see map pp70-1]

The **12½-mile (20km)** Bradford Link route is uneven, with patches of pure beauty interspersed with the occasional, less-impressive stretches where business parks and busy roads dominate. Bradford Council produce an excellent guide to the trail with four clear maps and four pages of detailed instructions; visit 🖳 dalesway.org/link_routes.htm and click on the Bradford council link. For further back-up, OS map Nos 288 and 297 cover the entire trail (as well as the first few miles of the Dales Way).

The walk starts at the ornate metal gates of **Bradford Cathedral** and ends, beautifully, with a crossing of Ilkley Moor, passing stone circles and ancient milestones along the way, before you drop down into the town centre to arrive at the railway station. The first part of the path between Bradford and Shipley is largely urban in nature, though even here there are some charming spots including **Boars Well Urban Wildlife Reserve** and some great views of the old mill buildings, which provided Bradford with so much of its wealth and status during its 19th-century heyday. (In fact, the original Bradford Link started at Shipley and was extended to Bradford's city centre only fairly recently.)

At **Shipley**, where refreshments are available, you join a canal towpath west for over a mile before heading north at Hirst Lock to reach Bingley Moor and the stone circle known as the **Twelve Apostles**. **Ilkley Moor** follows in short order, and soon the town itself is reached.

## LEEDS LINK                                       [see map pp70-1]

Though perhaps the least appealing of the three links, this is the official link path according to the Dales Way Association. At **21 miles (33.8km)** it's also the longest and many people may want to divide the hike, booking two nights in Leeds and taking advantage of the excellent public transport links to convey them back to the city after a day on the trail. The suburb of **Bramhope** is approximately halfway along the trail and well connected by bus; the **X84 bus** (see pp47-9) stops there en route between Leeds and Ilkley.

One of the problems with the route is the amount of time you spend walking out of Leeds itself. Indeed, it's only when you reach the reservoir at **Eccup** – around 6½ miles (10.5km) from the start of the walk at the **stone statue of Henry Marsden** (on **Monument Moor**) – that you feel as if you've entered the countryside (though to be fair, the trail does its best to stick to the greener parts of the city as it makes its way northwards, including lovely **Adel Woods**).

Highlights of this link include the red kites that fly above Eccup, and the gorgeous **Chevin Forest Park**, about five miles further north, with its excellent birdlife and timid roe deer. Towards the end of the trail you finally get to fill your lungs with pure, unpolluted countryside air as you enjoy the wide-open expanse of the **Burley** and **Ilkley Moors**, culminating in a visit to the famous **Cow and Calf Rocks** on the edge of Ilkley town.

OS map Nos 288, 289 and 297 will be required to cover the whole trail.

# ROUTE GUIDE & MAPS

## Using this guide

The route guide has been divided into stages but these should not be taken as rigid daily stages since people walk at different speeds and have different interests. The route summaries below describe the trail between significant places and are written as if walking the path from south to north, from Ilkley to Bowness.

To enable you to plan your own itinerary, practical information is presented clearly on each of the trail maps. This includes walking times in each direction, places to stay and eat, as well as shops where you can buy supplies. Further service details are given in the text; note that the hours stated for pubs relate, for the most part, to when food is served; most venues serve drinks outside these hours. For **trail profiles** of the various stages see the **colour overview maps** at the end of the book.

For an overview of this information see the suggested itineraries (p31) and the town and village facilities table (p32).

### TRAIL MAPS  [see key map inside cover; symbols key p168]

### Scale and walking times

The trail maps are to a scale of 1:20,000 (1cm = 200m; $3^1/_8$ inches = one mile). Each full-size map covers about two miles but that's a very rough estimate owing to the variety of terrain.

Walking times are given along the side of each map; the arrow shows the direction to which the time refers. Black triangles indicate the points between which the times have been taken. These times are merely a tool to help you plan and are not there to judge your walking ability. After a couple of days you'll know how fast you walk compared with the time bars and can plan your days more accurately as a result. **See note on walking times in the box below**.

---

❑ **IMPORTANT NOTE – WALKING TIMES**

Unless otherwise specified, **all times in this book refer only to the time spent walking**. You should add 20-30% to allow for rests, photos, checking the map, drinking water etc, not to mention time simply to stop and stare. When planning the day's hike count on 5-7 hours' actual walking.

## Up or down?

The trail is shown as a **dashed red line**. An arrow across the trail indicates the gradient; two arrows show that it's steep. Note that the arrow points towards the higher part of the trail. If, for example, you are walking from A (at 80m) to B (at 200m) and the trail between the two is short and steep it would be shown thus: A— — — >> — — – B. Reversed arrow heads indicate a downward gradient. Note that the *arrow points uphill*, the opposite of what OS maps use on steep roads.

## GPS waypoints

The numbered GPS waypoints refer to the list on p169.

## Other features

Features are marked on the map when they are pertinent to navigation. To avoid clutter, not all features have been marked each time they occur.

## ACCOMMODATION

Accommodation included in the guide is either on or within easy reach of the path. Many B&B proprietors based a mile or two off the trail will offer to collect walkers from the nearest point on the trail and take them back the next morning.

Details of each place are given in the accompanying text. The number of **rooms** of each type is given at the beginning of each entry, ie: **S** = single, **T** = twin room, **D** = double room, **Tr** = triple room and **Qd** = quad. Note that many of the triple/quad rooms have a double bed and either one/two single beds, or bunk beds, thus in a group of three or four, two people would have to share the double bed but it also means the room can be used as a double or twin.

**Rates** quoted for B&B-style accommodation are **per person (pp)** based on two people sharing a room for a one-night stay; rates are usually discounted for longer stays. Where a single room **(sgl)** is available the rate for that is quoted if different from the rate per person. The rate for single occupancy **(sgl occ)** of a double/twin may be higher, and the per person rate for three/four sharing a triple/quad may be lower. At some places the only option is a **room rate**; this will be the same whether one or two people (or more if permissible) use the room. See pp29-30 for more information on rates.

Your room will either have **en suite** (bath or shower) facilities, or a **private** or **shared** bathroom, or shower room, just outside the bedroom.

The text also indicates whether the premises have: **wi-fi** (WI-FI); if a **bath** (☞) is available either as part of en suite facilities, or in a separate bathroom – for those who prefer a relaxed soak at the end of the day; if a **packed lunch** (Ⓛ) can be prepared, subject to prior arrangement; and if **dogs** (🐕 – see also pp170-1) are welcome, again subject to prior arrangement, either in at least one room (many places have only one room suitable for dogs), or at campsites. The policy on charging for dogs varies; some charge an extra £5-20 – a fee that usually covers their entire stay whether it's for just one night or much longer, while others may require a refundable deposit against any potential damage or mess.

# The route guide

## ILKLEY   [see map p79; Map 1, p83]

The starting point for the 'official' Dales Way is Ilkley (🖳 ilkley.org), an attractive place of wide streets and handsome architecture. Best known as a Victorian spa town, Ilkley actually boasts some ancient origins. The Mesolithic carvings in the hills around the town are testimony to that, including some 250 'cup and ring' marks and a curved swastika carved on the rocky outcrops above the town which are estimated to be at least 11,000 years old.

The Romans moved in during the 1st century AD and built a fort (believed by some to be called Olicana), near to the modern town centre; a person from Ilkley is still called an Olicanian. And there are three crosses in All Saints' Church at the northern end of the main boulevard, Brook St, that date back to the 7th-century Saxons.

The town had to wait until the 19th century, however, to enjoy its heyday when the springs at Wheatley, a mile to the east, were developed by the Victorians into the huge Ben Rhydding Hydropathic Establishment; this has now been demolished, though Wheatley is now called Ben Rhydding in its honour. But where once folk used to flock to Ilkley to take the waters, now they arrive to drink the beer, with both the Ilkley and Wharfedale breweries located in town. For details of Ilkley's Food & Drink and Literature festivals see box p14.

Ilkley is a friendly place and, facilities-wise, there's pretty much everything a walker could want, including some fine places to eat, though accommodation options are slim. But with Ilkley Moor to the south and the Wharfe snaking away to the north, it's a rare walker who doesn't want to pull on their boots, strap themselves into their backpack – and get on the trail as soon as they can.

### Services

There's a small **tourist information centre** (☎ 01943 602319, 🖳 www.visitbradford .com/Ilkley.aspx; Apr-Sep Mon-Sat 9.30am-12.30pm & 1-4.30pm, rest of year Mon-Sat 10am-12.30pm & 1-4pm), at the top of the town opposite the railway station, while within the station itself is the **post office** (Mon-Fri 9am-5.30pm) and a **supermarket**, M&S Simply Food (Mon-Fri 8am-8pm, Sat to 7pm, Sun 11am-5pm).

A little further east on Station Rd is a large Tesco (Mon-Sat 6am-midnight, Sun 10am-4pm), and on the main drag, Brook St, there's a Co-op (daily 6am-11pm). This same road also hosts a branch of the **chemist's**, Boots (Mon-Sat 8.30am-5.30pm, Sun 11am-4pm), the **boot repairers** Timpson (Mon-Sat 9am-5.30pm), and an **outdoor/trekking shop**, Mountain Warehouse (Mon-Sat 9am-5.30pm, Sun 10.30am-4.30pm), for those who've forgotten their boots altogether.

There's an **ATM** outside Barclays Bank on Brook St.

### Transport

Ilkley is a stop on Northern Rail's **train** services from both Leeds and Bradford; see box p45. Ilkley **bus** station, on Station Rd, is a stop on the X52, X84 (journey time from Leeds over an hour) & 962. Services with stops on/near the Dales Way include Nos 74, 74A, 873, 874, 875 & 884; see pp47-9 for details.

### Where to stay

Ilkley rather lets itself down on the accommodation front, with no campsites, bunk barns or hostels within its borders and a dearth of B&Bs in the town centre too. If you're having trouble don't forget Addingham, just a few miles along the trail and with a couple of good options.

A few hundred metres east of the tourist information centre, off both Station Rd and Cowpasture Rd, at No 1 Tivoli Place, is ***One Tivoli Place Guesthouse*** (☎ 01943 431394, 🖳 osbornehouse.net; 3D/2T, all en suite; ▼; WI-FI; Ⓛ). It's a pleasant place, a Victorian terrace surrounded by high hedges and the new owners have fully refurbished the rooms; one now even has a Jacuzzi! Rates are £35-60pp (sgl occ £65-100). Evening meals are available upon request.

***The Crescent / Rooms by Bistrot Pierre*** (☎ 01943 811250, 🖳 bistrotpierre.co.uk; 11D or T, all en suite; ▼; WI-FI), on Brook St, offers B&B for £50-75pp (sgl occ room rate). Food is available in the 'bistrot' and also The Crescent's bar but that was closed at the time of writing.

Opposite All Saints' Church, on Church St, is ***The Black Hat*** (☎ 01943 607214, 🖳 blackhatilkley.co.uk; **fb**, 2D or T/4D/1Tr, all en suite; ▼; 🐕 bar only; Ⓛ; WI-FI), a pub that also has rooms. B&B costs from £35-45pp (sgl occ room rate) and food (Mon-Thur noon-8pm, Fri & Sat to 9pm, Sun to 6pm) is available daily.

Perhaps the best choice for walkers, just 200 yards from the start of the trail and overlooking the Wharfe, ***The Riverside Hotel*** (Map 1; ☎ 01943 607338, 🖳 ilkley-riversidehotel.com; **fb**; 1S/7D/3T/1Qd, all en suite; 🐕; Ⓛ; WI-FI) is a lovely spot. The hotel has been run by the same family since 1971. Rooms aren't cheap (B&B from £57.50pp, sgl/sgl occ £75/90), but they are smart and comfortable and come with views of either the river or Ilkley Moor. Note, it can get a little busy in the daytime, particularly at weekends when the sun is shining and the world and his wife seem to want to hang out by the riverbank here.

## Where to eat and drink

There are several choices for those who want to head off on the trail early in the morning and are looking for something to nibble on before they go, including branches of those ubiquitous cafés, ***Costa*** (Mon-Fri 7.30am-5pm, Sat 8am-5pm, Sun 9am-5pm) and ***Caffe Nero*** (🐕; Mon-Sat 7am-6.30pm, Sun 8am-6pm), with the latter allowing dogs inside.

If you want to avoid the high-street chains, ***La Stazione*** (🖳 www.lastazione.co.uk; **fb**; daily 7am-4.45pm), at the entrance to the railway station, also boasts an early opening time. ***Loafer Bakery*** (Mon-Sat 7.15am-2pm) charges just £4.50 for their large takeaway 'breakfast in a box', which includes toast, bacon, egg, sausage, black pudding, mushrooms, tomatoes and beans. Nearby on Brook St there's also a branch of the bakery chain ***Greggs*** (Mon-Sat 7am-5.30pm, Sun 8am-5pm).

For something with a bit more panache, ***Betty's*** (🖳 bettys.co.uk; daily 9am-5pm) is an elegant café-tearoom with antique décor, and a back terrace overlooking the town. The patisserie at the front sells all sorts of delicious baked goods, while the licensed café out back serves an ever-changing menu of fresh, healthy breakfasts (£6-12) and lunches (£11-15), including plenty of veggie and vegan options. Sandwiches cost £6 to £10, and there are various choices of afternoon tea.

There are also several great speciality choices on Church St. ***Veggie*** (☎ 01943 600245, 🖳 theveggiecafe.co.uk; **fb**; Tue-Thur 11am-4pm, Fri & Sat 11am-4pm & 5-9pm) employs lovely smiling staff who exude the joy of vegetarianism. Their veggie mezze (£9) is a great way to sample the range of fare on offer and their marinated portobello mushroom burger is delicious

**Symbols used in text** (see also pp75-6)
🐕 Dogs allowed; if for accommodation this is subject to prior arrangement (see p171)
▼ Bathtub in, or for, at least one room WI-FI means wi-fi is available
Ⓛ packed lunch available if requested in advance
**fb** signifies places that post their current opening hours on their Facebook page

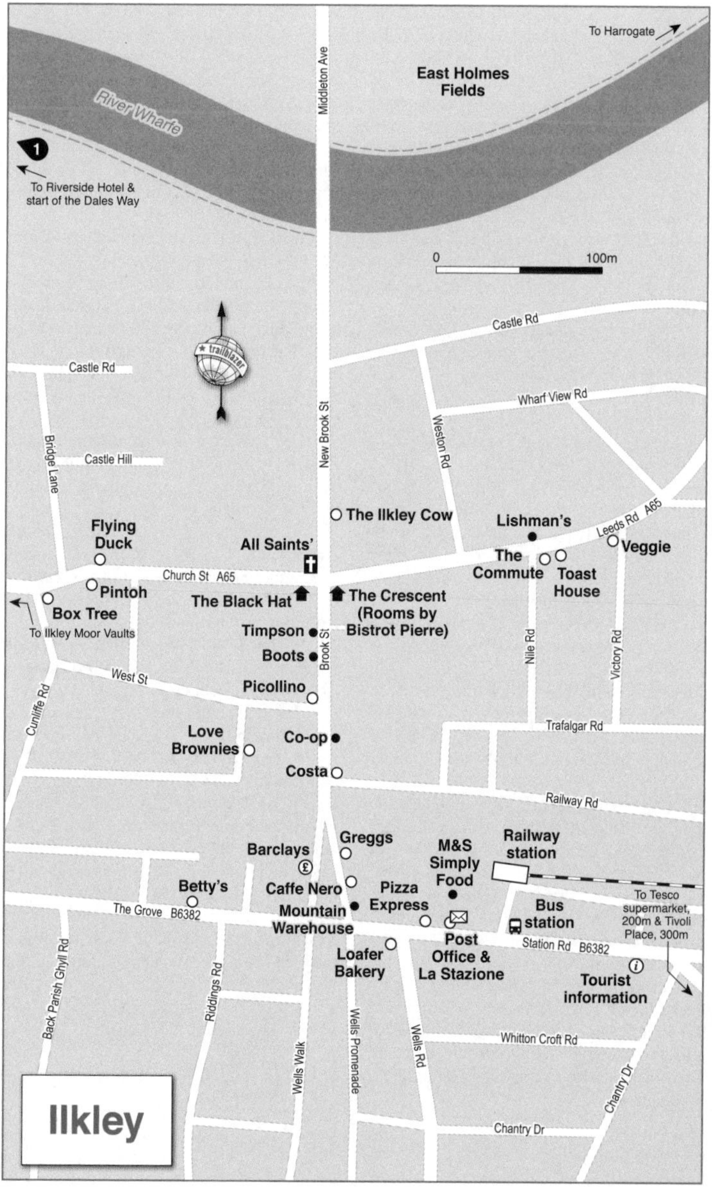

To Harrogate

East Holmes
Fields

River Wharfe

1
To Riverside Hotel &
start of the Dales Way

Middleton Ave

0        100m

Castle Rd

Castle Rd

Wharf View Rd

Weston Rd

Castle Hill

New Brook St

Bridge Lane

○ The Ilkley Cow

Lishman's ●

Flying
Duck
○

Leeds Rd  A65

All Saints'
✝

Veggie ○

Church St  A65

The
Commute ○○

Toast
House

○ Pintoh
Box Tree

The Black Hat ↑   ↑ The Crescent
(Rooms by
Bistrot Pierre)

To Ilkley Moor Vaults

Timpson ●

Boots ●

Nile Rd

Victory Rd

Brook St

West St

Picollino ○

Cunliffe Rd

Love
Brownies ○

Co-op ●●

Trafalgar Rd

Costa ○

Railway Rd

Barclays
£

Greggs ○

M&S
Simply
Food ●

Railway
station

Betty's ○

Caffe Nero ○
Mountain
Warehouse ●

Pizza
Express ○

Bus
station 🚌

To Tesco
supermarket,
200m & Tivoli
Place, 300m

The Grove  B6382

Loafer ○
Bakery

Post
Office &
La Stazione ✉

Station Rd  B6382

ⓘ

Tourist
information

Black Parish Ghyll Rd

Riddings Rd

Wells Walk

Wells Promenade

Wells Rd

Whitton Croft Rd

Chantry Dr

Chantry Dr

Ilkley

ROUTE GUIDE AND MAPS

(£8.95) – or you can stick to the regular sandwiches (£6.75) and paninis (£7.75). Close by, *Toast House* (🖳 toasthouse.co .uk; **fb**; Tue-Fri 9am-3pm, Sat to 1pm) is an unusual place, where you can order two slices of toast with various toppings, or a toast-based lunch (eg beetroot & mint dip with feta on two slices of sourdough toast). But you can also find a range of porridges, granola and the like, plus home-made soups. They also have a refill station where locals can fill up their own containers with produce rather than buying yet another piece of plastic.

Next door, *The Commute* (☎ 07932 060389, 🖳 shop.thecommuteyorkshire .com/cafe; **fb**; 🐾; daily 8am-5pm) is a cyclist-friendly café offering good-quality coffee, pastries, sandwiches and soups. Their banana bread is recommended.

Opposite, *Lishman's* (☎ 01943 609436; Mon-Sat 8am-4.30pm) is a first-class butcher's (they even offer butchery courses) which also does a nice byline in sausage rolls and also hot pork sandwiches with apple sauce (and even crackling if requested) for less than £3.

Hidden away in a car park off Brook St, *Love Brownies* (☎ 01943 262726, 🖳 lovebrownies.co.uk; Mon-Sat 9am-5pm, Sun 10am-4pm, winter hours may vary) has all your cakey cravings covered, does tea and coffee, and sells a range of boxed brownie selections for trail-walking sugar boosters.

For evening meals (or just a lunchtime pint, for that matter), the friendly pub *Ilkley Moor Vaults* (Map 1; ☎ 01943 607012, 🖳 www.ilkleymoorvaults.co.uk; **fb**; WI-FI; 🐾; Wed-Fri noon-2.30pm & 5.30-9pm, Sat & Sun noon-9pm) is highly recommended. Known locally as 'The Taps', it lies above the start of the trail on Stockeld Rd, and serves cask ales and delicious pub grub using locally sourced ingredients wherever possible. The menu and specials board change frequently but there are standard pub dishes and vegan/vegetarian/gluten-free options.

Back near the town centre, *The Ilkley Cow* (☎ 01943 602030, 🖳 theilkleycow.co .uk; Mon-Thur 5.30-9.30pm, Fri noon-2.30pm & 5.30-10pm, Sat noon-10pm, Sun to 8pm) is a serious steakhouse where you can stock up on calories ahead of your 81-mile walk, or celebrate having just finished with a slap-up meal. A 10oz sirloin steak with chunky chips, flat mushroom & roasted tomatoes will set you back £23.95.

Real ale aficionados should head to the *Flying Duck* (☎ 01943 609587, 🖳 thefly ingduck.co.uk; **fb**; food Tue-Fri noon-2.30pm, Sat & Sun to 5pm), a Grade II-listed building dating from 1709 that's home to Wharfedale Brewery (see box p23). They also do decent lunchtime pub food. Note the pub is closed on Mondays (apart from bank holidays).

For Thai food, head across the road to *Pintoh* (☎ 01943 816229, 🖳 pintoh.co.uk; Mon-Fri 5-10pm, Sat to 11pm, Sun 5-9pm) where most mains cost £11-15.

At 11 Station Plaza is a branch of *Pizza Express* (daily 11.30am-10pm). For something more genuinely Italian, try *Picollino* (☎ 01943 605827, 🖳 piccolinorestaurants .com/our-restaurants/ilkley; Sun-Wed to 10pm, Thur-Sat to 11pm) a friendly, elegant restaurant on Brook St with a roof terrace for that extra Mediterranean feel.

The place with the best reputation for fine dining in Ilkley is the Michelin-starred, flower-fronted *Box Tree* (☎ 01943 608484, 🖳 theboxtree.co.uk; Wed-Sat 6-9pm, Fri & Sat noon-1.20pm, Sun noon-2.30pm), where celebrated chef and stock-cube ambassador Marco Pierre White trained (though Simon Gueller is now executive chef). The pricing is fairly simple, with six courses for £90 (three-course lunch £45, Sun lunch £55) and the food is, of course, terrific. The menu frequently changes, but may include the likes of cured salmon, fillet of beef and mandarin soufflé. An alternative vegetarian menu is also available.

## STAGE 1: ILKLEY TO BURNSALL                    [MAPS 1-7]

Traditionally, the destination for walkers at the end of their first day on the Dales Way is Grassington, and with its superior choice of B&Bs, eateries and other facilities, it does at first sight seem a sensible choice. But there is no getting away from the fact that walking over 16 miles on the first day is, as sports commentators are wont to say, 'a big ask'. Furthermore, by attempting to hike all that way in one day you're leaving yourself little time to savour the sights and settlements – Addingham church and its ancient stone cross, magnificent Bolton Abbey, the pubs at Appletreewick and pretty Burnsall – that you'll encounter along on the way.

So for this reason, this guidebook is breaking with tradition and recommending that you actually reduce your ambitions on this first stage. If you're camping, this means stopping at Appletreewick, which at 12 miles (19.6km) from the trail's start is a sensible distance for the first day (and you get the chance to enjoy the best pub of the whole trail, the characterful Craven Arms, too). While those relying on B&Bs and pubs for their accommodation can choose to end their first day either in Appletreewick, or a mile further on in Burnsall (**13¼ miles/21.5km; 5¾hrs**), another lovely spot and one with everything a walker would want. In both cases, Grassington, around 3½ miles (5.7km) further on from Burnsall, can then be treated as an early lunch stop the next day.

As for the highlights on this first stage, well the magic really starts once you cross the boundary into the Yorkshire Dales National Park and are confronted by the fabulously photogenic **Bolton Abbey**, an enigmatic ruin set against a backdrop of mighty mature woodland. Thereafter the Way takes you on a stroll through **Strid Wood**, the longest unbroken stretch of woodland on the entire trail (and boy, is it lovely!) before embarking on an unchallenging amble along the banks of the Wharfe, past aqueduct, angler, wildflowers and white waters, to **Appletreewick**, whose main pub, Craven Arms, is just a few minutes from the path. **Burnsall**, with a wider choice of B&B-style accommodation, is a mere mile of pleasingly unproblematic promenading further along the trail.

### The route

The first half of this stage can best be summed up as 'pleasant'. Not 'jaw-dropping' or 'spellbinding' – those adjectives are best saved for later in the walk, when the sights and scenery truly justify them. Instead, this initial section is an attractive but unremarkable hike, necessary to convey you from the hubbub of Ilkley to the delights of the Dales.

The trail is not without interest – and this begins right at the start with the lovely 17th-century humpbacked **Old Bridge** (Map 1) at Ilkley. A hostage to both kismet and climate, its exterior ravaged by time, it nevertheless stands stoically and silently, bent but unbowed. Which is, coincidentally, how you'll be looking once the Dales Way has finished with you.

The start of your odyssey begins at the bridge's southern end, and initially feels more like a Sunday afternoon stroll than a long-distance trail, the path dodging a course between back garden and riverbank, through sheep fields and wild meadows alive with birdsong and butterflies as it follows, more or less, the line of the Wharfe to Addingham's venerable church.

## ADDINGHAM                         [Map 2, p84]

The chances are you'll see little of Addingham (🖥 addingham.info) save its churchyard, through which the Dales Way passes, and a couple of outlying streets. In one sense this is a bit of a shame, for the village itself is said to have more listed buildings than any in the Dales, even though it actually lies outside the boundary of the national park.

On the other hand, the centre of Addingham, Main St, is a 5- to 10-minute walk from the path and, given that you've not long left Ilkley, you probably won't want or need to visit Addingham proper. If you do wish to, on joining North St (after the church), cross the road and walk down Church St until you hit Main St, where you should turn right to reach the centre. Here you'll find several of these venerable listed buildings, most of which date back to the 18th and 19th centuries when Addingham was a mill town. Many of the listed buildings are the former residences either of the mill owners or the simple terraced cottages of those who worked for them.

Also on Main St is a Co-op **supermarket** (daily 7am-10pm), with a free-to-use **ATM** outside it, and three pubs, one of which offers accommodation.

*The Craven Heifer* (☎ 01943 831548, 🖥 cravenheifer-addingham.co.uk; 7D, all en suite; ✆; WI-FI) has gorgeous, individually designed **rooms** (B&B from £42.50pp, sgl occ room rate) and a menu (**food** Mon-Fri noon-3pm & 5-9pm, Sat noon-9pm, Sun to 5pm) with dishes from £13 (lamb en croûte with fondant sweet potatoes £18). On Sunday evenings they have a quiz night (£2; from about 7pm); light snacks are served.

The second pub is *The Fleece* (☎ 01943 830397, 🖥 the-fleece.com; 🐾 bar area; **fb**) a traditional Yorkshire taproom serving good ales, a lot of gin, and cracking **food** (Mon-Thur noon-9pm, Fri & Sat to 10pm, Sun to 8.30pm; lunchtime/evening mains £8-12/13-19).

Between the two is *The Swan Inn* (☎ 01943 430003, 🖥 swan-addingham.co.uk; **fb**; 🐾) serving cask ales and pub **food** (Mon-Sat noon-3pm & 5-8pm, Sun noon-7pm) such as fish & chips (£11/14); the menu may also include mushroom ragôut (£11.95) and black-bean beef chilli (£14.25). Don't miss the miniature doll's house replica of the pub, built lovingly by the pub's family owners during Covid lockdowns.

The Nos 62, 74/74A **bus** services call in along Main St. On Sundays/bank holidays the 873, 874 & 884 services also stop here. See pp47-9 for details.

But as pleasant as Addingham undoubtedly is, most walkers content themselves with just a quick peek inside **St Peter's Church** (🖥 stpetersaddingham.org.uk) before heading out. Parts of the current church date back to the 15th century, though Christians have been worshipping on this site for well over a thousand years, as the discovery in 1947 of an ancient stone cross and several Anglo-Saxon burial sites goes some way to proving. The cross is usually on display on the left-hand side of the church, although it sometimes gets removed when the church is being redecorated.

After Addingham, the path hugs the river more closely, bisecting caravan park and cow field, diverting only to cross the busy B6160 to **Farfield Friends' Meeting House** (Map 3). *(cont'd on p86)*

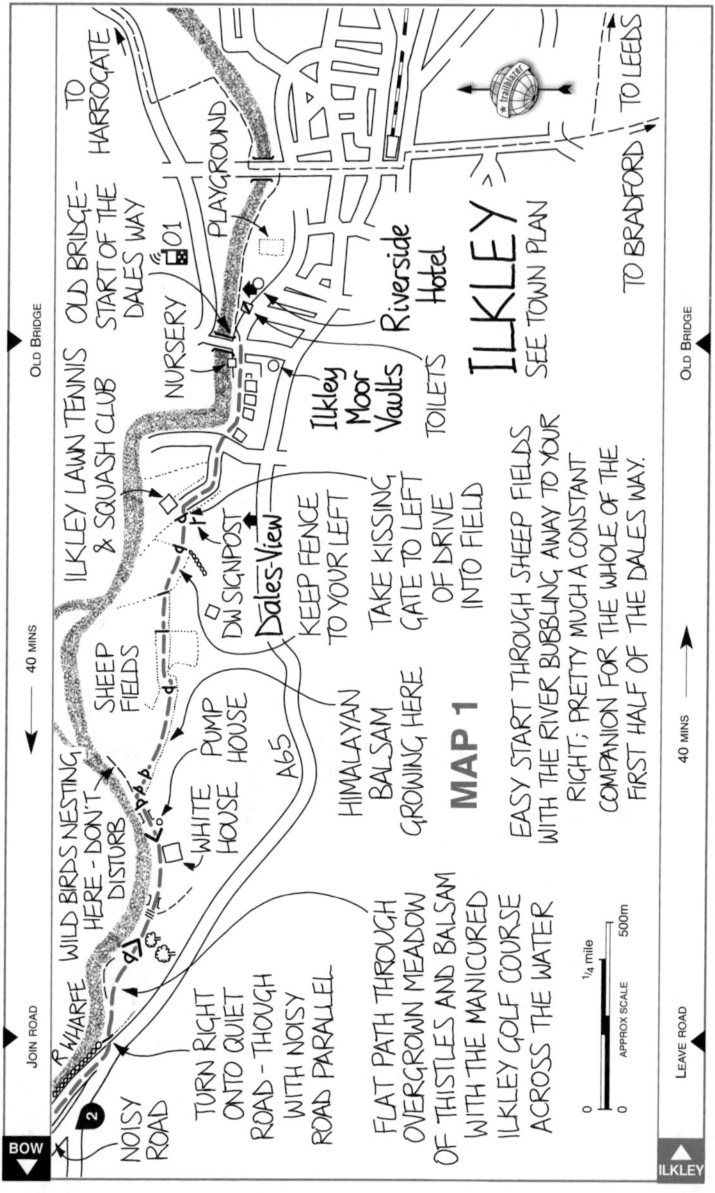
BOW
JOIN ROAD
OLD BRIDGE
40 MINS
NOISY ROAD
2
R WHARFE
TURN RIGHT ONTO QUIET ROAD - THOUGH WITH NOISY ROAD PARALLEL
FLAT PATH THROUGH OVERGROWN MEADOW OF THISTLES AND BALSAM WITH THE MANICURED ILKLEY GOLF COURSE ACROSS THE WATER
WILD BIRDS NESTING HERE - DON'T DISTURB
WHITE HOUSE
PUMP HOUSE
SHEEP FIELDS
A65
HIMALAYAN BALSAM GROWING HERE
MAP 1
EASY START THROUGH SHEEP FIELDS WITH THE RIVER BUBBLING AWAY TO YOUR RIGHT; PRETTY MUCH A CONSTANT COMPANION FOR THE WHOLE OF THE FIRST HALF OF THE DALES WAY.
DW SIGNPOST
Dales-View
KEEP FENCE TO YOUR LEFT
TAKE KISSING GATE TO LEFT OF DRIVE INTO FIELD
ILKLEY LAWN TENNIS & SQUASH CLUB
NURSERY
OLD BRIDGE - START OF THE DALES WAY
01
PLAYGROUND
Ilkley Moor Vaults
Riverside Hotel
TOILETS
ILKLEY
SEE TOWN PLAN
TO HARROGATE
TO BRADFORD
TO LEEDS
trailblazer
APPROX SCALE
0
1/4 mile
0
500m
LEAVE ROAD
40 MINS
ILKLEY

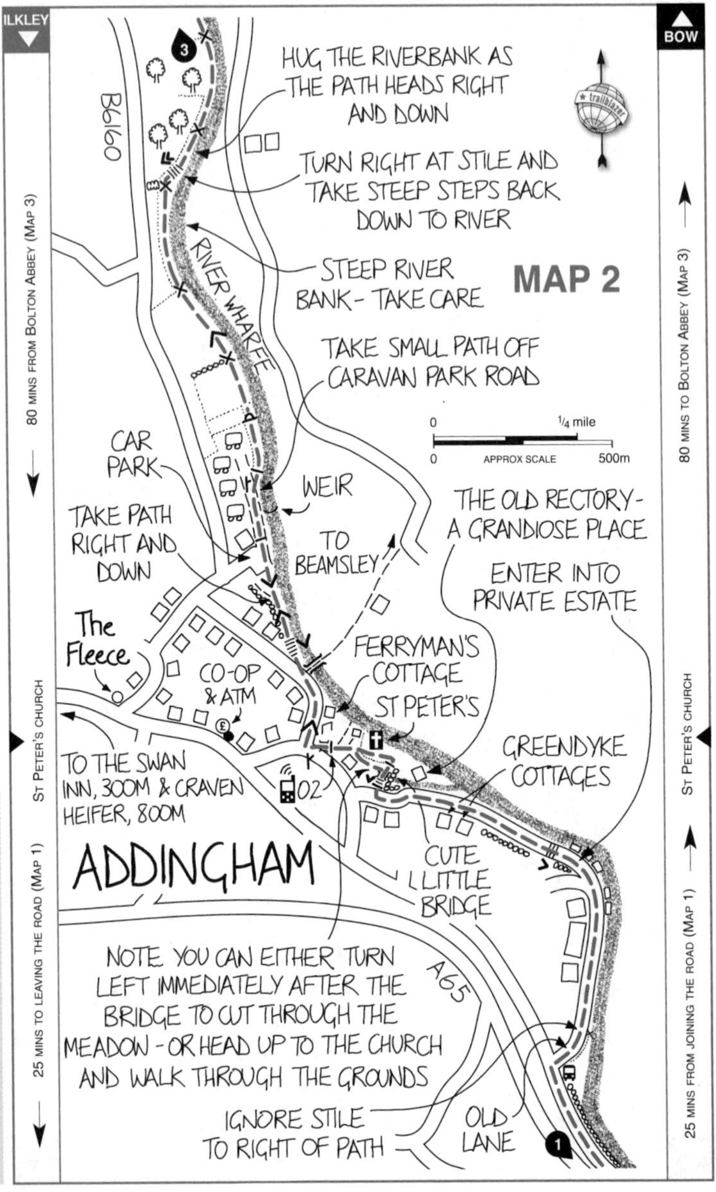


ROUTE GUIDE AND MAPS

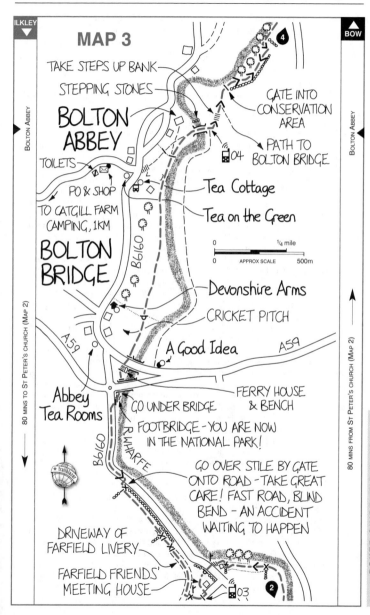

MAP 3

ILKLEY ▼

▲ BOW

TAKE STEPS UP BANK
STEPPING STONES

BOLTON ABBEY

GATE INTO CONSERVATION AREA

PATH TO BOLTON BRIDGE

TOILETS

PO & SHOP

TO CATGILL FARM CAMPING, 1KM

BOLTON BRIDGE

Tea Cottage

Tea on the Green

04

0   ¼ mile
0   APPROX SCALE   500m

Devonshire Arms

CRICKET PITCH

A Good Idea

A59

A59

FERRY HOUSE & BENCH

Abbey Tea Rooms

GO UNDER BRIDGE

FOOTBRIDGE - YOU ARE NOW IN THE NATIONAL PARK!

GO OVER STILE BY GATE ONTO ROAD - TAKE GREAT CARE! FAST ROAD, BLIND BEND - AN ACCIDENT WAITING TO HAPPEN

DRIVEWAY OF FARFIELD LIVERY

FARFIELD FRIENDS' MEETING HOUSE

03

2

B6160

R.WHARFE

BOLTON ABBEY

BOLTON ABBEY

← 80 MINS TO ST PETER'S CHURCH (MAP 2)

80 MINS FROM ST PETER'S CHURCH (MAP 2) →

trailblazer

ROUTE GUIDE AND MAPS

*(cont'd from p82)* The building is undecorated and tranquil, its simplicity masking its importance historically for the Quaker movement (see box below). The Meeting House provides as good a place as any to make peace with your God before you tackle the most dangerous stretch of walking on the whole trail, as you join the pavement-less B6160 on a blind downslope in the road.

If after that you need a stiff drink to settle your nerves, after walking under the A59 turn left on the road and call in at the super-smart 17th-century

---

❑ **THE QUAKERS AND FARFIELDS FRIENDS' MEETING HOUSE**

The Religious Society of Friends started life back in the middle of the 17th century when a young man, George Fox, from Leicestershire, became dissatisfied with the established Church of England and its teachings. In particular, George believed that the ordained clergy of the Church were unnecessary, even an obstruction, hindering the relationship between a believer and his God and that one could communicate with Him without their intervention. An egalitarian group, Quakers believe that there is something of God in everybody and thus one needs neither clergy nor their rites and rituals in order to pray and speak with their Lord. Even the church buildings themselves were deemed by Fox to be unnecessary, for one could just as easily pray in a field or orchard as in a chapel or church.

Unfortunately, for the first few decades his followers faced wholesale persecution; the English Civil War (1642-51) was still fresh in many people's minds and any dissent or deviation from the orthodox was viewed as unsettling and potentially dangerous. Indeed, George himself was brought before the magistrates in 1650 on charges of religious blasphemy. It was during this trial that the judge, on being told by Fox to 'tremble at the word of the Lord', dubbed him and his religious group 'Quakers' – a nickname that stuck and was eventually adopted by the Society itself.

The Toleration Act of 1689 gave the Friends a little more religious freedom – as long as they pledged allegiance to the king – and it was in this year that **Farfield Friends' Meeting House** was built, the land having been given to the society by the tenants of Farfield Hall, the Myers family, who were followers. As is typical of the movement, the building lacks any sort of ornamentation – in stark contrast to the ruins of Bolton Priory nearby. Attend a Friends' meeting today (note it's not called a 'service') and you'll find no priests, no singing nor set prayers; just a group of like-minded individuals sitting in a circle in noiseless contemplation, the silence broken only when one of the members feels compelled to speak.

The seats you see around the walls at Farfield today are the original 17th-century benches, though the ones in the centre are from a meeting house in Skipton and date back 'only' to 1761. The elaborate tombs outside are something of an anomaly for such a humble, unostentatious sect and house the members of the Myers family – the benefactors who gave the land to the Friends. The hall is today in the care of the Historic Chapels Trust, who replaced the roof in 1998, though the meeting hall has not actually been used regularly by the Quakers for over 150 years.

Incidentally, later on in the walk, just after Sedbergh, you will pass **Brigflatts** (Map 26), which perhaps holds an even more prominent position in the history of the Quaker movement. For it was here in 1652 that Fox repaired to after he had had his 'great vision' atop Pendle Hill – which Quakers often count as the beginning of their story. Subsequently a meeting house was built here in 1675 (the second oldest in the UK after one in Hertford but older even than the one at Farfield), a simple whitewashed affair that you can visit to this day.

*Devonshire Arms Hotel & Spa* (☎ 01756 718100, 🖳 devonshirehotels.co.uk/
devonshire-arms-hotel-spa; 40D or T, all en suite; 🞂; WI-FI; 🐾) in **Bolton
Bridge**. Rates for B&B start at around £120pp (sgl occ £220), while a three-
course lunch at their Brasserie and Bar (food daily noon-3pm & 5-9pm) will set
you back a cool £38. For more flaccid thirst quenchers, *Abbey Tea Rooms* (☎
01756 710797; 🐾; **fb**; daily 9.30am-4pm) is just across the road. Alternatively,
if you're here over the weekend, turn right and head over the bridge to *A Good
Idea* (☎ 01756 711272; Fri-Sun 10am-5.30pm), a weekend-only farm shop
which sells hot and cold drinks and sausage rolls as well as fresh fruit.

That said, in terms of choice and setting, you're better off waiting until you
get to the lovely tearooms at Bolton Abbey, beckoning you ahead....

## BOLTON ABBEY   [Map 3, p85]

It's hard not to love Bolton Abbey (🖳
boltonabbey.com; see website for opening
hours) and the neighbouring village that
shares its name. This is one of those rare
places where the modern world has to make
concessions for the ancient one, rather than
the other way round. If that sounds hard to
believe, take the Sunday bus (see p88) that
runs through the village and watch as the
driver is forced to stop, remove the wing
mirror so that the bus can squeeze through
an ancient stone arch, then re-attach it once
through.

Considering there can't be more than
half a dozen buildings in Bolton Abbey

village, there are more services here than
anyone has a right to expect. There's a **post
office** for a start (Mon 9am-12.30pm, Tue-
Sat 10am-12.30pm), which is part of a large
souvenir **shop** (Mon 9am-5.30pm, Tue-Sun
10am-5.30pm) next to the car park. Though
it's mostly souvenirs, the shop does also
sell a few snacks and cold drinks. There are
**toilets** next door.

There's no accommodation in the centre of the village but there is a well-
equipped **campsite**, called *Catgill Farm* (☎
01756 710247, 🖳 www.catgillfarm.co.uk;
WI-FI reception area; 🐾; Apr-end Oct),
about 1km west of the post office along the

---

### ❏ THE PRIORY OF BOLTON ABBEY

Bolton Abbey is, despite the name, technically actually a priory rather than an abbey.
Originally founded in 1154 by the Augustinian order, it has suffered down the centuries from raids by the Scots and, most devastatingly, from the Dissolution of the
Monasteries in 1540, which left most of the eastern end of the structure in ruins. The
western half of the site, however, has served as the parish church since around 1170
and survived the Dissolution's devastation. Much of the intact church you see today
is Gothic in style but with Victorian embellishments, including the stained-glass windows by celebrated artist August Pugin.

It's difficult to look upon the ruins of Bolton Abbey today and not be inspired, and
down the years the priory has been the subject of several paintings by JMW Turner and
a long narrative poem by William Wordsworth, *The White Doe of Rylstone*, which
starts with the deer entering the churchyard to lie down on a particular grave.

The dukes of Devonshire have owned the estate since the 18th century. The current owner is the septuagenarian Peregrine Andrew Morny Cavendish, the 12th Duke
of Devonshire and the son of Dowager Duchess 'Debo', the youngest of the notori-
ous Mitford sisters who enjoyed a certain level of fame as the public face of the
Duke's main family seat, Chatsworth, about which she wrote and in whose restoration she played a key role.

pavement-less but quiet road. It's a decent place with nice people running it, and a pop-up breakfast coffee shop (daily but hours vary) selling hot drinks and pastries. Expect to pay £12 for a hiker and tent (includes shower facilities); booking is recommended in the peak season.

In their determination that no artery should go unclogged, this cholesterol-laden village boasts two wonderful **tearooms** close to the post office.

***Tea on the Green*** (☎ 01756 711834, 🖥 teaonthegreen.org; **fb**; WI-FI; 🐾; Tue-Sun 10am-3pm) operates a 'field to fork' philosophy, meaning that they serve local produce wherever possible. The menu includes sandwiches (from £7) and toasted teacakes (£2.60) with lashings of butter. Dog treats and a bowl of water are thoughtfully provided by the front door for all passers-by.

Opposite, ***Tea Cottage*** (☎ 01756 710495, 🖥 teacottageboltonabbey.co.uk; **fb**; summer daily 10am-4pm, winter days/hours variable; WI-FI; 🐾 in 'dog' room and outside) is an even more traditional tearoom. The inside is very quaint and olde-worlde, but there is also some wonderful outdoor space, including a covered area with blankets and, again, dog treats and a bowl of water provided free of charge. What's more, it's only from outside that you can truly appreciate the cottage's magnificent setting as you overlook the abbey grounds while munching on a scone with jam & clotted cream (£3.50), or fruit cake with Wensleydale cheese (£2.95). The nearest defibrillator, by the way, is at the New Inn in Appletreewick.

The 74/74A **bus** services call here and on Sundays/bank holidays the 873 & 874; for details see pp47-9.

So far, so-so. But Bolton Abbey is more than just a lovely place to get indigestion. As you've already discovered it also confirms that you are now very much in the national park (and have been since you crossed the small footbridge prior to passing under the A59). And isn't it strange how, almost as soon as you enter the park, the scenery becomes that much prettier, the grass that little bit more lush, the trees mightier and, overall, the landscape that much more attractive. It's as if someone flicked the pretty switch.

So when you finally manage to extricate yourself from your chair at one of Bolton Abbey's tearooms and waddle back down to the path, you're in for a treat! Taking the lovely footbridge at the eastern end of the ruins (or, for adrenaline junkies in search of a cheap hit, the stepping stones that lie parallel to it), there now follow two stretches of divine wood walking, first on one side of the Wharfe and then an even more gorgeous stretch on the other, western side. Between the two is the large **café** known as ***Cavendish Pavilion*** or, as Dales Way veterans call it, the 'Cav Pav' (Map 4; ☎ 01756 710245, 🖥 devonshire hotels.co.uk/cavendish-pavilion; WI-FI; **fb**; daily 10am-5pm, to 4pm in winter), a bright, airy place with loads of outdoor seating where dogs are welcome, strong coffee and plenty of sandwiches, cakes and ice creams. Too big, perhaps, to be charming, there are nevertheless several things here that you may find useful, including a **gift shop-cum-tourist office** (open same times as the café), some **toilets** and a **phone**.

The stretch of woodland walking after the pavilion takes you through **Strid Wood**, named after the small but deadly section of violent rapids that lie at their centre. Before you get there, however, you'll come to **Flying Shavings**, where the owner, universally known as 'The Bodger', runs wood-turning courses using local materials. If nothing else, you have to admire the location of his office!

MAP 4

0 — ¼ mile
0 — APPROX SCALE — 500m

R. WHARFE

FLYING SHAVINGS - WOOD-CARVERS

A GLORIOUS - AND EASY - STROLL THROUGH LOVELY STRID WOOD

LOOK OUT FOR DIPPERS, GOOSANDERS AND, OF COURSE, KINGFISHERS

WOODEN CHAIRS

B6160

STONE CHAIR

BEACH

FORD SMALL STREAM OR TAKE FOOT-BRIDGE

TAKE PATH SIGNPOSTED FOR WHEELCHAIR USERS

STRID WOOD

FALLOW FIELD

SHOP & TOURIST INFO

TOILETS

05 Cavendish Pavilion

COIN TREE

BOLTON ABBEY'S WELLY WALK - ROPE & TREE-CLIMBING & OTHER CHILDREN'S ACTIVITIES

3

60 MINS FROM AQUEDUCT (MAP 5)
BRIDGE BY CAVENDISH PAVILION
35 MINS TO BOLTON ABBEY (MAP 3)

60 MINS TO AQUEDUCT (MAP 5)
BRIDGE BY CAVENDISH PAVILION
35 MINS FROM BOLTON ABBEY (MAP 3)

As for the Strid itself, you'll read enough warnings on the information boards dotted about the place but just to reiterate: no matter how narrow The Strid looks, don't even think of jumping across it. The ground can be slippery, the consequences of any mistake are often fatal – and if you've been indulging at the Bolton Abbey's tearooms, you're probably not as mobile as you were at the start of the walk.

A little further along from the Strid itself and a couple of hundred metres off the path, on the B6160, lies the ***Strid Wood Tearooms*** (Map 5; ☎ 01756 711745, 🖥 stridwoodtearooms.co.uk; **fb**; daily 9.30am-4pm; 🐾; WI-FI), a cheerful place catering more to the passing motorist than the walker, though it has a decent menu, with their pasties particularly recommended. It has a big outside **toilet block**, too, though note that camping is not allowed anywhere near here – even though many a walker would consider it an ideal spot. There is a campsite, but it's for motorhomes and caravans only. For those who've had enough, the same **bus** services (74, 74A 873 & 874; see pp47-9) that serve Bolton Abbey also call here, 5-6 minutes earlier or later depending, of course, on which way they're heading.

## ❏ THE STRID

Given the deadly reputation of this small, 20m-long section of rapids (Map 5) in the heart of the forest that took its name, and the legends that have grown up around it, your first impression maybe that it all looks a little, well, tame. Indeed, you may well be thinking that, with one decent-sized stride, you'll be safely on the other side. But I strongly advise you not to test this hypothesis.

For the fact of the matter is that for all the noise and fury of the foaming surface, the real danger lies under the rocks. Undertows drag you into underwater caverns from where the force of the water ensures there's no escape. It would be an unpleasant way to go.

The roll call of those who have perished at the Strid is lengthy, though the most famous remains The Boy of Egremond (sometimes spelt Egremont), the son of Alizia de Romille, the lady of Skipton Castle in the 12th century. The tragedy is recounted in a 19th-century poem by Samuel Rogers, which was illustrated by JMW Turner.

*In tartan clad and forest-green,*
*With hound in leash and hawk in hood,*
*The Boy of Egremond was seen.*
*Blithe was his song, a song of yore*
*But where the rock is rent in two,*
*And the river rushes through,*
*His voice was heard no more!*
*'Twas but a step! the gulf he passed;*

*But that step – it was his last!*
*As through the mist he winged his way,*
*(A cloud that hovers night and day,)*
*The hound hung back, and back he drew*
*The Master and his merlin too.*
*That narrow place of noise and strife*
*Received their little all of Life!*

In her grief, Lady Alizia is said to have given the Augustinians at nearby Embsay some land near the Strid on which to build Bolton Abbey (though as the Boy of Egremond was a signatory to this transfer, this version of events seems unlikely). It is said, however, that shortly before the Strid claims its next victim the ghostly apparition of a white horse is seen nearby.

More delights await as you finally leave the wood behind for good, for in a matter of metres you're confronted by the 19th-century crenellated **Barden Aqueduct** where on sunny days you may be treated with the sight of kingfishers dazzling the banks of the lazy river, blissfully unaware of the chaos that awaits just a little way downstream at the Strid. Surprisingly, the aqueduct is actually still in use, carrying the waters from Nidderdale, 15-20 miles away, towards Leeds. You'll see no sign of this, however, for the pipework is buried between the path that you take to cross it and the tops of the arches underneath.

Once across the Wharfe the water runs down inside the bridge abutment at the far (north-eastern) end, and continues its subterranean way towards the feeder reservoirs for Bradford and Leeds. Don't forget to look up too, to appreciate the lovely vista as the river ahead sweeps right towards Barden Bridge, with the ruin of Barden Tower overseeing everything.

## BARDEN BRIDGE       [Map 5]

The main thing of interest to the Dales Way walker here is the **ice cream van** that's often parked here during the summer. If you were to cross the bridge – which was largely rebuilt in 1659 to replace a much earlier crossing – and head up the hill (take the

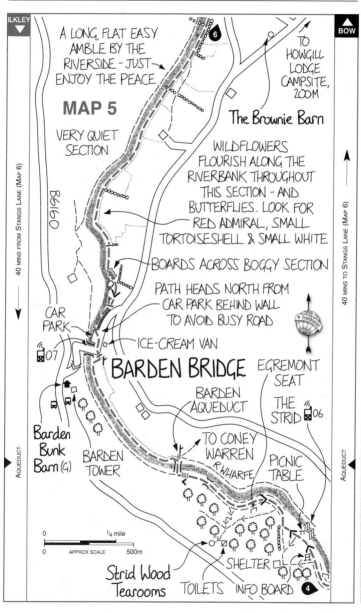

ILKLEY ▼

▲ BOW

A LONG, FLAT EASY AMBLE BY THE RIVERSIDE – JUST ENJOY THE PEACE

TO HOWGILL LODGE CAMPSITE, 200M

**MAP 5**

VERY QUIET SECTION

The Brownie Barn

WILDFLOWERS FLOURISH ALONG THE RIVERBANK THROUGHOUT THIS SECTION – AND BUTTERFLIES. LOOK FOR RED ADMIRAL, SMALL TORTOISESHELL & SMALL WHITE

B6160

40 MINS FROM STANGS LANE (MAP 6)

40 MINS TO STANGS LANE (MAP 6)

BOARDS ACROSS BOGGY SECTION

PATH HEADS NORTH FROM CAR PARK BEHIND WALL TO AVOID BUSY ROAD

★ trailblazer

CAR PARK

07

ICE-CREAM VAN

BARDEN BRIDGE

EGREMONT SEAT

BARDEN AQUEDUCT

THE STRID 06

AQUEDUCT

Barden Bunk Barn (G)

BARDEN TOWER

TO CONEY WARREN

R WHARFE

PICNIC TABLE

AQUEDUCT

0    ¼ mile
0    APPROX SCALE    500m

Strid Wood Tearooms

SHELTER

TOILETS    INFO BOARD    4

ROUTE GUIDE AND MAPS

stile on the left about halfway up to avoid the road), you come to **Barden Tower**, once a 15th-century hunting lodge (the name 'Barden' is said to be a corruption of the Anglo-Saxon for 'Valley of the Wild Boar') which was later turned into a lavish private residence by the 10th Lord Clifford (1454–1523), who preferred it to his family seat at Skipton Castle. The main building is now a ruin and off-limits but the grounds play host to the 24-bed *Barden Bunk Barn* (🖥 thebarnatbarden.com) which, unfortunately, is only for **groups** of eight or more.

The 74/74A **bus** services stop by the tower (see pp47-9).

The stretch from Barden Bridge to Burnsall and beyond can accurately be described as classic Dales Way terrain. This is walking at its most serene and care-free, the ground flat and easy, the scenery absorbing, and with little to disturb the tranquillity. Your soundtrack on this stretch will be that of birdsong, and of the river bubbling lazily on your left; while keeping you company are the riverbank wildflowers that nod gently on the breeze and the butterflies – the small tortoiseshell, large and small whites, and maybe even the odd peacock and red admiral – that flit between them (assuming, of course, that the weather will be good when you take this path – otherwise, the reality that greets you may be less serene than the picture painted here).

It's all very straightforward and, in the right climate, idyllic. So much so, you may want to stop here to give yourself a chance to take it all in, and luckily there are one or two options about a mile from Barden bridge on **Stangs Lane**. The first is a simple **mobile home** (Map 6; ☎ 01756-720294; sleeps 5) just before you hit the road, in which a handwritten sign is displayed in the window offering it for £120 for the weekend (£350 for a week) – though they may, if bookings allow, offer it for less time. As you reach the road you'll also notice a footpath that takes you up to *Howgill Lodge* (off Map 6; ☎ 01756 720655, 🖥 howgill-lodge.co.uk; WI-FI), a camping and glamping site which has four en suite timber **lodges** (from £175 per night for two adults), sleeping up to six people, with their own log-burners, private patio and hot tub. However, they have a two-night minimum stay policy unless there is a one night gap in their bookings. They also offer **camping** (Apr to end Oct; 🐾 if under close control) from £10pp per night for hikers and including use of shower and toilet facilities

Nearby, at Howgill Barn, is *The Brownie Barn* (Map 5; ☎ 01943 262726, 🖥 lovebrownies.co.uk/pages/brownie-barn; WI-FI; 🐾; fb; daily 9am-5pm), run by the Love Brownies team you may have met in Ilkley, and a perfect pick-me-up for tired walkers. There's indoor and outdoor seating, strong coffee, fresh smoothies and, of course, hundreds of hand-made brownies (from £2.50).

Back on the path, and after passing some rapids that interject a brief note of sound and fury on an otherwise peaceful stretch, it's not long before the trail delivers you to the tiny but lovely village of **Appletreewick**.

## APPLETREEWICK                [Map 6]

Little more than a one-street village, Appletreewick – often shortened to Ap'wick by the locals – boasts a fair history for a place of less than 250 souls.

The most celebrated son is Sir William Craven, whose meteoric career saw him Sheriff and Lord Mayor of London at the beginning of the 17th century, and whose

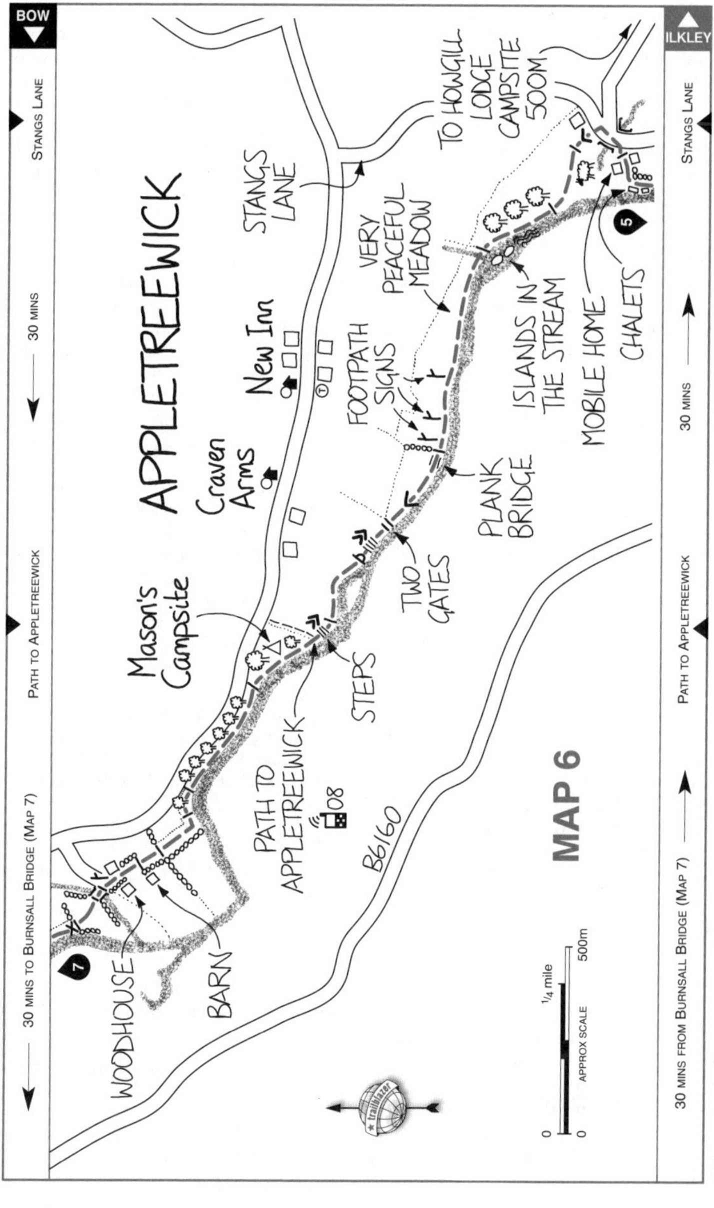

BOW ▼

▲ ILKLEY

STANGS LANE

30 MINS

PATH TO APPLETREEWICK

30 MINS TO BURNSALL BRIDGE (MAP 7)

APPLETREEWICK

STANGS LANE

New Inn

Craven Arms

Mason's Campsite

PATH TO APPLETREEWICK

B6160

STEPS

TWO GATES

FOOTPATH SIGNS

VERY PEACEFUL MEADOW

TO HOWGILL LODGE CAMPSITE 500M

PLANK BRIDGE

ISLANDS IN THE STREAM

MOBILE HOME CHALETS

5

WOODHOUSE

7

BARN

MAP 6

¼ mile

500m

APPROX SCALE

STANGS LANE

30 MINS

PATH TO APPLETREEWICK

30 MINS FROM BURNSALL BRIDGE (MAP 7)

ROUTE GUIDE AND MAPS

life is believed by some to have been the basis for the Dick Whittington legend. On his return from London, Sir William spent some of his fabulous wealth enriching the area (in 2000 *The Sunday Times* named him as one of the 100 richest people who have lived in England since 1066, with a personal fortune in today's terms of around £6.3 billion). It was he who was responsible for building Burnsall bridge (Map 7) and the nearby school too, and he also repaired St Wilfrid's Church in Burnsall. More recently (in 2009), Appletreewick was awarded the title of 'Britain's Friendliest Town to Drive Through', a result based upon UK-wide data collected on road-rage incidents, driver communication, average speeds and so on.

Today, the village plays host to two pubs, a **phone box** (outside The New Inn), one very good campsite and .... not much else, though the 74A **bus** service stops by The New Inn (see pp47-9).

The **campsite** is *Mason's* (☎ 01756 720275, 💻 masonscampsite.co.uk; 🐾; WI-FI; mid May to end Oct), a very popular place, unsurprisingly so given its location (by the river, near a great pub and abutting the Dales Way) as well as the quality of the facilities on site (the showers are particularly lovely). They have also adopted the concept of glamping in a big way, with **yurts** (sleeping two people) and a **safari tent** (sleeping up to six people) available (£155-185). For walkers arriving on foot, the price is more digestible – from £10pp.

As for the **pubs**, at the eastern end of town is *The New Inn* (☎ 01756 720252, 💻 appletreewick.pub; 1T/5D or T, all en suite; 🐾; WI-FI), a friendly place with recently renovated rooms where rates are from £55pp (sgl occ rates on request) including

continental breakfast (cooked £9.95 extra). The **food** (Wed-Sat noon-7pm, Sun to 5pm) may include veg lasagne (£11.95) and steak & ale pie (£15.95), but what really marks this place out is its 16 real ales all from local brewers.

However, as good as the grub is here, it suffers by comparison to the 16th-century *Craven Arms* (☎ 01756 720270, 💻 craven-cruckbarn.co.uk; WI-FI; 🐾; **fb**; food daily noon-8pm), back down the hill. Indeed, this is pretty much the most fascinating pub on the trail, built with stone-flagged floors and real oak beams and equipped with a large open fire and pleasant beer garden – and all of it still lit by gaslight. Always the centre of the village, until 1926 the Court Leet was still held here to deal with local minor crimes, the wrong-doers being punished in the stocks that still stand to the left of the building. The main focus here, though, is the fine food and good beer – areas in which they truly excel. The menu may include mains such as pan-fried fillet of salmon with crushed new potatoes (£16.95) and also 'Craven classics' such as steak & ale pie (£15.95) and also a couple of vegetarian/vegan options. The only criticism is that it gets so busy you need to get here early to secure a table. That, and the fact that the dishes tend to be tasty rather than hearty; though, to be fair, the puddings are of the same quality as the mains that preceded them and can top up any holes left unfilled by the main course.

There is no accommodation in the pub but they do have three heated **shepherd huts** (💻 shepherdhuts@craven-cruckbarn .co.uk; 2D/1Tr; from £75 per hut) with en suite shower rooms.

The river meanders a lot in this section, drifting here and there as if reluctant to head downstream, like a schoolchild on his way to an exam for which he hasn't revised. Soon, however, you leave the river for a brief stroll through farm and fields on the way to lovely **Burnsall**.

❏ **IMPORTANT NOTE – WALKING TIMES**

All times in this book refer only to the time spent walking. You will need to add 20-30% to allow for rests, photography, checking the map, drinking water etc.

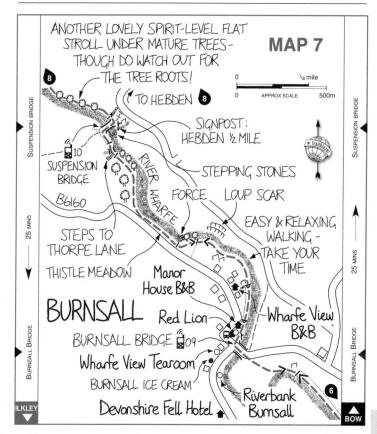

ANOTHER LOVELY SPIRIT-LEVEL FLAT STROLL UNDER MATURE TREES—THOUGH DO WATCH OUT FOR THE TREE ROOTS!

MAP 7

0 ¼ mile
0 APPROX SCALE 500m

TO HEBDEN

SIGNPOST: HEBDEN ½ MILE

SUSPENSION BRIDGE

10 SUSPENSION BRIDGE

B6160

RIVER WHARFE

STEPPING STONES

FORCE   LOUP SCAR

EASY & RELAXING WALKING — TAKE YOUR TIME

STEPS TO THORPE LANE

THISTLE MEADOW

Manor House B&B

BURNSALL

Red Lion

Wharfe View B&B

BURNSALL BRIDGE 09

Wharfe View Tearoom

BURNSALL ICE CREAM

Devonshire Fell Hotel

Riverbank Burnsall

SUSPENSION BRIDGE

25 MINS

BURNSALL BRIDGE

25 MINS

BURNSALL BRIDGE

ILKLEY

BOW

## BURNSALL [Map 7]

Though bisected by the B6160, the main road that runs along the length of the Wharfe from Addingham to Buckden and beyond, Burnsall is one of the most exquisite villages on the Dales Way. It can be quite beautiful at times, particularly in the late evening when the bridge glows a pale honey hue in the evening light, or during the day when kids splash about in the water while on the nearby green the parents gently sizzle and get sozzled under the scorching sun.

The 74/74A and Sun/bank holiday 874 **bus** services call here; for details pp47-9.

For accommodation, there are a few options. About 100m past the primary school, *Wharfe View B&B* (☎ 01756 720643, 🖳 burnsall.net; 2T both en suite, 2Qd shared facilities; 🐾; WI-FI; ℒ; from £42.50pp, sgl occ £55) has amiable hosts and large rooms. The two 'quad' rooms can actually sleep up to five people.

Dominating the centre of the village, *The Red Lion* (☎ 01756 720204, 🖳 red lion.co.uk; 14D or T, all en suite; 🐾; 🐕; WI-FI in the public areas; ℒ) was originally a ferryman's inn built in the 16th century (ie before the bridge was built) and remains the focus of village life today. B&B costs £65-90pp (sgl occ £120-170. Some of the rooms are a little small. The owners also run the Victorian *Manor House* (8D/3D or T, all en suite; 🐾; WI-FI in public area; B&B £55-65pp, sgl occ rates on request), just over 100m away, with most of the rooms boasting river and village views. In addition they also have **four cottages** (2D or T) in the village.

On the outskirts of town is the Edwardian *Devonshire Fell Hotel* (☎ 01756 729000 option 3, 🖥 devonshireho tels.co.uk/devonshire-fell-burnsall; 8D/4D or T/4Tr, all en suite; 🐾; WI-FI; 🐕) Another place named in honour of the local aristocrats, the hotel's bold décor is said to have been chosen by the Duchess of Devonshire herself. Rates vary greatly according to demand and season but start at around £70pp (from £125 for sgl occ) for B&B. Check online for special offers.

For **food**, there's *Riverbank Burnsall* (☎ 07711 530156, 🖥 riverbankburnsall .com; **fb**; approx 9am-3pm but days/hours vary so check on Google or contact them), a small, friendly, riverside café selling bacon rolls, tea, coffee and cakes as well as occasionally wood-fired pizza.

For something slightly more formal, *Wharfe View Tearoom* (☎ 01756 720237, 🖥 wharfe-view-cafe.business.site; Mon-Wed 9am-3pm, Sat & Sun to 4pm) does a good Yorkshire cheese on toast and a home-made steak & potato pie, though they accept only cash. Next door *Burnsall Ice Cream* (daily 11am-6pm) sells, er..., ice creams.

*The Red Lion* (see Where to stay; Sun-Thur 10am-7pm, Fri & Sat to 8.30pm) has classics, such as steak & ale pie (£14.50), sharing plates (from £13) and sandwiches (from £7) but also some more unusual dishes such as sautéed seabass fillets, seaweed gnocchi, roasted chestnuts, clementine purée, sea purslane & lemon foam (£18.50). The riverside seating out back by the path is lovely on a warm summer's evening.

## STAGE 2: BURNSALL TO BUCKDEN VIA GRASSINGTON
### MAPS 7-13

Up to now the Dales Way has stuck with limpet-like tenacity to the valley floor, hugging the riverbank closely and avoiding, where possible, any hint of a slope or gradient.

On this **14¾-mile (23.4km; about 6hrs)*** section, however, the path shows what treats await those who head for the heights. True, the first part of this stage, to Grassington, couldn't have been flatter if God had used a spirit level. The last stretch from Kettlewell to Buckden covers familiar riparian terrain, too – and both of these stretches are lovely in their own way.

But it's the middle section, from Grassington to Kettlewell, that will stick in your mind the longest. Free of the valley walls that have been hemming you in and the vast shadows they cast, you are now able to savour Yorkshire's very own Big Sky Country. It's bracing, there's little shelter, and it can be quite windswept and lonely; but there's no denying its beauty, the isolation is glorious – and the views down the valley frequently verge on the breathtaking.

Logistically, there are plenty of options for this stage. The 874 **bus** service (Sun/bank hols only; see pp47-9) bumbles along between Burnsall and Buckden, and there are several places to stop and eat on the way – or indeed, stop altogether for the day if the whim takes you, with Grassington and Kettlewell both directly en route and Hebden and Starbotton both just off it.

*(You need to add another 200m to take you from the trail to Buckden itself)

## The route

What a lovely – and gentle – way to start a stage. Heading round the back of the Red Lion on a path so flat that it's even accessible for wheelchairs, the trail continues its love affair with the Wharfe for this first stretch to Grassington, passing **Loup Scar** (Map 7), a limestone escarpment and the final resting place of poor Dr Petty, the victim of homicidal Tom Lee (see box p98). This stretch of the river up to the bridge is popular with anglers, canoeists, kingfishers and those who just want to spend a sunny summer afternoon splashing around. It's a very pretty stretch, with the springy old suspension bridge at **Hebden** (which is not the same as Hebden Bridge, a town about 40 miles to the south) and its accompanying stepping stones a particular highlight.

### HEBDEN                    [Map 8, p99]

Where the path turns left (west) after the bridge (see Map 7), those in need of sustenance can continue straight on to Hebden and *The Old School Tea Room* (Map 8; ☎ 01756 753778, 🖳 theoldschooltearoom .com; **fb**; WI-FI; well-behaved 🐾; Mon-Fri 10am-5pm, Sat & Sun 9am-5pm) where if the weather's right you can sit in their lovely garden and watch their pygmy goats play. It's pretty much the most charming tearoom on the walk, the only drawback being that it's the best part of 1½ miles (2.4km) from the trail.

Nearby, for accommodation, *Court Croft* (☎ 01756 753406; 2T en suite, 1T private bathroom; ☎; WI-FI; 🐾; Ⓛ) sits next to the church on Church Lane and is decent value with **B&B** costing £40-45pp (£45-50 sgl occ).

*North Barn* (☎ 01756 752816, 🖳 northbarnhebden.com; 2D or T, both en suite; ☎; WI-FI; Ⓛ) lies a little further north on Brayshaw Lane at the end of a farm track. Rates are from £40pp (sgl occ room

rate), with evening meals (£19.95) if booked in advance; bring your own wine.

Still further north, just off the B6265, *Orchard House* (off Map 8; ☎ 01756 752597, 🖳 orchardhousehebden.co.uk; 1D private bathroom/1D or T en suite; ☎; WI-FI) is at the far (northern) end of the village and charges from £37.50 (sgl occ room rate). Nearby, at the far northern end of Hebden – though simultaneously its spiritual centre – *The Clarendon* (☎ 01756 752446, 🖳 clarendoninn.co.uk; 5D/1T, all en suite; 🐾; WI-FI; Ⓛ) is an award-winning pub with rooms (B&B £50-70pp, sgl occ room rate), and the place to go in the evenings for **food** (Mon & Tue 6-9pm, Wed-Sat noon-2.30pm & 6-9pm, Sun noon-6.45pm); mains start from around £12 and range from pub classics such as gammon, eggs, chips & peas to more adventurous offerings such as pheasant burger with truffle mayonnaise, or Whitby cod cheeks with mussels.

The 74A **bus** service (see pp47-9) stops by The Clarendon.

Back at the bridge, on the northern side of the Wharfe the path becomes slightly quieter but no less level as you amble beneath a row of mighty chestnut trees. A further set of stepping stones to the left of the path, before you reach the fish farm, leads to **Linton**'s **St Michael and All Angels Church**, Norman in origin though much restored over the centuries. Back on the trail and sticking to the path through open, saturated sheep fields, eventually you turn right up a dreamy little country lane lined by two impressive stone walls. The lane leads all the way to Grassington, the town that marks the border between Lower Wharfedale and Upper Wharfedale. Before you do so, however, turn left at the stile to admire the view of **the weir** from the bridge.                    *(cont'd on p100)*

## ❏ THE TALE OF TOM LEE

The year was 1779 and the main protagonist of the story is a hot-headed young man in his late 20s. On the face of it life was pretty sweet for young Tom Lee. Married, with a good business as a blacksmith in the centre of pretty Grassington, there would have been many at that time who looked upon his situation with more than a degree of envy. They would also probably have resented the fact that such blessings had fallen to one who so little deserved it, for Tom Lee had a reputation as an intimidating bully, with a legendary temper that could be as hot as the metal that he worked with all day.

Things started to go very wrong for Tommy when he tried to hold up and rob the 'running postman', whose job it was to deliver the wages of the local lead miners to the counting house at Yarnbury, 1½ miles away. The attack, which occurred on Grassington's Moor Lane, failed largely because of the efforts of the postman himself who successfully fought back against his assailant, with Tom Lee receiving a bullet in the shoulder for his troubles.

Badly injured, Tommy sought the help of the local doctor, a cheerful middle-aged gentleman who went by the name of Dr Petty. Clearly a man of probity, Dr Petty adhered to the principle of patient/doctor confidentiality, and made no attempt to tell the authorities about Tom Lee's injuries – even though the attack on the running postman was by now common knowledge amongst the townsfolk – and such an assault was punishable by death.

Unfortunately for Dr Petty, this decision not to grass on the Grassington blacksmith was to have fatal consequences. For while the good doctor had saved the young man's life by treating his wounded shoulder, in return Tom Lee hatched a plot to kill Dr Petty, presumably because he couldn't live with the knowledge that all the doctor had to do was tell someone about his injuries and arrest – and execution – was sure to follow. Which was how it came to pass that, a few months later, the good doctor could be found lying wounded on the ground (near the path of the modern Dales Way; see p97), having been dragged from his horse by Tom who had been hiding behind a drystone wall. Under the light of the moon, he then set about beating the doctor to death, raining blow after sickening blow down upon his victim with a heavy cudgel, before dragging the limp body of Dr Petty into the undergrowth to cover his crime.

As the previous episode with the postman had already shown, however, Tom's wickedness was matched only by his incompetence. Returning to the scene of the crime with his young apprentice, Bowness, to bury the body, they quickly realised that the doctor was still – just – alive. This time Tommy made sure, killing the doctor 'again' before burying the body in a nearby peat bog. (Several weeks later Tommy moved the body for a second time, on this occasion with the help of his wife to the River Wharfe and Loup Scar, near Burnsall. Incidentally, the nearby lane is still called Skull Lane to this day.) Though the body was eventually discovered, and suspicion immediately fell upon Tom Lee, initially no charges were brought against him due to lack of evidence. Indeed, it was only three years later that his apprentice, Bowness, unable to live with the guilt any longer, went to the authorities to confess. Tom Lee was immediately arrested, tried, convicted and hanged, his body then suspended by chains in Grass Wood, near the scene of the murder.

Today, the life and crimes of Tom Lee are recounted in song, poem and play. You may, quite properly, think his rather unsavoury deeds unworthy of such celebration. But while nobody would describe the Dales Way as 'murderous', there is nevertheless a certain symmetry between the short, brutal life of Tom Lee, which was eventually ended by Bowness – and the short (and just occasionally brutal) Dales Way – which also, of course, ends by Bowness.

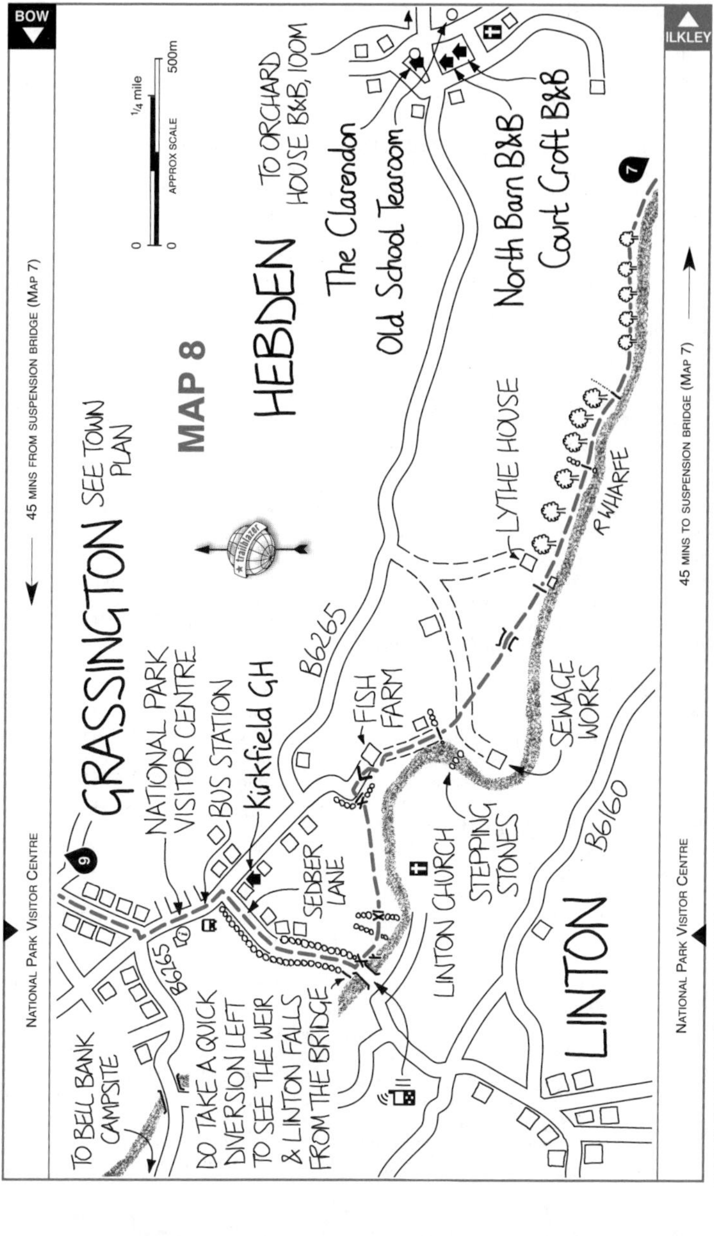

NATIONAL PARK VISITOR CENTRE

45 MINS FROM SUSPENSION BRIDGE (MAP 7)

¼ mile
0 500m
APPROX SCALE

GRASSINGTON SEE TOWN PLAN

MAP 8

HEBDEN

TO ORCHARD HOUSE B&B, 100M

The Clarendon
Old School Tearoom

North Barn B&B
Court Croft B&B

LYTHE HOUSE

R.WHARFE

SEWAGE WORKS

B6265

FISH FARM

Kirkfield GH

BUS STATION

NATIONAL PARK VISITOR CENTRE

SEBER LANE

TO BELL BANK CAMPSITE

B6265

DO TAKE A QUICK DIVERSION LEFT TO SEE THE WEIR & LINTON FALLS FROM THE BRIDGE

LINTON CHURCH
STEPPING STONES

LINTON

B6160

NATIONAL PARK VISITOR CENTRE

45 MINS TO SUSPENSION BRIDGE (MAP 7)

ROUTE GUIDE AND MAPS

## GRASSINGTON

You have to have a sneaking admiration for a place that decides not to cover up the fact that its most famous son is a murderer (see box on p98), but opts instead to celebrate it openly and fervently. Visit the smart glass bus shelter, for example, by the National Park Centre and you'll find a poem recounting Mr Lee's deeds etched into the glass, while head to the town centre and you'll find his former home is even marked with a plaque. But this is Grassington, Wharfedale's largest town and a lovely looking place, with a great character and, refreshingly for a tourist hotspot, a wonderful sense of community too.

The town's somewhat sedate façade also hides a rather lengthy and lively history that stretches back at least 1500 years, for the Romans farmed these slopes for grain way back in the 4th and 5th centuries AD. Since medieval times, however, Grassington has gone downhill – quite literally, for the remains of the medieval town lie in fields above the modern Grassington, as you'll see when you continue on the Dales Way to Kettlewell (see p104).

The current town prospered on the back of the lead-mining industry, which had been carried out in the local hills since the 15th century. As the mining industry thrived at the end of the 17th century so more people were attracted to the town and Grassington became a wild and rather lawless place during most of the 18th and early 19th centuries. No surprise, then, that the local police force is said to have been the first in the UK to have been armed! This was also the era of Tom Lee, his grisly acts adding even more notoriety to the town.

Eventually, as the mining industry died so the workforce drifted away, leaving only a few hardy souls and a couple of grand buildings behind, such as the Mechanics Institute at the top of town, donated in the 1870s by concerned benefactor, the Duke of Devonshire, after whom it is now named.

The town enjoyed a renaissance in the middle of the 20th century, thanks largely to the tourist industry; these days it's awash with Gore-Tex in the warmer months as hikers come from all around to explore the surrounding hills. This summer influx helps to keep the town's economy thriving and ensures, too, that there are plenty of B&Bs, cafés and pubs to serve the weary walker. However, being used as a location for filming the anniversary series (and now a second series) of *All Creatures Great and Small* (see p41) meant several businesses and private homes changed their identity and represented the book's fictional village Darrowby in the 1930s: The Stripey Badger bookshop became a grocer and The Devonshire's frontage was The Drovers Arms.

You can find more about the history of the town and its local environment by visiting **Grassington Folk Museum** (🖥 grassingtonfolkmuseum.org.uk; Mar-end Oct daily 2-4.30pm, but only if volunteer staff are available; free, but donations welcome), on the main square (which is called, rather unimaginatively, The Square). Exhibits include some locally panned gold and a few mesolithic arrow points and scrapers.

Even though Grassington is not at the end of a stage in this book it's only a few easy miles from Burnsall and many will say that the extra effort is definitely worth it.

### Services

The **National Park Visitor Centre** (🖥 www.yorkshiredales.org.uk; late Mar to end Oct daily 10am-5pm; weekends only in winter 10am-4pm) sits on the Dales Way at the start of town, next to the main bus stop. Full of useful info, it's a great place to sort out the rest of your trip, find out about bus services and buy souvenirs. Lots and lots of souvenirs. By the way there is a fee of 20p to use the **toilets** next door – rather annoying if you've been saving yourself on the walk for this moment!

Another option for tourist information is **The Hub** (Grassington Hub & Community Library; ☎ 01756 752222, 🖥 discovergrassington.co.uk; Mon-Fri 10am-12.30 & 1.30-4pm, Sat 9.30am-1pm).

Moving to the centre you'll find the **post office** (Mon-Fri 9am-5.30pm, Sat to 4.30pm) inside a general store (daily 10am-5pm), while down the hill is a small

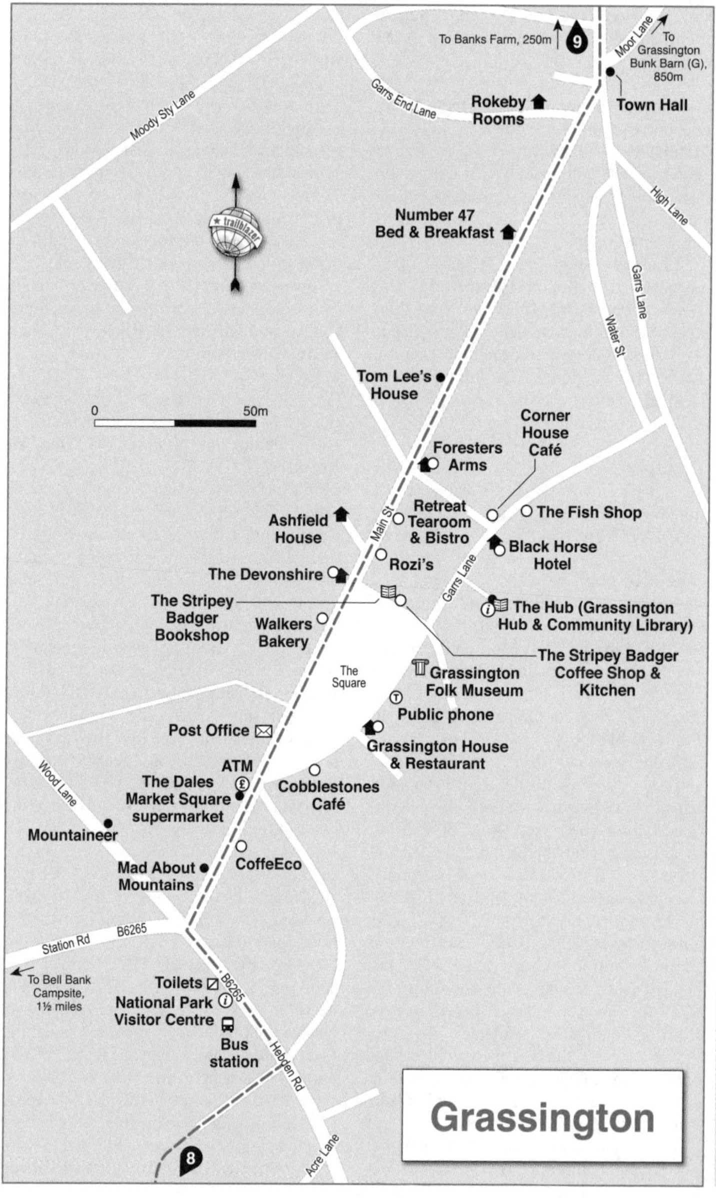

To Banks Farm, 250m  **9**

Moor Lane
To
Grassington
Bunk Barn (G),
850m

Garrs End Lane

**Rokeby
Rooms**

**Town Hall**

Moody Sty Lane

High Lane

**Number 47
Bed & Breakfast**

Garrs Lane

Water St

*trailblazer*

0        50m

**Tom Lee's
House**

**Corner
House
Café**

**Foresters
Arms**

**Retreat
Tearoom
& Bistro**

○ **The Fish Shop**

**Black Horse
Hotel**

**Ashfield
House**

Main St

**The Devonshire** ○

**Rozi's**

Garrs Lane

**The Hub (Grassington
Hub & Community Library)**

**The Stripey
Badger
Bookshop**

**Walkers
Bakery**

**The Stripey Badger
Coffee Shop &
Kitchen**

The Square

**Grassington
Folk Museum**

**Public phone**

**Post Office** ⊠

**Grassington House
& Restaurant**

**ATM
£**

**The Dales
Market Square
supermarket**

○ **Cobblestones
Café**

**Mountaineer** ●

**Mad About ●
Mountains**

○ **CoffeEco**

Station Rd    B6265

B6265

← To Bell Bank
Campsite,
1½ miles

**Toilets** ☒
**National Park** ⓘ
**Visitor Centre**

**Bus
station**

Hebden Rd

Acre Lane

**8**

# Grassington

ROUTE GUIDE AND MAPS

**supermarket**, The Dales Market Square (daily 8am-9pm), with a free-to-use **ATM** outside it.

Reflecting the popularity of Grassington amongst walkers, there is not one but two **outdoor stores**: Mad About Mountains (Mon-Sat 9am-5.30pm), by the supermarket; and, round the corner on Wood Lane, Mountaineer (🖳 mountaineer shop.co.uk; daily 10am-4pm), which sells camping stove gas.

The **bookshop** (daily 10am-4.30pm) adjacent to The Stripey Badger (see Where to eat) is run by the same business; their stock includes local guidebooks and maps.

There's plenty of accommodation but during **Grassington Festival** and **Dickens Festival** (see box on p14) rooms may be a little harder to come by.

### Transport

[See pp47-9 for details]  Grassington is a stop on several **bus** routes: the 72/72A/ 72B, 74/74A and 874/875.

### Where to stay

There are **no campsites** in Grassington: the nearest one (**Bell Bank**; ☎ 01756 752321; 🐾 £10/14 for one/two people and a tent but no children; showers and toilets; nice people; Apr-end Oct) is almost two miles away across the river on Skirethorns Lane in **Threshfield** (the 72/72A/874 bus services call here; see pp47-9).

There are **no hostels** in Grassington either and what's more, the local **Grassington Bunk Barn** (☎ 01756 753882, 🖳 grassingtonbunkbarn.co.uk; 1 x 2-bunk bed en suite, 3 x 6-, 2 x 12- bunk bedrooms; shared facilities; WI-FI; 🐾 ), about 800m above the town on Moor Lane (opposite the junction with Edge Lane), usually only accept **group bookings** (from £410 per night) but individuals may stay during the week for £26 per night if there is a gap. Cooking facilities are available.

As such, a **B&B** is pretty much your only option in Grassington, and they fill up fast. At the top of town, friendly **Banks Farm** (off Map 9; ☎ 07766 257555, 🖳 banksfarmgrassington.co.uk; 1D en suite, 1D private bathroom; 🛏; 🐾 ; WI-FI; ⓛ);

rates from £45pp, sgl occ £65; 10% discount for walkers and cyclists), is pretty much the last house on Chapel St before Bank Lane so is right on the Dales Way.

Further downhill is **Rokeby Rooms** (☎ 01756 753839 or ☎ 07855 925048, 🖳 grassington.wixsite.com/rokebyrooms; 2D, both en suite; 🛏; WI-FI; ⓛ), a pretty former 17th-century farmhouse off the northern end of Main St on Garrs End Lane. It has elegantly decorated rooms and a delightful flower-filled garden which guests are free to use. Breakfast is not offered, though there's no shortage of options in town, so you needn't go hungry. Room-only rates are from £55pp (sgl occ £75; room rate at weekends).

Moving down the hill, on the same side of Main St and also dating from the 17th century is **Number 47 Bed & Breakfast** (☎ 01756 752069, ☎ 07734 110521, 🖳 www.number47.co.uk; 1D or T private bathroom; 🛏; WI-FI; ⓛ); they charge from £45pp (sgl rates on request). They also have a very small single which they are happy to let for a group of three people and cycle storage is available.

Tucked away down its own private cul-de-sac off Main St is the 17th-century, Grade II listed **Ashfield House** (☎ 01756 752584, 🖳 ashfieldhouse.co.uk; 4D/3D or T, garden suite; all en suite; 🛏; WI-FI; ⓛ); a supremely smart place that was once just a row of humble lead-miners' cottages. B&B rates are from £60pp (sgl occ rates on request), but rise to over £100pp (based on two sharing) for the garden suite.

Ashfield House's position as the smartest address in Grassington has two real challengers. Firstly, no review of the town's accommodation can be complete without **Grassington House** (☎ 01756 752406, 🖳 grassingtonhouse.co.uk) 8D/1D or T, all en suite; 🛏; WI-FI; ⓛ); after all, it was their decision back in the late 19th century to change their home from a private residence to a boarding house which kicked off the tourist industry here. The place itself is very salubrious and comfy – as you'd expect from a hotel that's had over a hundred years to get it right. The rooms are all individually furnished and the rates are also varied, with B&B ranging from £72.50 to £97.50pp (sgl occ £127.50-137.50).

Finally, in addition to the B&Bs, there are the **pubs**. ***The Devonshire*** (☎ 01756 752525, 🖳 thedevonshiregrassington.co.uk; **fb**; 4D or T/4Qd, all en suite; ☕; WI-FI; 🐕; Ⓛ; B&B costs from £55pp, sgl occ rates on request) is large and centrally located. Also on Main St, the noisy ***Foresters Arms*** (☎ 01756 752349, 🖳 forestersarmsgrassington.co.uk; **fb**; 3D/1T/1D or T/2Tr, all en suite; ☕; 🐕; WI-FI; Ⓛ) currently gets the lion's share of guests. This 18th-century former coaching inn is down-to-earth and remains the most popular place to eat at night (see Where to eat) so there's not far to crawl back to bed afterwards. B&B costs from £45pp (sgl occ £65). ***Black Horse Hotel*** (☎ 01756 752770, 🖳 blackhorsehotelgrassington.co.uk; 4T/8D/2Tr/1Qd, all en suite; ☕; 🐕; WI-FI) has smart rooms for a pub and provides a decent, albeit more expensive alternative (B&B from £51.25pp, sgl occ £72.50). There is a minimum 2-night stay here at weekends.

On Hebden Rd (B6265) south of the town centre is ***Kirkfield Guest House*** (Map 8; ☎ 01756 752385, 🖳 kirkfieldguesthouse.co.uk; 1Qd/1Tr both en suite, 1T/1Tr shared facilities; ☕; WI-FI; Ⓛ). Guests have access to a private TV lounge and they also have a drying room. B&B costs from £40pp (sgl occ from £50).

### Where to eat and drink

While Grassington can't quite feed you round the clock, it certainly does its best. Those in need of an early morning fix of caffeine and cholesterol should find that ***Walkers Bakery*** (🖳 www.walkers-bakery.co.uk; Mon-Sat 8am-3pm) is often open much earlier than advertised and seems happy to serve you. There's no seating inside but for those wanting to set off on the trail early, they do a good selection of pastries, filled rolls and the like.

If caffeine is your drug of choice, you certainly won't be suffering withdrawal symptoms in Grassington. At the southern end of The Square, ***CoffeEco*** ☎ 01756 751835; 🐕; **fb**; Thur-Tue 9am-5pm), where both dogs and muddy boots are welcome, serves coffee carrying the Fairtrade mark and the food is locally sourced where possible.

On the northern side of The Square, and also very welcoming, ***The Stripey Badger Coffee Shop & Kitchen*** (☎ 01756 753583, 🖳 thestripeybadger.co.uk; WI-FI; 🐕; **fb**; Wed-Sun 10am-4.30pm) does great coffee, tasty breakfasts (try the bacon croissant melt, £5.25) and hearty soups (£4.95). Their cakes are also well worth sampling.

Also on The Square, ***Cobblestones Café*** (☎ 01756 752303; **fb**; WI-FI; 🐕; Mon-Wed 10am-3pm, Sat to 4pm) is another dog-friendly option with paninis, scones, hot chocolate and the like, plus a decent full English breakfast.

Continuing up the hill the family-run ***Corner House Café*** (☎ 01756 752414, 🖳 cornerhousegrassington.co.uk; **fb**; WI-FI; 🐕; daily 10am-4pm) does cakes, bakes, omelettes and toast, plus grilled paninis and burgers.

Also in the café mould, the ***Retreat Tearoom & Bistro*** (☎ 01756 751887, 🖳 retreatgrassington.co.uk; 🐕; **fb**; daily 10am-4pm, winter hours may vary) is very popular. Again, they welcome muddy boots. They don't have wi-fi, but do have great coffee and a sizeable menu of healthy breakfasts (£2.80-7.95), sandwiches (from £5.80) and lunchtime options (£5-11). Their weekend **bistro** (Mar-Nov Fri & Sat 6.15-8.15pm) offers more grown-up mains (from £13.95) plus a wine menu.

Other than the bistro, evening options are restricted to takeaways and pubs. For takeaway there's ***Rozi's*** (☎ 01756 753342, 🖳 rozisgrassington.co.uk; daily 5-11.30pm), an Indian restaurant where you can eat in or takeaway, or ***The Fish Shop*** (☎ 01756 751863; **fb**; summer Tue-Thur noon-1.30pm & 4-7pm, Fri & Sat same but to 8pm, winter Tue & Wed 4-7pm, Thur-Sat noon-1.30pm & 4-7pm) at 6 Garrs Lane.

For pubs, ***Foresters Arms*** (see Where to stay; food Mon-Sat noon-2.30pm & 5.30-8pm, Sun noon-7pm) is very popular with walkers and locals alike, which is always a good sign. Their reputation for serving huge portions of grub is justifiable, with mains costing £11.95-12.95, although the sandwiches are cheaper.

There's also **Black Horse Hotel** (see Where to stay; food Mon-Thur noon-2.30pm & 5.30-9pm, Fri & Sat noon-9pm, Sun noon-8pm) again offering traditional English fare but with evening mains costing £12-16. **The Devonshire** (see Where to stay; food Mon-Sat noon-8.45pm, Sun to 7.45pm) also serves standard pub food,

including weekend roasts, with mains costing £10-16.

**Grassington House** (see Where to stay Grassington House; food Wed & Thur noon-8pm, Fri & Sat noon-8.30pm, Sun to 7.30pm) plays host to the town's most refined dining option; mains at its restaurant may include baked monkfish (£19.95), Yorkshire lamb (£24.50) and pan-seared wood-pigeon breast (starter £7.25).

It's after Grassington that things – literally – begin to look up. You can tell from the fact that you leave Grassington from the top end of the village that the riparian walking you've been used to thus far on the trail is, for the moment at least, suspended. Yet in spite of the bleak, lonely nature of this section, curiously the area is rich in archaeological treasures with plenty of tell-tale signs that man once lived and worked here – and died up here too.

The evidence that man once lived up here can be found in the **medieval village of Grassington** (Map 9), which you come upon almost as soon as you leave the modern-day version. To the layman there's little remarkable about these first few fields that you cross, save that they seem a bit more lumpy than usual. But when seen from the air a clear series of enclosures and building platforms can be discerned, etched into the pasture. The area has yet to be fully surveyed, but a small dig in the 1960s uncovered a *midden* (an old dump for kitchen waste) containing pottery from the 14th century as well as a few rectangular buildings built in a row, one with a paved floor.

A little way along is proof that man died and was buried up here too. A turf-covered **burial cairn**, situated to the left of the path before the kiln, dates back to the early Bronze Age, around 4000 years ago. Excavated in 1892 by the local vicar, the cairn consisted of a central chamber that contained the bones of at least five individuals, as well as several flint arrowheads and an early Bronze Age beaker.

As for the evidence that man worked here too, well about half a mile further on the path passes a **lime kiln** on the left, dating back to about the mid 19th century. These kilns were used to super-heat limestone, producing quicklime which was then spread on the fields to improve the fertility of the soil by controlling the acidity. The limestone could also be used for mortar in buildings.

These days, of course, where man has finally moved out, the cows have moved in, and it is their disconcerting, unblinking gaze that will follow your progress now as you cross field after field, finally ending up overlooking a tall **communications mast** – proof that modern man hasn't abandoned these uplands altogether. Don't make the mistake, as so many do on this stage, of heading down the slope here on Scot Gate Lane, a path that leads to Conistone and Kilnsey but which will entail either a long schlep back up the slope to rejoin the path or a section of roadside trudging up the valley to the next destination, Kettlewell. Unless, of course, you specifically want to…

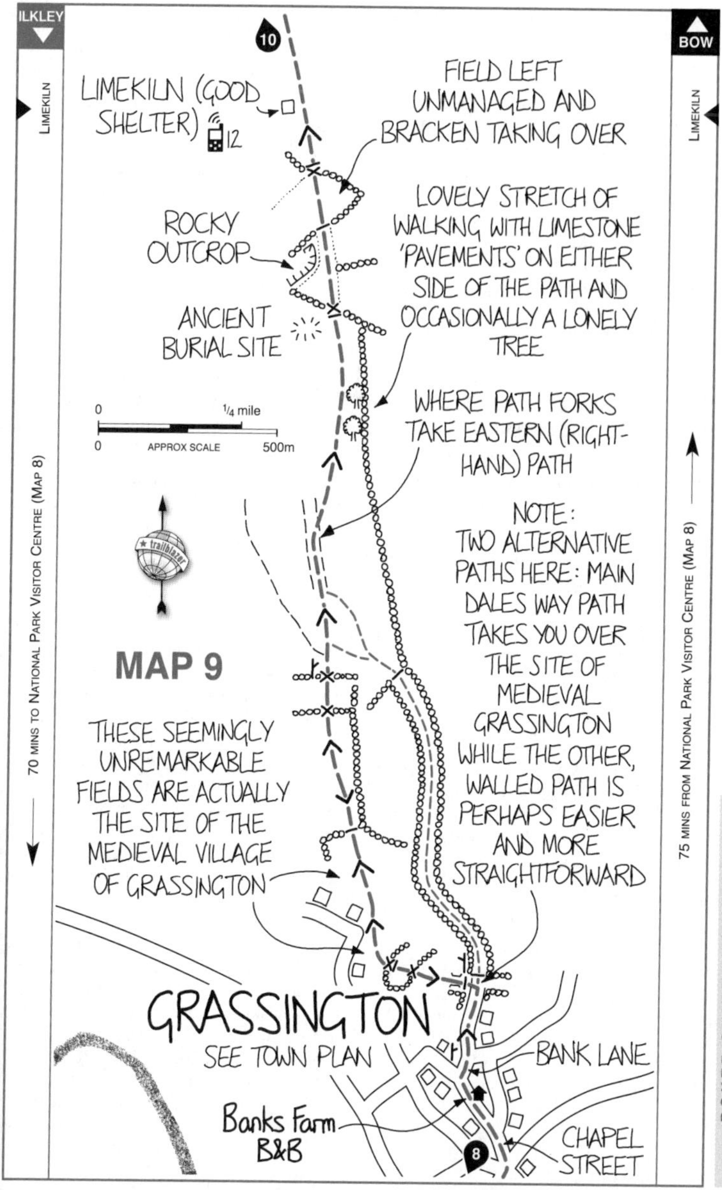

ILKLEY ▼

LIMEKILN ►

**10**

LIMEKILN (GOOD SHELTER) 📱12

ROCKY OUTCROP

ANCIENT BURIAL SITE

0 ¼ mile
0 APPROX SCALE 500m

▲ trailblazer

**MAP 9**

THESE SEEMINGLY UNREMARKABLE FIELDS ARE ACTUALLY THE SITE OF THE MEDIEVAL VILLAGE OF GRASSINGTON

FIELD LEFT UNMANAGED AND BRACKEN TAKING OVER

LOVELY STRETCH OF WALKING WITH LIMESTONE 'PAVEMENTS' ON EITHER SIDE OF THE PATH AND OCCASIONALLY A LONELY TREE

WHERE PATH FORKS TAKE EASTERN (RIGHT-HAND) PATH

NOTE: TWO ALTERNATIVE PATHS HERE: MAIN DALES WAY PATH TAKES YOU OVER THE SITE OF MEDIEVAL GRASSINGTON WHILE THE OTHER, WALLED PATH IS PERHAPS EASIER AND MORE STRAIGHTFORWARD

**GRASSINGTON**
SEE TOWN PLAN

Banks Farm B&B

**8**

BANK LANE

CHAPEL STREET

BOW ▲

LIMEKILN ►

← 70 MINS TO NATIONAL PARK VISITOR CENTRE (MAP 8)

75 MINS FROM NATIONAL PARK VISITOR CENTRE (MAP 8) →

ROUTE GUIDE AND MAPS

## CONISTONE & KILNSEY    [Map 10]

Two small settlements (Conistone and Kilnsey) sit snugly in the valley, hidden from the trail a steep mile away.

Conistone (⌨ kilnseyandconistone.co .uk) lies on the eastern side of the Wharfe and is, unfortunately, perhaps best known for the Mossdale Caverns tragedy, where six cavers were drowned in 1967 in what remains the most deadly speleological incident in the UK. A plaque marks the entrance to the caverns, which have been closed to cavers since the tragedy.

There's little for the trekker in Conistone – though it's pretty enough – but

across the water in **Kilnsey** is Kilnsey Park Estate (off Map 10; ⌨ kilnseypark.co.uk), just off the B6160, with its own *café* (daily 9am-5pm). The estate actually dates back to the 1100s, when it was farmed by the monks from nearby Fountains Abbey, though these days it's better known for its trout farm and its meadows, in which grow the UK's rarest orchid, the lady's slipper orchid (see pp64-5).

The limited 72A/72B, 874 & 875 **bus** services stop in Kilnsey; see pp47-9.

For those who don't want to drop all that way to Conistone, keep instead to the high ground and the trail and you will eventually find yourself, after a period of valley-top tramping, descending via wood and field to the outskirts of Kettlewell. Within sight of the village (Map 11), however, a rather nasty surprise awaits, with a lengthy series of stiles, gates, gaps and ladders across a series of narrow fields standing between you and your destination. It's like an agrarian version of the Olympic 110m hurdles, except there's only sheep as spectators and there are no medals for those who complete the course…just the chance of a well-earned cup of tea.

## KETTLEWELL    [see map p109]

*The charm of Kettlewell is an abiding charm, and to those of us whose life is spent amid the hurley-burley of city life, the village seems the peculiar abode of peace and quiet beauty; its limestone terraces, with their fringes of hazel and rowan coppices give to the district a characteristic beauty. But the special glory of Kettlewell is not that of colour, but of line. Situated at the junction of the main valley of the Wharfe valley, which descends from the Coverhead Pass, Kettlewell is the converging point of many contour lines, and to the eye which delights in the flow and ripple of sky line there is a beauty in Kettlewell which is all its own.*
    **Frederic William Moorman** (1872-1918), Professor of English Language and Literature at Leeds University. Moorman, incidentally, died in a drowning accident and was succeeded in the post by one JRR Tolkien.
    Kettlewell is where Wharfedale and Coverdale meet, a cosy little village where

the houses are huddled cheek-by-jowl on the valley floor while the sheer slopes of the fells rise loftily above. The name is believed to derive from the Anglo-Saxon 'Cetel Wella', which means a bubbling spring or stream, and in 1997 workmen digging near the village uncovered the skeleton of a woman that dates back to this era, being about 1400 years old. Like Grassington, however, Kettlewell only grew really prosperous with the establishment of the lead-mining industry that flourished in these parts back in the 17th and 18th centuries.

    These days it's tourism that brings in the bucks, with walkers and cyclists in particular making up the majority of visitors. Most of them use the village as a base, of course, to explore the surrounding hills but if you've got a spare few minutes do visit the pretty local church, **St Mary's**, a 19th-century edifice built on the site of an original 12th-century Norman church.

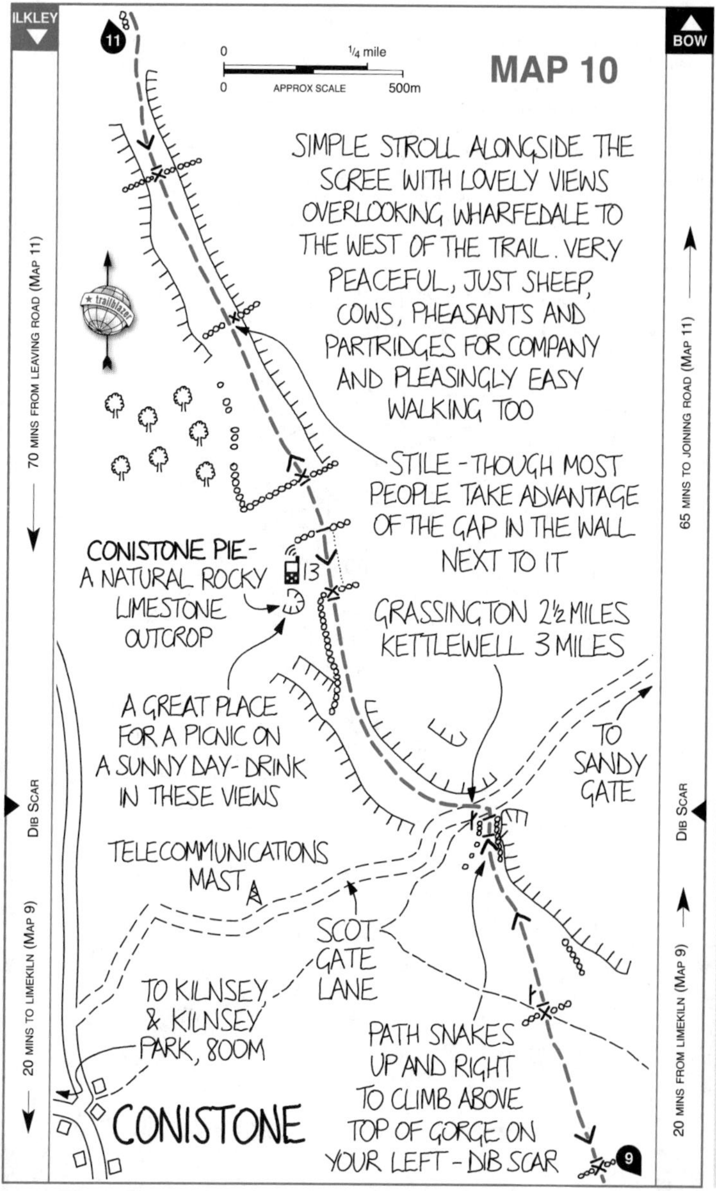

**MAP 10**

0 ———— ¼ mile
0 ———— 500m
APPROX SCALE

ILKLEY ▼

BOW ▲

(11)

70 MINS FROM LEAVING ROAD (MAP 11)

65 MINS TO JOINING ROAD (MAP 11)

★ trailblazer

SIMPLE STROLL ALONGSIDE THE SCREE WITH LOVELY VIEWS OVERLOOKING WHARFEDALE TO THE WEST OF THE TRAIL. VERY PEACEFUL, JUST SHEEP, COWS, PHEASANTS AND PARTRIDGES FOR COMPANY AND PLEASINGLY EASY WALKING TOO

STILE - THOUGH MOST PEOPLE TAKE ADVANTAGE OF THE GAP IN THE WALL NEXT TO IT

CONISTONE PIE - A NATURAL ROCKY LIMESTONE OUTCROP

13

GRASSINGTON 2½ MILES
KETTLEWELL 3 MILES

A GREAT PLACE FOR A PICNIC ON A SUNNY DAY - DRINK IN THESE VIEWS

TO SANDY GATE

TELECOMMUNICATIONS MAST

SCOT GATE LANE

DIB SCAR

DIB SCAR

20 MINS TO LIMEKILN (MAP 9)

20 MINS FROM LIMEKILN (MAP 9)

TO KILNSEY & KILNSEY PARK, 800m

CONISTONE

PATH SNAKES UP AND RIGHT TO CLIMB ABOVE TOP OF GORGE ON YOUR LEFT - DIB SCAR

(9)

## Services

**Kettlewell village store** (🖳 kvsonline .co.uk; Mon-Sat 9am-3pm, Sun to noon) is very much the heartbeat of the village. There is no tourist information in town but the people who run the store seem to be able to answer any questions you may have. In the absence of any ATM in the village the store's **cashback facility** is also very handy. The pubs here usually also offer cashback.

## Transport

[See pp47-9] Kettlewell is a stop on the Nos 72A/72B, 874 & 875 **bus** routes.

## Where to stay

There is an excellent **campsite**, called *Kettlewell Camping* (☎ 07930 379079, 🖳 kettlewellcamping.co.uk; £10pp; 🐕 on lead; mid Mar to end Oct), well located on the edge of the village and a short way off the trail. There's a smart and spotless toilet

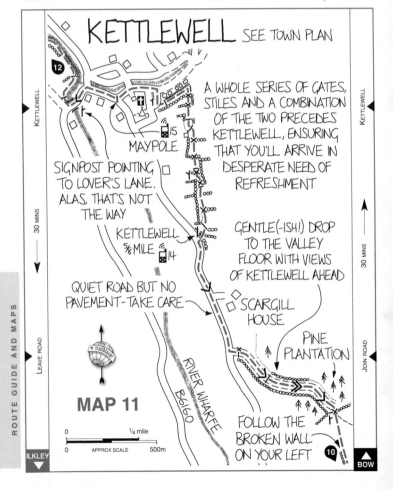

ROUTE GUIDE AND MAPS

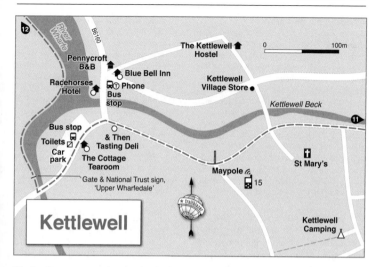

**Kettlewell**

block where you can have a lovely hot shower, and there's even access to a fridge, should you need one.

The village also plays host to one of the oldest **hostels** in the YHA network, having taken in guests for over 75 years. *The Kettlewell Hostel* (☎ 01756 760232, 🖳 yha.org.uk/hostel/yha-kettlewell or 🖳 the kettlewellhostel.co.uk; WI-FI; ⓛ; Feb-Nov for individual bookings; WI-FI) is an independent family-run hostel affiliated with the YHA. There are 42 beds across 11 rooms (2x2-, 4x3-, 2x4-, 1x5 & 2x6-bed room, shared facilities); the communal areas include a large dining room, lounge with wood-burning stove, garden, self-catering kitchen and drying room. The hostel also has a large second-hand bookshop. Home-cooked evening meals and breakfasts are available as well as packed lunches if requested the night before. The hostel is fully licensed. Check-in is from 4pm. Private rooms cost from £59 for two sharing; they hope to be able to offer dorm beds (from £25) in 2022 but at the time of research couldn't confirm this. There is a discount of up to 15% for current members of the YHA .

Sadly there are only two **B&Bs** left in Kettlewell. Friendly and helpful

*Pennycroft* (☎ 01756 760845, 🖳 penny croft.co.uk; 1D en suite; ●; WI-FI; ⓛ; from £42.50pp, sgl occ £70) sits right next to the pubs and boasts of serving the 'best breakfast in the Dales'.

*The Cottage Tea Room* (☎ 01756 760405, 🖳 www.kettlewelltearooms.co.uk; 2D, both en suite; ●; 🐾; WI-FI) has two neat and tidy rooms for B&B, and welcomes guests with a glass of sherry and a chocolate; the breakfast room is also a residents' lounge. Rates are from £57.50pp (sgl occ room rate).

Otherwise, you'll have to stay in one of the pubs. Hopefully open again after a refurb, following a severe flood in 2020, *Racehorses Hotel* (☎ 01756 760233, 🖳 racehorseshotel.co.uk; 5D/9D or T, all en suite; ●; WI-FI; ⓛ; 🐾; B&B rates £55-60pp, sgl occ from £90) dates back to the mid 1700s according to the date above the large fireplace. It's a big place for such a small village, though it's rather overshadowed by the even older and more popular *Blue Bell Inn* (☎ 01756 760230, 🖳 blue bellkettlewell.com; 2T/4D, all en suite; 🐾; WI-FI; ⓛ; B&B from £55pp, sgl occ £90) where dogs are given just as warm a welcome as their owners.

## Where to eat and drink

As its name suggests *The Cottage Tea Room* (see Where to stay; food daily 9am-5pm) is more of a traditional tearoom than a café. It stands opposite the car park on the way out of the village, and serves decent teacakes, but also does coffee and hot food. Due to Covid they installed a marquée and the tea room may continue to be in this.

Newer on the scene is the unusually named *& Then Tasting Deli* (fb; Wed-Sun 10am-4pm), a cute, stone-walled café-cum-deli with excellent coffee as well as sandwiches, melts, Yorkshire cheeses, cold meats, pasties, croissants and home-made flapjacks. They do wine and beer, too.

*Blue Bell Inn* (see Where to stay; Mon-Sat noon-3pm & 5-9pm, Sun noon-7pm), employs nice little touches such as the miniature glasses by each of the beer pumps, which allow you to 'try before you buy'; they also give a warm welcome to people's dogs. The menu includes their famous Blue Bell Meat & Potato Pie (£14.65), which is large enough to take up most of a table. You won't go hungry here!

Another option, *Racehorses Hotel* (see Where to stay: food Mon-Fri noon-2pm, Sat & Sun to 3pm, daily 6-9pm), opposite, is not a bad choice either, with more typical pub-grub mains starting at around £10.

Leaving Kettlewell, note the garage on the right by the car park, which played a small but integral role in the 2003 film *Calendar Girls*. In the movie, a calendar of topless 'glamour models' on the wall of the garage provides the inspiration for the WI (Women's Institute) ladies to get their kit off for charity; see p41. Thereafter, things settle down into a pattern more familiar with Dales Way walkers as the trail once again adheres more or less to the river, passing through yet more archetypal Dales fields and pasture meadows, each separated from its neighbour by an old drystone wall.

After 2¼ miles (3.5km) a bridge conveys those seeking rest or refreshment across the water to teeny-tiny **Starbotton**.

## STARBOTTON                    [Map 12]

Those for whom the Dales Way is little more than a glorified pub crawl may wish to take the bridge across the Wharfe to the 70-house hamlet of Starbotton and the very decent, 400-year-old *Fox and Hounds* (☎ 01756 760269, 🖳 foxandhoundsstarbotton .co.uk; 3D/1T, all en suite; ◔; 🐾; Ⓛ; WI-FI). **B&B** rates are from £40pp (sgl occ £70) and they serve good **food** (Wed-Sat noon-3pm & 5.30-8pm, Sun noon-6.30pm) and have a selection of real ales. They are always closed on Mondays and Tuesdays.

At the far (northern) end of the village, *Sweetbriar Cottage* (☎ 01756 761307, 🖳

sweetbriarcottage.co.uk; 1Qd, private bathroom; ◔; 🐾; WI-FI; Ⓛ) is a converted 18th-century farmhouse. The **B&B** room has a double bed and bunk beds (for up to four adults) as well as its own private lounge; rates are from £50pp (sgl occ £75).

They also offer **camping** for £7.50pp, with toilets and a tap, but no showers. Breakfast is also available for campers if requested in advance.

The 72A/72B **bus** services call here; see pp47-9.

---

### 💻 IMPORTANT NOTE – WALKING TIMES

All times in this book refer only to the time spent walking. You will need to add 20-30% to allow for rests, photography, checking the map, drinking water etc.

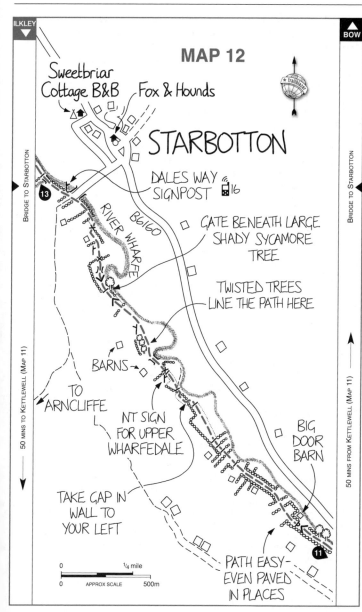

ILKLEY ▼

BOW ▲

**MAP 12**

Sweetbriar Cottage B&B

Fox & Hounds

## STARBOTTON

DALES WAY SIGNPOST 📱16

B6160

RIVER WHARFE

GATE BENEATH LARGE SHADY SYCAMORE TREE

TWISTED TREES LINE THE PATH HERE

BARNS ⟶

TO ARNCLIFFE

NT SIGN FOR UPPER WHARFEDALE

TAKE GAP IN WALL TO YOUR LEFT

BIG DOOR BARN

PATH EASY – EVEN PAVED IN PLACES

13

11

BRIDGE TO STARBOTTON

BRIDGE TO STARBOTTON

50 MINS TO KETTLEWELL (MAP 11)

50 MINS FROM KETTLEWELL (MAP 11)

0 — ¼ mile
0 — 500m
APPROX SCALE

ROUTE GUIDE AND MAPS

Back on the western side of the bridge, the call of Buckden continues to lure you onward, the path still flirting with the Wharfe. At one point you pass a copse of incongruous **redwoods**, the living remnants of a 19th-century estate, planted by local landowner Sir John Ramsden in 1850 – though now, like everything else round here, property of the National Trust.

As trail and river diverge you'll notice the surrounding land becoming boggier (though thankfully not the path itself) and sedges and other moisture-loving plants dominate the fields, evidence of the fact you're now on a floodplain that is still occasionally inundated after heavy rain.

### BUCKDEN                    [Map 13]
The serene village of Buckden (🖳 buckden .org) can feel like the final outpost of civilisation: in all probability your mobile phone signal will have abandoned you back down the valley before Kettlewell; the bus also stops following your path here. And after here there's just one more pub, a church, and a few scattered farmhouses providing lonely but lovely accommodation before the inn at Cowgill is reached in the neighbouring valley of Dentdale, over 16 miles (25.7km) away. What's more, the nearest shop from here isn't until Dent, almost 22 miles (35.4km) and one very long day's walk further along the trail. So stock up in Buckden and plan well, for there's little help along the way for the next 20 miles and more.

The **village shop** (☎ 01756 760257; Mon & Tue & Thur-Sat 8am-4pm, Sun 9am-4pm) is reasonably well stocked, but does sometimes close early if it's pelting down with rain. The owner also provides tea and coffee. At the time of research the **phone box** outside wasn't working.

The 72A/72B, 874 & 875 **bus** services stop by and opposite Buck Inn; for details see pp47-9.

For **accommodation**, you can pitch a tent or sleep in a heated wooden camping pod at *Buckden Camping* (☎ 07786 896985, 🖳 buckdencamping.co.uk; ✻; WI-FI). Tent pitches cost £11.50/16 for one/two people. Furnished heated camping pods, which can sleep up to three adults or two adults with up to three children, cost £50-

55 for two plus £3 for each extra person. They come with mattresses, but you need your own bedding. Shower and toilet block facilities are available. Note that advance booking in the summer months is essential.

Frustratingly for most walkers, the National Trust-owned **Town Head Bunk Barn** (🖳 nationaltrust.org.uk/holidays/town-head-barn-yorkshire) is for groups only.

For **B&B**, there are two choices: the highly recommended *West Winds* (☎ 07790 692938, 🖳 westwindsbuckden.co.uk; 1S or T/1D, private facilities; WI-FI; ⓛ) where you'll receive complimentary tea and cake on arrival, and a great breakfast to set you on your way the following day. B&B rates are from £40pp (sgl £50, sgl occ £55).

The other option is the village pub, *The Buck Inn* (☎ 01756 761933, 🖳 the buckinn.com; 1S/1T/4D, all en suite; ✻; WI-FI; ⓛ). It's certainly the spiritual centre of the village and a warm welcome is pretty much guaranteed. The rooms were revamped in 2018 after the pub was fully refurbished and are smart, bright and modern. Rates are from £47.50pp (sgl/sgl occ £85). This is also the only **place to eat** but fortunately it's a cosy, welcoming place and both the **food** (daily noon-2.30pm & 6-8.30pm) and the real ales are excellent. Mains cost £12-14 and include the likes of steak & ale pie, hunters' chicken, and butternut squash & chickpea curry. Homemade ciabatta sandwiches with chips (£6.95) are also available until 2.30pm.

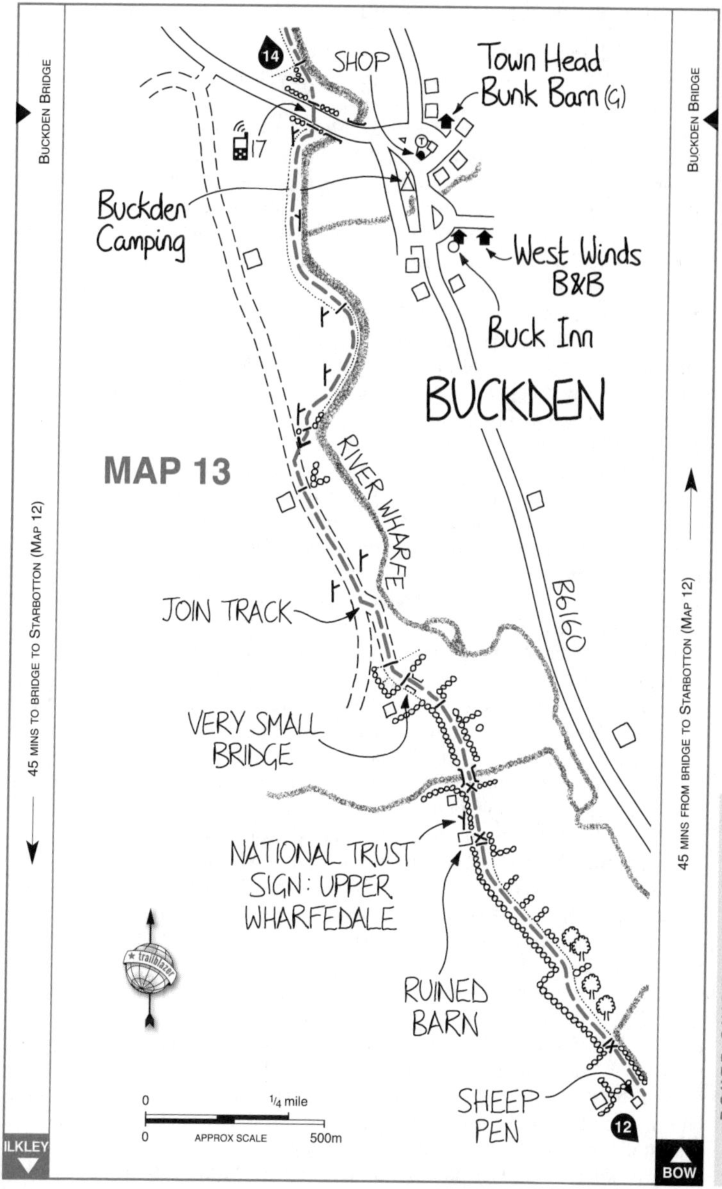

BUCKDEN BRIDGE

BUCKDEN BRIDGE

14

SHOP

Town Head
Bunk Barn (G)

17

Buckden
Camping

West Winds
B&B

Buck Inn

BUCKDEN

RIVER WHARFE

MAP 13

B6160

JOIN TRACK

VERY SMALL
BRIDGE

NATIONAL TRUST
SIGN: UPPER
WHARFEDALE

RUINED
BARN

SHEEP
PEN

12

45 MINS TO BRIDGE TO STARBOTTON (MAP 12)

45 MINS FROM BRIDGE TO STARBOTTON (MAP 12)

ILKLEY

BOW

trailblazer

0          1/4 mile
0    APPROX SCALE    500m

ROUTE GUIDE AND MAPS

## STAGE 3: BUCKDEN TO COWGILL                    MAPS 13-22

If by this point you've had enough of Wharfedale — its effortlessly ravishing riparian landscapes; its delightful kingfishers with their acrobatics and dazzling iridescent plumage; its lovely locals with warm welcomes and lashings of home-cooked food — then it will be with a sigh of relief that you'll learn that today is the day that you wave farewell to the Wharfe. Where you actually do so, however, is open to debate. For one thing, soon after you leave Buckden, the valley you follow is actually renamed **Langstrothdale**, even though the river you are following is still the Wharfe. Then, at Beckermonds, 4 miles (6.3km) further on, the river is joined by another tributary, **Green Field Beck** (Map 16), and many people cite *this* spot as the place where the River Wharfe actually begins. But that's not the end of the matter: for though, officially, the waterway you follow upstream of Beckermonds is called Oughtershaw Beck, others will maintain that it's still called the Wharfe, and only at Nethergill (see p120) do Wharfe and Way finally separate for the last time, with the river bending north to its source at boggy Fleet Moss.

Confused? Well, you're not alone. Suffice to say, whatever the correct version, your farewell to the Wharfe is a fairly protracted one. Nor is this the only reason that this is such a red-letter day. For it is on this stage that you pass the halfway point (occurring near Winshaw House on the regular route, or somewhere on the approach to Wold Fell from Newby Head Gate on the Alternative (High Level) route; see pp125-30 for details). The high point of the entire trail, at 522m (or 574m on the Alternative route), is also conquered. This is also where the path turns from being one heading generally northwards, though with a slightly westward drift, to being a more westerly path with a slightly northerly leaning. What's more, if you manage to reach Dentdale before the end of the stage (which is one of the few valleys round here that's named after one of the villages within it rather than the river that runs through it, which is called the Dee; Wensleydale, incidentally, is another) then you're also in a new county, Cumbria – even though you won't actually be leaving the Yorkshire Dales National Park for a couple of days yet!

But such accomplishments are not gained easily and for many this **17¾-mile (29km; 7hrs)** stage to Cowgill – or it's **17 miles (27.3km)** to The Sportsman's Inn – is the hardest walk of the entire Way. This is particularly true if the weather's against you, for there are lots of exposed stretches and little shelter en route. Furthermore, with the nearest proper village not until Dent, 22 miles away, and with some tricky walking in between, the average Dales Way walker is usually compelled to find somewhere en route to bed down for the night. For some, that could be one of several isolated farmhouses that earn a little extra by offering B&B, or a place to camp. For others, there are a couple of places away from the route that can put you up for the night. The Station Inn (see p130) at Ribblehead, for example, near the mighty viaduct, is a sensible choice, even though it's about 1½ miles (2.4km) from the path along a busy-ish road, for it divides the walk into two manageable chunks: 12½ miles (20km) from Buckden to Far Gearstones plus 1½ miles (2.4km) to Ribblehead on the

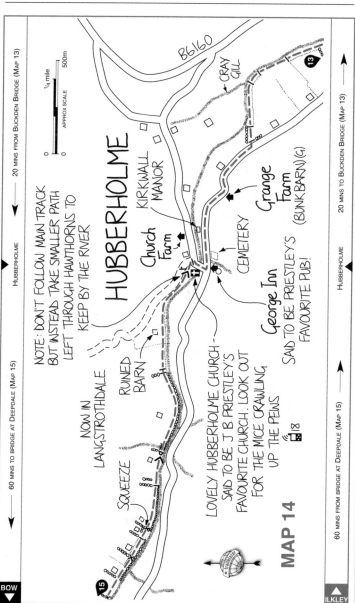

← 60 MINS TO BRIDGE AT DEEPDALE (MAP 15)

HUBBERHOLME

← 20 MINS FROM BUCKDEN BRIDGE (MAP 13)

B6160

CRAY GILL

0 ¼ mile
0 500m
APPROX SCALE

HUBBERHOLME

KIRKWALL MANOR

NOTE: DON'T FOLLOW MAIN TRACK BUT INSTEAD TAKE SMALLER PATH LEFT THROUGH HAWTHORNS TO KEEP BY THE RIVER

Church Farm

Grange Farm (BUNK BARN) (G)

CEMETERY

George Inn
SAID TO BE PRIESTLEY'S FAVOURITE PUB!

NOW IN LANGSTROTHDALE

RUINED BARN

SQUEEZE

LOVELY HUBBERHOLME CHURCH – SAID TO BE J B PRIESTLEY'S FAVOURITE CHURCH. LOOK OUT FOR THE MICE CRAWLING UP THE PEWS

MAP 14

13

20 MINS TO BUCKDEN BRIDGE (MAP 13) →

HUBBERHOLME

60 MINS FROM BRIDGE AT DEEPDALE (MAP 15) →

15

BOW ▼

▲ ILKLEY

ROUTE GUIDE AND MAPS

first day, then 1½ miles (2.4km) back to Far Gearstones and 10 miles (16km) to Dent.

But whatever your destination on this stage, an early start is recommended; in all probability you've got a lot of miles to cover and, if something does go wrong, it's good to have plenty of daylight to sort yourself out.

## The route

The start of this stage is mundane enough (though to describe it as such probably says more about how you've been spoilt with the scenery and walking thus far and less about the quality of this stretch!) as you once again follow the river upstream. A significant moment occurs about 10 minutes from Buckden Bridge, however, as **Cray Gill** joins the Wharfe from the north – and the valley you follow is renamed **Langstrothdale** (though it is still the River Wharfe that will be accompanying you). Soon afterwards you join a road, Dubbs Lane, that leads all the way to **Hubberholme**.

### HUBBERHOLME          [Map 14, p115]

Though it may sound like someone breaking wind in the bath, the name Hubberholme is actually derived from the Norse for Hunberg's Homestead, which gives you an idea of the ancient origins of this village. It's a tiny place, little more than a pub, church and a couple of farmsteads squashed together by the river which is, for most of the day at least, by far the noisiest element.

Hubberholme's pub and church have an interesting relationship. Indeed, The George Inn started off life as the vicarage back in the 17th century, and the pub's tradition of having a lit candle on the bar dates back to a time when the vicar of the church would put a candle in his window to let his parishioners know that he was home. That candle later found secondary employment as the centrepiece of the **Hubberholme Parliament**.

Taking place on the first Monday of each year, the parliament is an auction where local farmers bid for the rights to 16 acres of pasture held by the church, with the proceeds traditionally going to the poor of the parish. The auction ends only when the candle finally burns itself out, with the vicar himself acting as auctioneer, overseeing the proceedings from the House of Lords (or the dining room as it's more commonly called), while the farmers themselves stay in the House of Commons (ie the bar).

As for the **church** itself, it still revels in the endorsement it received from author JB Priestley, who described it as 'one of the smallest and most pleasant places in the world'. You can see why Priestley, who was born in nearby Bradford, was so captivated, for it remains the most characterful and absorbing church on the entire path. Do pay a visit (it's usually open), looking out in particular for the altar, rescued in 1862 from the pub where it was seeing service as the bar and returned to the church. The keen-eyed amongst you may also wish to seek out the mice carved into the pews by the famous Mouseman of Kilburn, the carpenter Robert Thompson. The mice are said to commemorate a time when the church was flooded after the Wharfe broke its banks and rodents got into the chapel. Priestley's ashes incidentally, were scattered in the churchyard after his death in 1984, and there's a memorial plaque dedicated to him in the church.

The pub also likes to claim that it was Priestley's favourite watering hole, and it wouldn't be a surprise if this, too, were true. *The George Inn* (☎ 01756 760223, 🖳 thegeorge-inn.co.uk; **fb**; 2D/3D or T/1Tr, all en suite; 🛏; 🐾; WI-FI residents only) is a throwback to a less cacophonous age, with a lovely lack of piped music and gaming machines inside. B&B costs from £52.50pp (sgl occ £90). The **food** (summer Wed-Sun noon-2.30pm, Wed-Sat 6-8pm,

BOW ▼

MAP 15

LOOK FOR SIGN-POST UNDER SYCAMORE BY FARMHOUSE

SIGNPOST: BECKERMONDS 2¼ MILES, DEEPDALE 1 MILE

14

ILKLEY ▲

SIGNPOST INDICATES THAT YOU NEED TO KEEP TO THE WALL THROUGH THE FIELD

DEEPDALE

ANOTHER LIMEKILN - THE SECOND ON THE TRAIL

SIGNPOST TO BECKERMONDS

YOCKENTHWAITE

STONE CIRCLE - ANCIENT OR A VICTORIAN COPY

ROUGH BUT REASONABLE STONE TRACK

NEWHOUSE COTTAGE

FOLLOW BACK GARDEN WALL UP PAST TREE TO GATE LEADING ONTO DRIVE

Low Raisgill B&B

TRACK GOES THROUGH GATE TO LEFT - THE PATH, HOWEVER, CONTINUES BY THE RIVER

16

0    ¼ mile

0    500m

APPROX SCALE

IT'S A LOVELY WALK THIS, THOUGH WITH LITTLE SHELTER ALONG THE WAY. NOTE HOW THE WHARFE IS SHRINKING IN SIZE BEFORE YOUR EYES AS YOU HEAD UPRIVER. NOTE HOW THERE ARE NO VILLAGES HERE - JUST ISOLATED FARMS. NO PUBLIC TRANSPORT EITHER. IT'S ALMOST EERILY PEACEFUL

60 MINS FROM HUBBERHOLME (MAP 14) — BRIDGE AT DEEPDALE ▶ 35 MINS TO BECKERMONDS (MAP 16)

60 MINS TO HUBBERHOLME (MAP 14) — BRIDGE AT DEEPDALE ▶ 35 MINS FROM BECKERMONDS (MAP 16)

ROUTE GUIDE AND MAPS

Sun & Mon to 7.30pm, winter hours variable) is good too with hot and cold sandwiches (from £6.95), soups and a choice of
at least seven different pies (though full
selection only on Mon) alongside the usual
pub-grub favourites (most mains from
£13.95). Note, the pub is closed on
Tuesdays year-round.

There's also **B&B** at the 16th-century
***Church Farm*** (☎ 07833 702055, ☎ 01756
760240 or ▣ churchfarmhubberholme.co
.uk; 1D or T en suite/1T private bathroom;
☛; WI-FI; from £43pp, £70 sgl occ), a short
distance down Stubbing Lane. The **bunk
barn** at **Grange Farm** (☎ 01756 760259)
is for groups only.

The trail continues on its riparian route with the Wharfe now to its left, taking you past ruined barns and ruminating sheep to **Yockenthwaite** (Map 15), an
isolated, chilly huddle of houses. Fans of British children's TV programmes in
the 1990s may recognise the name as one of the main characters in *The
Rottentrolls*, narrated by Martin Clunes. (Kettlewell, Little Strid and Penyghent
are just some of the other characters in the show, and all the names used are
taken from place names from this corner of the Dales.)

Though there's no accommodation in Yockenthwaite itself, you can leave
the path to cross the river here and make your way back down to *Low Raisgill
B&B* (☎ 01756 760351, ▣ lowraisgill.co.uk; 1S private bathroom, 2D/1T all en
suite; ☛; WI-FI; (Ⓛ)) with genial hosts and a lovely location. There are Aga-
cooked breakfasts, a wood burner in the dining room and lifts offered to and
from the pub for evening meals. B&B costs £55-60pp (sgl/sgl occ from
£70/100-110). However, they have a minimum 2-night stay policy.

Continuing on the trail from Yockenthwaite, a fine **lime kiln**, the chamber
of which is more complete even than the restored one you saw outside
Grassington, lies directly on the path. Of even more interest, further along you
come to a **stone circle**, two dozen or so stones placed in a slight oval by the
path. The current consensus amongst academics is that rather than conforming
to the official definition of a stone circle, this is actually a **ring cairn**, a construction most commonly seen in Wales and Cornwall but which can also be
found in neighbouring Derbyshire to the south. (The distinction between stone
circles and ring cairns is minor, though one difference is that the stones that
form a ring cairn tend to be lower.) Whatever it's called, the actual purpose for
the Bronze Age people who constructed it about 4000 years ago is still very
much open to debate to this day.

Continuing on, weather permitting you'll love the next stretch of easy
strolling, the open expanse of moor on either side and the far-reaching views
providing a welcome contrast to the more enclosed scenery of much of what's
gone before. The trail decides to cross back to the southern bank at **Deepdale**,
though this is not to the detriment of the walk, which seems to grow lovelier
with every step around here. Herons stand sentinel on the old stone barns, kings
of all they survey, while the river, now a shallow shadow of its downstream self,
bubbles merrily away on your right.

At lovely **Beckermonds** (Map 16) the two sources of the Wharfe – Green
Field Beck and Oughtershaw Beck – unite for the first time, after which you are
faced with one of the longest stretches of road walking on the trail, a schlep of

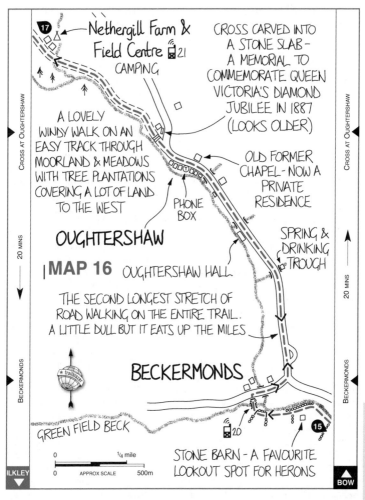

**17** Nethergill Farm &
Field Centre 📱21
CAMPING

CROSS CARVED INTO
A STONE SLAB –
A MEMORIAL TO
COMMEMORATE QUEEN
VICTORIA'S DIAMOND
JUBILEE IN 1887
(LOOKS OLDER)

A LOVELY
WINDY WALK ON AN
EASY TRACK THROUGH
MOORLAND & MEADOWS
WITH TREE PLANTATIONS
COVERING A LOT OF LAND
TO THE WEST

OLD FORMER
CHAPEL - NOW A
PRIVATE
RESIDENCE

PHONE
BOX

OUGHTERSHAW

SPRING &
DRINKING
TROUGH

**MAP 16**  OUGHTERSHAW HALL

THE SECOND LONGEST STRETCH OF
ROAD WALKING ON THE ENTIRE TRAIL.
A LITTLE DULL BUT IT EATS UP THE MILES

BECKERMONDS

📱20

GREEN FIELD BECK

STONE BARN - A FAVOURITE
LOOKOUT SPOT FOR HERONS

**15**

* trailblazer

0        ¼ mile
0    APPROX SCALE    500m

CROSS AT OUGHTERSHAW

20 MINS

BECKERMONDS

CROSS AT OUGHTERSHAW

20 MINS

BECKERMONDS

ILKLEY ▼

BOW ▲

ROUTE GUIDE AND MAPS

over a mile – though thankfully you'll rarely encounter traffic on the way save
for summer weekends. The road takes you through the hamlet of **Oughtershaw**,
at the end of which the path leaves the road, just by the old stone cross carved
to celebrate Queen Victoria's Diamond Jubilee in 1887 (the spring you passed
on the road before Oughtershaw commemorates the same event).

Things are starting to feel very remote now, the landscape opening up with
every stride but revealing little for those seeking civilisation. There are, how-

ever, two path-side options for those who've had enough for the day. First up is *Nethergill Farm* (☎ 01756 761126, 🖥 nethergill.co.uk; WI-FI; 🐾), an eco-farm with an emphasis on rewilding and increasing bio-diversity, which has a study/nature barn attached. They usually have chickens and sometimes a local farmer's Belted Galloway cattle graze on their land. They have two lovely **self-catering cottages**, sleeping four people each, but there's a minimum stay of three nights at the weekend or four nights midweek and seven nights in the high season. Of more use to passing hikers is the fact that you can **camp** here for £10pp; they are happy for campers to use the nature barn overnight and the facilities (a toilet, washbasin, microwave and water heater). Campers can also spend the evening in the nature barn or use the microwave to heat up one of the frozen Mindful Chef meals (£7) the owners have for campers who are short on supplies. The nature barn (generally summer 10am-5/6pm, winter hours earlier) is open if they are around and walkers can use the kitchen and toilet. They operate on an honesty system and ask for donations for drinks and flapjacks, which go towards running costs.

About a mile further along the track, *Swarthghyll Farm* (Map 17; ☎ 01756 760466, 🖥 swarthghyll-farm.co.uk; WI-FI; small 🐾) is a lovely place to rest your corns. They offer superior self-contained, **self-catering accommodation** in four flats surrounding a courtyard (2D/1T/1Qd). Rates are £42.50-47.50pp in the double or twin flats, sgl occ £75-85, and it's £165 for the four-bed courtyard flat. Note that breakfast is not included. Like Nethergill Farm, they also allow walkers to **camp** (£10pp) in one of their fields, with the added bonus of being able to use the hot shower they have in an outhouse, which also has a microwave, toilet and a washing-up sink. On the northern side of the courtyard is a bunkhouse but it's reserved exclusively for the use of groups.

From here it's a simple matter of traversing field after boggy field, ascending slowly, crossing the **watershed** and reaching **Breadpiece Barn** (Map 18), one of the few barns on the Way to have been honoured with a name. Thereafter dodging both bog and bull you make your way to isolated **Cam Houses**, where a final decision needs to be made: do you want to stick to the official, traditional Dales Way route? Or would you rather spice things up with a stroll on the Alternative (High Level) route which, as the name suggests, is higher. If the latter, it's time you turned to p125; while to stick to the main trail, read on.

One of the hardest things about the regular route is finding where it starts from Cam Houses: if you find yourself heading on the main drive straight up the hill, suffice to say, you've gone wrong. Instead, you need to go through the series of gates by the side of the **main barn**. Locate this trail correctly and it's not long before you find yourself striding through **Cam Woodland**, though this corner of the pine plantation is now largely felled. From here it's a mere skip to join the **Pennine Way** and the **Cam High Road**; the cairn that marks the mile-long union of the two, incidentally, also marks **the high point of the entire Dales Way**. Cam High Road is actually an old Roman Road (you can probably tell this by how straight it is) that once linked Ingleton with the fort at Bainbridge.

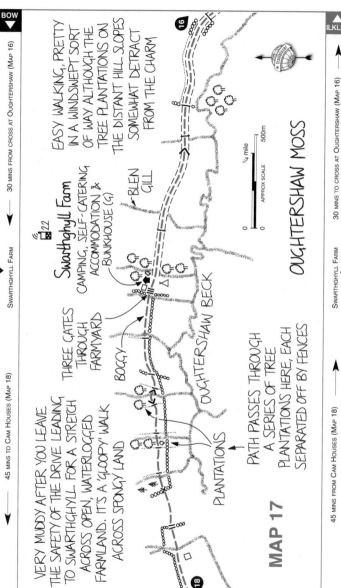

BOW ▼

30 MINS FROM CROSS AT OUGHTERSHAW (MAP 16)

↑ ILKLEY

EASY WALKING, PRETTY IN A WINDSWEPT SORT OF WAY ALTHOUGH THE TREE PLANTATIONS ON THE DISTANT HILL SLOPES SOMEWHAT DETRACT FROM THE CHARM

16

🛜📷22

Swarthghyll Farm
CAMPING, SELF-CATERING ACCOMMODATION & BUNKHOUSE (4)

BLEN GILL

OUGHTERSHAW BECK

OUGHTERSHAW MOSS

¼ mile
500m
0
0
APPROX SCALE

THREE GATES THROUGH FARMYARD

BOGGY

VERY MUDDY AFTER YOU LEAVE THE SAFETY OF THE DRIVE LEADING TO SWARTHGHYLL FOR A STRETCH ACROSS OPEN, WATERLOGGED FARMLAND. IT'S A 'CLOOPY' WALK ACROSS SPONGY LAND

PATH PASSES THROUGH A SERIES OF TREE PLANTATIONS HERE, EACH SEPARATED OFF BY FENCES

PLANTATIONS

MAP 17

18

← 45 MINS TO CAM HOUSES (MAP 18)

SWARTHGHYLL FARM

30 MINS TO CROSS AT OUGHTERSHAW (MAP 16) →

↑

← 45 MINS FROM CAM HOUSES (MAP 18)

SWARTHGHYLL FARM

ROUTE GUIDE AND MAPS

The descent from here is steady and easy, allowing you to peruse the messages that are doubtless coming into your mobile phone after you've been without a signal for a day or more. Do look up temporarily, at least, to enjoy the views, not least the staggering sight of the Ribblehead Viaduct across the valley from the junction known as **Cam End** (Map 19), where the Pennine Way diverts off left.

---

### ❏ THE SETTLE TO CARLISLE RAILWAY LINE AND THE VIADUCTS ON THE DALES WAY

Guaranteed to fill the memory banks of both cranium and camera, the huge viaducts that one passes by, under and alongside during the walk are the most distinguishing features of the latter half of the Dales Way. As one gazes in wonder at their sheer size and grandeur, one can only imagine the levels of cooperation and teamwork that must have been required to get these huge projects completed. Ironic, then, that without man's more petty, self-serving instincts, these monolithic wonders of the Industrial Age might never have been required at all!

For behind the viaducts' construction is a disagreement between the two main rail companies in the region in the middle of the 19th century, the London & North Western Railway (LNWR) and the Midland Railway. The former had control of the main line between London and Scotland. The latter wanted access to it but their own network only went as far as Ingleton. From Ingleton, the line did continue to Low Gill and a union with the main London–Scotland line – but this section was under the ownership of LNWR, who were loath to allow Midland Railway trains on their tracks. Indeed, the relationship between Midland and LNWR were in such a parlous state that the two networks even built their own stations at Ingleton, a mile apart from each other, and passengers were forced to walk between the two in order to continue their journey.

So the Midland Railway decided to build its own railway – and the idea of the Settle–Carlisle line was born. Work began on the line in 1870 and during the course of its construction over 6000 navvies were employed, each labouring on some of the toughest terrain in England and, as you may have already experienced, under some of the worst weather conditions the British Isles could throw at them!

Camps for the workers were set up right by the course of this new railway, with names like Jericho and Sebastopol – the Crimean War of the 1850s still being fresh in people's minds at this time. These unofficial 'townships' came complete with schools, post offices and chapels, with scripture readers employed by the Midland Railway to warn workers against the demon drink. The remains of one of these camps, **Batty Green**, where over 2000 lived and worked, can be seen by the arches of Ribblehead Viaduct.

An estimated 100 workers were killed during the construction of the 73-mile (117.5km) Settle and Carlisle (as the Settle to Carlisle Railway is sometimes called). Nor was it just industrial accidents that one had to watch out for: a plaque in the church at Chapel-le-Dale near Ribblehead is dedicated to the 80 souls who lost their lives in a smallpox outbreak at Batty Green; in total there are over 200 burials of men, women and children in the church graveyard that date back to this time.

The railway was eventually opened to goods traffic in the summer of 1875 and passenger services followed the next year. For the first few decades the line was a success, though after the Second World War it appeared to be running out of steam, its greater gradients making it slower and thus less competitive than rival lines.

Unless you're staying at Station Inn at Ribblehead (see p130), you'll have to content yourself with this distant view of the viaduct right now. But don't despair – before the day is out you'll be walking under a second, just as mighty, viaduct and within sight of another, while within 48 hours you will be walking under two more! Incidentally, the stream at the bottom of the descent, running parallel to the B6255, is **Gayle Beck**, which is a major tributary of the Ribble

The Beeching Report of 1963 recommended its closure and by 1970 there were only two passenger services a day using the line. However, in the 1980s, as other lines became clogged with traffic, the line enjoyed an upturn in fortunes. This coincided with campaigns, mainly from railway enthusiasts, to keep the line open. Today, with eight of the original stations that were shut in 1970 now reopened, the line is fully operational once more with at least five passenger services in each direction each day; see ⊟ settle-carlisle.co.uk for a timetable.

### The viaducts

Central to the railway's construction were, of course, the viaducts necessary to enable the line to cross such undulating terrain. In total there are 22 viaducts, each one built in just four years between 1870 and 1874. The most famous of these is the **Ribblehead Viaduct**, also known, more correctly, as the **Batty Moss Viaduct**. With a 400m span, it's the longest on the railway and rises 32 metres above the mire of Batty Moss.

Linking Ribblehead with the neighbouring viaduct at Dent Head is **Blea Moor Tunnel**, over 1½ miles (2.4km) long and the longest of the 14 tunnels on the line. As for **Dent Head Viaduct** (Map 20), it was actually built above a marble quarry, from which the massive blocks used in its construction were hewn. At 182 metres long, Dent Head's span may be less than half of Ribblehead's but it *can* match its neighbour's 30m+ height – something you'll appreciate as you walk underneath it on entering Dentdale. Even higher, **Arten Gill Viaduct**, to the north of Dent Head, reaches a height of 35m and is visible from the path, particularly when descending past Dent railway station on the Alternative (High Level) Route (see pp130-3). If you're on the regular route, look east near where the road and path cross the Dee at a place called **Stone House** (Map 21).

### So what are the other viaducts on the Dales Way?

The other two enormous viaducts visited on the Dales Way (and in both cases you walk right underneath them) are part of the original Ingleton to Lowgill line that roughly follows the course of the Lune River and was owned by LNWR. In other words, it's the 19-mile (30.5km) line that connected the Midland network (that stopped at Ingleton) with the main line running between London and Scotland. As such, these viaducts are actually older than those mentioned above. **Lune Viaduct**, for example, more properly called **Waterside Viaduct**, was built between 1857 and 1861; that at **Lowgill**, as you leave the Dales National Park, in 1859. The lovely **iron bridge across the Rawthey River** (see Map 26) that you pass after the mill at Birks is part of the same line.

Due to the disagreement between LNWR and Midland and the subsequent building of the Carlisle and Settle Line, this line remained a minor branch line before eventually closing in 1967.

River. This in turn flows west to Preston and the Irish Sea, whereas up to now every river encountered on the route has eventually found its way east to the North Sea – incontrovertible proof that you have now crossed the watershed of England! For the Alternative (High Level) route see opposite and for the continuation of the main route see p130.

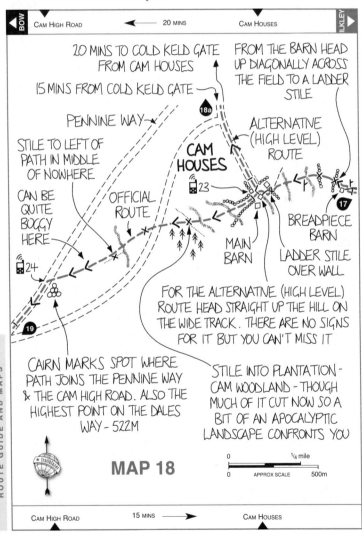

BOW ◄

CAM HIGH ROAD  ◄——  20 MINS  CAM HOUSES  ► ILKLEY

20 MINS TO COLD KELD GATE FROM CAM HOUSES

FROM THE BARN HEAD UP DIAGONALLY ACROSS THE FIELD TO A LADDER STILE

15 MINS FROM COLD KELD GATE

PENNINE WAY

18a

ALTERNATIVE (HIGH LEVEL) ROUTE

STILE TO LEFT OF PATH IN MIDDLE OF NOWHERE

CAM HOUSES

23

CAN BE QUITE BOGGY HERE

OFFICIAL ROUTE

24

19

17

BREADPIECE BARN

MAIN BARN

LADDER STILE OVER WALL

FOR THE ALTERNATIVE (HIGH LEVEL) ROUTE HEAD STRAIGHT UP THE HILL ON THE WIDE TRACK. THERE ARE NO SIGNS FOR IT BUT YOU CAN'T MISS IT

CAIRN MARKS SPOT WHERE PATH JOINS THE PENNINE WAY & THE CAM HIGH ROAD. ALSO THE HIGHEST POINT ON THE DALES WAY - 522M

STILE INTO PLANTATION - CAM WOODLAND - THOUGH MUCH OF IT CUT NOW SO A BIT OF AN APOCALYPTIC LANDSCAPE CONFRONTS YOU

MAP 18

0        ¼ mile
0   APPROX SCALE   500m

ROUTE GUIDE AND MAPS

CAM HIGH ROAD  15 MINS ——►  CAM HOUSES

**Alternative (High Level) route**

Map 18; Map 18a; Map 18b, p127; Map 18c, p128; Map 21, p133

For those who crave both solitude and the opportunity to take a trail that one friend rightly describes as 'viewtastic', the Alternative (High Level) route is a terrific option. The only drawbacks are: i) you don't get the spectacular view

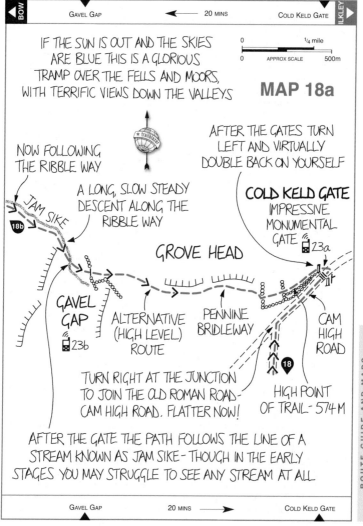

GAVEL GAP ← 20 MINS COLD KELD GATE

BOW / ILKLEY

IF THE SUN IS OUT AND THE SKIES ARE BLUE THIS IS A GLORIOUS TRAMP OVER THE FELLS AND MOORS, WITH TERRIFIC VIEWS DOWN THE VALLEYS

0 ¼ mile
0 APPROX SCALE 500m

**MAP 18a**

NOW FOLLOWING THE RIBBLE WAY

JAM SIKE
18b

A LONG, SLOW STEADY DESCENT ALONG THE RIBBLE WAY

AFTER THE GATES TURN LEFT AND VIRTUALLY DOUBLE BACK ON YOURSELF

**COLD KELD GATE**
IMPRESSIVE MONUMENTAL GATE 23a

GROVE HEAD

GAVEL GAP 23b

ALTERNATIVE (HIGH LEVEL) ROUTE

PENNINE BRIDLEWAY

CAM HIGH ROAD

TURN RIGHT AT THE JUNCTION TO JOIN THE OLD ROMAN ROAD - CAM HIGH ROAD. FLATTER NOW!

18

HIGH POINT OF TRAIL - 574 M

AFTER THE GATE THE PATH FOLLOWS THE LINE OF A STREAM KNOWN AS JAM SIKE - THOUGH IN THE EARLY STAGES YOU MAY STRUGGLE TO SEE ANY STREAM AT ALL

GAVEL GAP 20 MINS → COLD KELD GATE

ROUTE GUIDE AND MAPS

of Ribblehead Viaduct that you do on the official trail (though you do get several, oblique views of the other viaducts); ii) if you're staying in Lea Yeat at The Sportsman's Inn or the nearby campsite, you'll have to walk back up the hill for 20 minutes (though there is a second campsite in Cowgill); and iii) this high-level trail is very exposed and there's little shelter en route – unless, perhaps, you're willing to hunker down behind a drystone wall or beneath a particularly obliging cow.

That said, there are a couple of opportunities to rejoin the main route should the weather turn against you: at one point the trail drops to the B6255 and follows the Dent Rd, thus passing within waving distance of the official route, just a 5- to 10-minute walk away. Then, further on, after the path has rounded **Wold Fell** (Map 18b) there's the chance to drop down **Arten Gill** (Map 18c), underneath its magnificent **viaduct** and on to **Stone House** (Map 21) in Upper Dentdale.

Distance-wise, if you come off the High Level trail before Wold Fell and rejoin the official path on Dent Rd, you've actually shortened your walk by 1¾ miles compared to the official trail, ie **16 miles (24.5km)**, rather than 17¾ miles (28.5km) that you would have clocked up if you'd stayed on the official trail all the way to Lea Yeat. Stay on the Alternative (High Level) route until Arten Gill, and you've still shortened your walk when compared to the official trail, though only by half a mile now, the distance now being **17¼ miles (27.7km)** to Lea Yeat. While if you stay on to the very end and drop down to Lea Yeat via Dent railway station, you've actually walked three-quarters of a mile *more* than if you took the official trail, a magnificent **18½ miles (29.8km)** to Lea Yeat – and you've probably got to walk at least another three-quarters of a mile (1.2km) to get to your accommodation too! But trust us, if your pack's light and the weather's right, you'll think it's worth it. Expect the walk from Cam Houses to Lea Yeat bridge to take about **3 hours 25 minutes**.

From Cam Houses (Map 18) the path initially follows the farmhouse road out and up the slope, leaving it to head for the same Roman road, **Cam High Road**, that you would have joined if you'd stuck to the official trail; though this time you'll head north-east along it rather than south. This you leave after passing through the monumental gateposts at **Cold Keld Gate** (Map 18a), the path now following the **Pennine Bridleway** as it describes an almost hairpin bend to head virtually due west, passing the high point on the trail at 574m soon after. The terrain is cold, windswept, empty and landmarks are few; the path, however, is fairly clearly scoured into the ground.

Passing through a gate in a wall known as **Gavel Gap**, you join up with the Ribble Way which starts here (the source of the Ribble being nearby) to enjoy a steady descent along the line of **Jam Sike** and then **Long Gill** (Map 18b), the first being a tributary of the second, before leaving the waters altogether for the clear path leading down to **Newby Head** and the junction of the **B6255** with Dent Rd.

You're on the tarmac for less than three minutes, however, before you leave it again through a gate to head up **Wold Fell**; don't forget to look around you as you approach the summit for the three highest peaks of the Dales – Pen-y-ghent (694m), Ingleborough (723m) and, largest of the lot, Whernside (736m).

From the top you drop round to reach **Arten Gill**; the path down from here to Stone House is straightforward and walking under the viaduct is

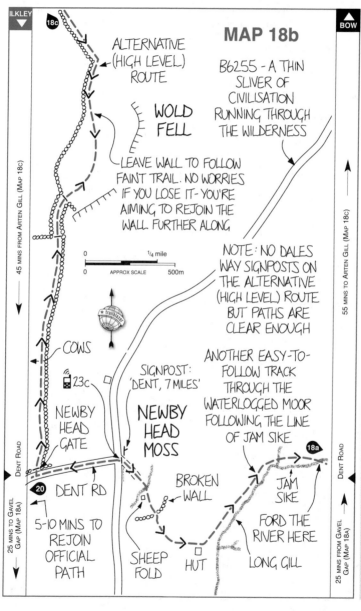

**MAP 18b**

ILKLEY ▼

18c

ALTERNATIVE (HIGH LEVEL) ROUTE

WOLD FELL

B6255 - A THIN SLIVER OF CIVILISATION RUNNING THROUGH THE WILDERNESS

LEAVE WALL TO FOLLOW FAINT TRAIL. NO WORRIES IF YOU LOSE IT - YOU'RE AIMING TO REJOIN THE WALL FURTHER ALONG

NOTE: NO DALES WAY SIGNPOSTS ON THE ALTERNATIVE (HIGH LEVEL) ROUTE BUT PATHS ARE CLEAR ENOUGH

0    ¼ mile
0    APPROX SCALE    500m

COWS

23c

SIGNPOST: 'DENT, 7 MILES'

ANOTHER EASY-TO-FOLLOW TRACK THROUGH THE WATERLOGGED MOOR FOLLOWING THE LINE OF JAM SIKE

NEWBY HEAD GATE

NEWBY HEAD MOSS

18a

JAM SIKE

DENT RD

20

BROKEN WALL

FORD THE RIVER HERE

5-10 MINS TO REJOIN OFFICIAL PATH

SHEEP FOLD

HUT

LONG GILL

BOW ▲

45 MINS FROM ARTEN GILL (MAP 18c)

DENT ROAD

25 MINS TO GAVEL GAP (MAP 18a)

55 MINS TO ARTEN GILL (MAP 18c)

DENT ROAD

25 MINS FROM GAVEL GAP (MAP 18a)

ROUTE GUIDE AND MAPS

always a thrill, but if time and weather are on your side, stay on the trail, which now follows an old drover's track known as **Galloway Gate**. This contours round **Great Knoutberry Hill** (aka **Widdale Fell**), with the fantastic prospect of Dentdale stretching below you and views north into neighbouring

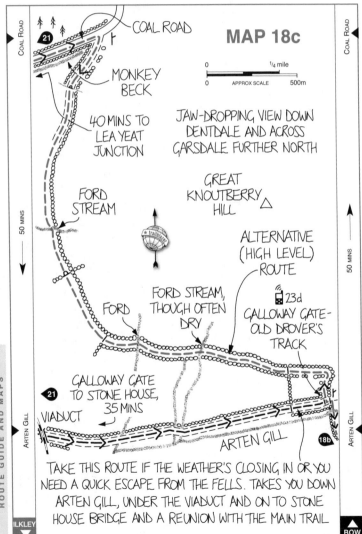

**MAP 18c**

COAL ROAD

COAL ROAD

0     ¼ mile
0    APPROX SCALE    500m

COAL ROAD

MONKEY BECK

40 MINS TO LEA YEAT JUNCTION

JAW-DROPPING VIEW DOWN DENTDALE AND ACROSS GARSDALE FURTHER NORTH

FORD STREAM

GREAT KNOUTBERRY HILL △

50 MINS

ALTERNATIVE (HIGH LEVEL) ROUTE

50 MINS

FORD

FORD STREAM, THOUGH OFTEN DRY

23d
GALLOWAY GATE - OLD DROVER'S TRACK

GALLOWAY GATE TO STONE HOUSE, 35 MINS

ARTEN GILL

VIADUCT

ARTEN GILL

18b

ARTEN GILL

TAKE THIS ROUTE IF THE WEATHER'S CLOSING IN OR YOU NEED A QUICK ESCAPE FROM THE FELLS. TAKES YOU DOWN ARTEN GILL, UNDER THE VIADUCT AND ON TO STONE HOUSE BRIDGE AND A REUNION WITH THE MAIN TRAIL

ROUTE GUIDE AND MAPS

ILKLEY ▼

BOW ▲

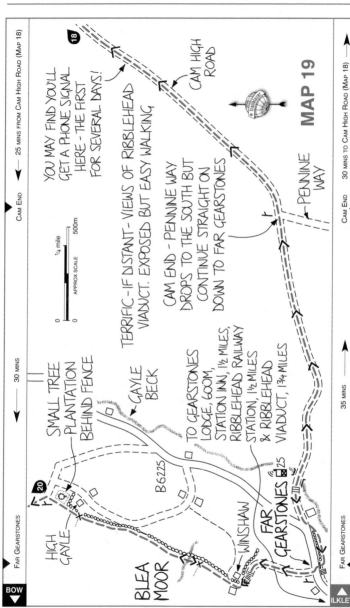

CAM END — 25 MINS FROM CAM HIGH ROAD (MAP 18)

18

CAM HIGH ROAD

YOU MAY FIND YOU'LL GET A PHONE SIGNAL HERE - THE FIRST FOR SEVERAL DAYS!

MAP 19

CAM END — 30 MINS TO CAM HIGH ROAD (MAP 18)

PENNINE WAY

TERRIFIC - IF DISTANT - VIEWS OF RIBBLEHEAD VIADUCT. EXPOSED BUT EASY WALKING

CAM END - PENNINE WAY DROPS TO THE SOUTH BUT CONTINUE STRAIGHT ON DOWN TO FAR GEARSTONES

1/4 mile

500m

APPROX SCALE

30 MINS

SMALL TREE PLANTATION BEHIND FENCE

GAYLE BECK

TO GEARSTONES LODGE, 600M, STATION INN, 1½ MILES, RIBBLEHEAD RAILWAY STATION, 1½ MILES & RIBBLEHEAD VIADUCT, 1¾ MILES

35 MINS

B6225

20

HIGH GAYLE

WINSHAW

FAR GEARSTONES

BLEA MOOR

FAR GEARSTONES

BOW

ILKLEY

ROUTE GUIDE AND MAPS

**Garsdale**. The track – and your time on the Pennine Bridleway – ends by **Monkey Beck** and **Coal Road** that leads down, down, down to **Dent railway station** (Map 21), England's highest, and beyond to **Lea Yeat** (Map 21) and a reunion with the official trail.

## FAR GEARSTONES & RIBBLEHEAD
### [Map 19, p129]

With so few amenities on this stretch of the Way, many people will happily walk the mile and a half along the B6255 from the path at Far Gearstones to *The Station Inn* (☎ 01524 241274, ☐ thestationinnribble head.com; 2T/4D, all en suite; ✟; WI-FI; (L)), which offers **B&B** accommodation (£42.50-55pp, sgl occ £75-90) as well as three **bunkhouses** (1 x 8-, 2 x 6-bed; £100-250 per night per bunkhouse) although they are usually only available for groups. However, if one is not booked individuals can stay for £30pp.

Back in the pub, the **food** (daily noon-9pm; mains £12-16) is all home-made and includes pasta, burgers and wholesome pies, while real ales sit alongside gin and tonics, hot chocolate and coffee on the drinks menu. The best thing, of course, is the pub's location, right next to Ribblehead

station and just a few hundred metres from the viaduct itself.

The adjacent field is owned by the National Trust but people have used it for **wild camping**; there are no facilities when the pub is shut, other than a simple water tap at the back.

Well before you reach The Station Inn (just 600m along the main road from the trail), is *Gearstones Lodge* (☎ 07590 679018, ☐ gearstones.com; WI-FI) which has a self-catering **cottage** sleeping up to six (1D, two bunk-beds) and goes for a very reasonable £60 per night (minimum two nights for advance bookings). They also have a bunkhouse but it's only for groups.

Northern Rail's Leeds to Carlisle **train service** calls at Ribblehead; the summer Sunday/bank holiday 830 **bus** service calls in at Far Gearstones and Ribblehead station. See pp47-9 for details.

*(Main route cont'd from p124)*  Back on the trail at **Far Gearstones**, the path picks its way across the road and up **Blea Moor**, opposite, bending round **Winshaw** (house) to head north-east for a couple of miles across often saturated ground to Dent Rd, which you then follow downhill under **Dent Head Viaduct** (Map 20; see box pp122-3) and for a couple of miles (the longest stretch of road walking on the entire Dales Way) to Cowgill, Cumbria – and the end of this stage (unless you decide, as many people do, to push on for another four miles to Dent, where there's much more in the way of accommodation).

## LEA YEAT
### [Map 21, p133]

Lea Yeat and its slightly larger neighbour, Cowgill (see p132), are little more than a few houses and farms as well as a pub stretched over a couple of miles of tarmac running down **Dentdale** (☐ dentdale.com).

Campers should continue to Cowgill but anyone wanting B&B can stop here.

*The Sportsman's Inn* (☎ 01539 625282, ☐ thesportsmansinn.com; 2D/2T, private facilities; ☛; (L)) is a bit of a landmark on the Dales Way if only because it's the only place to eat for miles around and

the publican's trademark gruffness seems to be all part of the character of the place. Dog owners please note they love dogs but don't accept them in the pub because of people's allergies. Still, you can't fault the **food** (daily 6-8.30pm at the time of research) with all mains both filling and well priced. Tables are kept for all guests staying but others should book. Rates for **B&B** are from £45pp (sgl occ £70), which is fairly reasonable given the lack of competition around here.

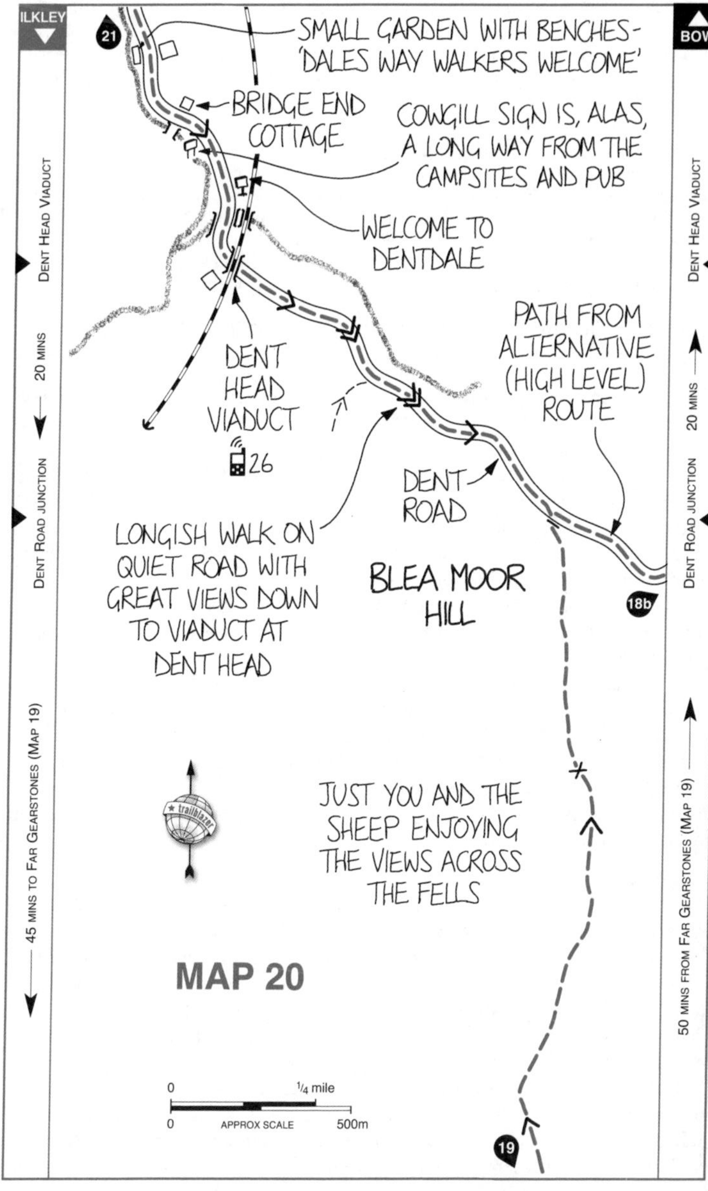

ILKLEY ▼

BOW ▲

SMALL GARDEN WITH BENCHES- 'DALES WAY WALKERS WELCOME'

BRIDGE END COTTAGE

COWGILL SIGN IS, ALAS, A LONG WAY FROM THE CAMPSITES AND PUB

WELCOME TO DENTDALE

PATH FROM ALTERNATIVE (HIGH LEVEL) ROUTE

DENT HEAD VIADUCT 📱26

DENT ROAD

LONGISH WALK ON QUIET ROAD WITH GREAT VIEWS DOWN TO VIADUCT AT DENT HEAD

BLEA MOOR HILL

JUST YOU AND THE SHEEP ENJOYING THE VIEWS ACROSS THE FELLS

MAP 20

0 ¼ mile
0 APPROX SCALE 500m

DENT HEAD VIADUCT — 20 MINS — DENT ROAD JUNCTION — 45 MINS TO FAR GEARSTONES (MAP 19)

DENT HEAD VIADUCT — 20 MINS — DENT ROAD JUNCTION — 50 MINS FROM FAR GEARSTONES (MAP 19)

ROUTE GUIDE AND MAPS

Above Lea Yeat is Dent railway station, the highest mainline station in England; it's a sweaty 15-minute ascent up from the main/only junction in Lea Yeat (and a good four miles from the village which it purports to serve). The station is a stop on Northern's Leeds to Carlisle service (see box p45). Some of the S1 **bus** services call at the station; for details see pp47-9.

## COWGILL   [Map 22, p134]
Often pronounced 'Ca'gil' by the locals – although, given the preponderance of precipitation in these parts, perhaps it would be more appropriate if it was pronounced 'Cagoule' – Cowgill has a **church** and a few S1 **bus** services (see pp47-9) stop here.

The only choice for accommodation is **camping** (for £7pp) at *Ewegales Camping* (☎ 01539 625440; 🐾) at the far end of Cowgill. It's a basic farm campsite (in a sheep field), but it does have simple shower and toilet facilities.

## STAGE 4: COWGILL TO MILLTHROP (FOR SEDBERGH)
### [MAPS 22-26]

This is a deliberately short stage – just **10½ miles (16.9km; 3½hrs plus approx 15 mins to Sedbergh)**, and even shorter if you ended up staying in Dent last night – but it's designed to allow you time to enjoy two of the loveliest settlements on the Dales Way – or rather, just off it, for one (Dent) lies 200m off the path and the other (Sedbergh) is half a mile/800m from it. Given your exertions of the previous stage (not to mention the 16-miler on the next one), it really is time to take it easy and revel in the local tearooms and taverns – establishments in which both Dent and Sedbergh excel.

The walking is straightforward and, unless encounters with cows intervene (for the first time on the walk there are as many bovines as ovines on this stage), you should find yourself dancing into Dent by lunchtime and strolling smugly into Sedbergh for afternoon tea. If you *do* want to push on further, there's accommodation (B&B, camping and glamping) at various spots along or near the River Lune (Maps 27 & 28) plus more options further on at Grayrigg and Patton Bridge (Map 30), but bear in mind that there are no pubs or shops nearby (though evening meals can usually be arranged in advance with your accommodation). Still, why not take it easy today? Put your feet up and save the sweaty stuff for tomorrow.

### The route
Assuming you stayed the night in Lea Yeat (Map 21), your first action of the day will probably be to continue along the same road that you finished on yesterday, swapping road for river only by the bridge where the trail diverts off the tarmac. Though you may walk in a different Dale, the trail soon follows a familiar pattern to what's gone before, sticking fast to the river through fields of sheep and cattle. After Ewegales Farm and its campsite, however, things take an unexpected turn, with road and river branching off to your right while you climb through fields towards **Little Towne** (Map 22) – which is certainly little, but ain't no town. Instead, it's a simple listed farmhouse set in what was until recently a felled tree plantation but now feels more like a nature reserve for wildflowers, with rosebay willowherb particularly prominent.   *(cont'd on p136)*

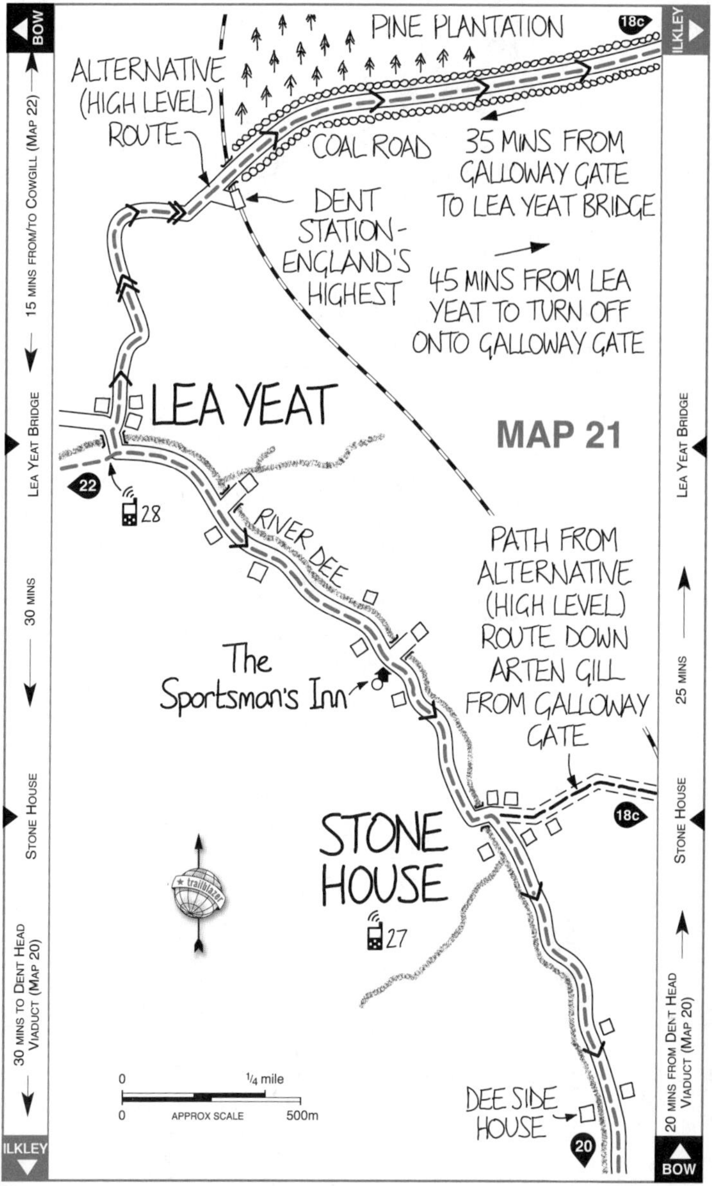
BOW
ILKLEY
15 mins from/to Cowgill (Map 22)
Lea Yeat Bridge
30 mins
Stone House
30 mins to Dent Head Viaduct (Map 20)
ILKLEY
Lea Yeat Bridge
25 mins
Stone House
20 mins from Dent Head Viaduct (Map 20)
BOW
PINE PLANTATION
18c
ALTERNATIVE (HIGH LEVEL) ROUTE
COAL ROAD
35 MINS FROM GALLOWAY GATE TO LEA YEAT BRIDGE
DENT STATION - ENGLAND'S HIGHEST
45 MINS FROM LEA YEAT TO TURN OFF ONTO GALLOWAY GATE
LEA YEAT
MAP 21
22
28
RIVER DEE
PATH FROM ALTERNATIVE (HIGH LEVEL) ROUTE DOWN ARTEN GILL FROM GALLOWAY GATE
The Sportsman's Inn
STONE HOUSE
18c
trailblazer
27
0 1/4 mile
0 APPROX SCALE 500m
DEE SIDE HOUSE
20

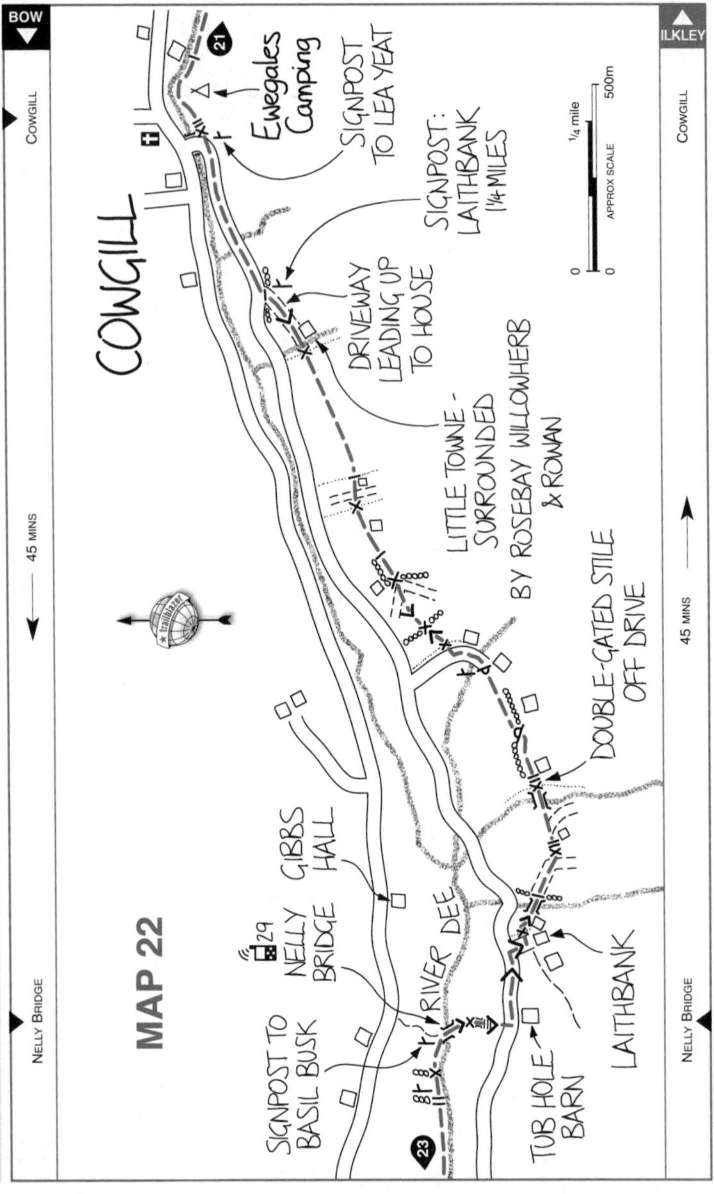

MAP 22

COWGILL

BOW ▼

ILKLEY ▲

Cowgill

Cowgill

Nelly Bridge

Nelly Bridge

21

Ewegales Camping

SIGNPOST TO LEA YEAT

SIGNPOST: LAITHBANK 1¼ MILES

DRIVEWAY LEADING UP TO HOUSE

LITTLE TOWNE - SURROUNDED

BY ROSEBAY WILLOWHERB & ROWAN

DOUBLE-GATED STILE OFF DRIVE

45 MINS

NELLY GIBBS BRIDGE HALL

29

RIVER DEE

SIGNPOST TO BASIL BUSK

48

23

TUB HOLE BARN

LAITHBANK

45 MINS

¼ mile

500m

0

0

APPROX SCALE

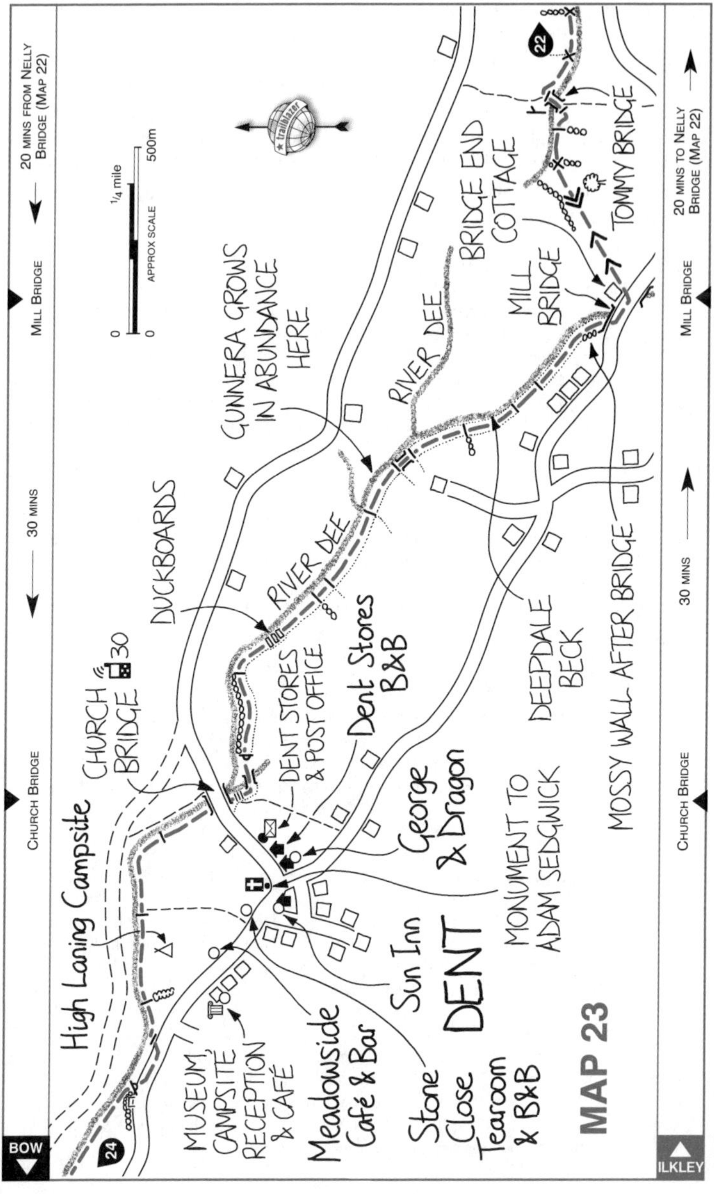

MAP 23

High Laning Campsite

Museum
Campsite Reception & Café

Meadowside Café & Bar

Stone Close Tearoom & B&B

Sun Inn
DENT

Monument to Adam Sedgwick

George & Dragon

Dent Stores & Post Office

Dent Stores B&B

Deepdale Beck

Mossy Wall after Bridge

Church Bridge

30 mins

Church Bridge

30 mins

Mill Bridge

Church Bridge

Duckboards

River Dee

River Dee

Gunnera grows in abundance here

20 mins from Nelly Bridge (Map 22)

Mill Bridge

Bridge End Cottage

Mill Bridge

Tommy Bridge

20 mins to Nelly Bridge (Map 22)

¼ mile

500m

APPROX SCALE

BOW

24

22

ILKLEY

*(cont'd from p132)*  Follow the waymarks and maps carefully on this section for there are lots of fields and farms to cross – though as long you find yourself contouring the valley side in a westerly direction, you shouldn't be too far off the trail. And besides, it's not long before the Dales Way loses its nerve and once again heads to the security of the riverbank, initially reuniting with the River Dee at **Nelly Bridge** before forsaking it at **Tommy Bridge** (Map 23) for a second waterway, **Deepdale Beck**, which you join at **Mill Bridge**. Beck and river unite soon afterwards and flow together beneath **Church Bridge**, with lovely **Dent** just a minute or two away.

## DENT                   [Map 23, p135]

Dent is a dreamy little place. A cobbled village of narrow, twisting streets, there's nothing of any major interest to compel you to take the two-minute diversion off the trail to get here – but, in all honesty, you'd be mad to miss it.

Do call in and you'll notice that for the first time the brochures and bus timetables tend to focus on the Lakes now, and the local paper on offer is probably the *Westmoreland Gazette*. It's a reminder that, while Dent was actually part of Yorkshire until 1974 (and though you're still in Yorkshire Dales National Park), you're no longer *actually* in Yorkshire; and Dent,

lying west of the Pennines, feels both geographically and in spirit more a part of Cumbria too.

Given its tiny size and isolation, Dent boasts an impressive history. Settled by the Vikings in the 10th century, Dent's main claim to fame is as the birthplace of celebrated geologist **Adam Sedgwick**, born in 1785, the man responsible for proposing the Devonian and Cambrian periods on the geological timescale. Today, a big lump of rock in the village centre, across from The George and Dragon pub, celebrates this fact. For around 500 years, from the 16th to the 20th centuries, Dent was also famous

### ❑ THE TERRIBLE KNITTERS OF DENT

For over 300 years, from the 16th to the 19th centuries, the people who lived and worked in the Yorkshire Dales became renowned for their talent for working with wool. The knitting industry here had, at its root, a school that was set up in York in 1590 to teach the children of the poor of the city to knit as a way of supplementing the household income. It wasn't a success and soon closed but a second school, based in Richmond, on the eastern edge of the Dales, did manage to thrive, and from there the craft spread throughout the rural districts.

Other knitting schools opened in various parts of the Dales, including four at Dent alone. The village's reputation as a centre for the knitting industry soon grew, and the people were dubbed the 'terrible knitters of Dent' – 'terrible' in this instance being used to mean something like 'furious' or 'obsessive' and refers to the sheer speed and skill with which they worked their needles and the fact that they pretty much knitted the whole time, whether at home, outdoors, sitting, walking... even at church! The whole family would join in too – fathers, mothers, grandmothers (of course), grandfathers and children.

Yet despite their fine reputations, the knitters made little money from their knitwear, and had to work long hours in order to earn enough to survive, sometimes working in very dark, cramped conditions in smoky, cold, dimly-lit rooms. Once the candles had burnt out or the hearth had been extinguished, the knitters would still carry on, knitting under their blankets to keep themselves warm.

for its 'terrible knitters' (see box opposite), about whom you can find out more at **Dent Village Museum and Heritage Centre** (☎ 01539 625800, 🖳 museumsintheyorkshire dales.co.uk; summer daily 9am-4pm, winter from 10am; £3.50), a real hotch-potch of a collection with a few animated mannequins scattered hereabouts to amuse the adults and scare the children.

Today, with the knitting industry all but expired the town depends on tourism for its survival and, for the past few years, has held **Dentdale Music and Beer Festival** at the end of June which helps bring in the hordes; see p14 for details.

## Services

What few services Dent has to offer are concentrated on its **Dent Stores** (☎ 01539 625209, 🖳 dentstores.co.uk; Mon & Tue & Thur-Sat 8.30am-5.30pm, Wed 8.30am-1pm, Sun 10am-4pm), where you'll find a part-time **post office** (Tue 9.30am-12.30pm). The store also offers a **cashback** service – useful, as there's no ATM here; up to £50 is available for those spending a minimum of £5. Hot drinks, sandwiches and snacks are available to take away.

## Transport

Dent is served by several infrequent **buses**, ie the S1, S3 & S4; see pp47-9.

Dent **railway station** (Map 21; see box on p45) is 4½ miles from Dent village, near Lea Yeat.

## Where to stay

Dent's **campsite**, called ***High Laning Caravan & Camping Park*** (☎ 01539 625239, 🖳 highlaning.com; walkers £10; 🐕), is at the far end of the village, opposite the museum, which is run by the same people. You get lovely flat grassy pitches and there are two shower and toilet blocks, though disappointingly they charge 50p for a shower.

Attached to the village store is ***Dent Stores B&B*** (see Services; 3D or T, all en suite; ☕; Ⓛ; WI-FI); the rooms are on the small side, but feel fresh and bright, decorated in whites and creams. **B&B** costs from £40pp (sgl occ £70) if booked direct.

The two village pubs also do B&B. Best value is ***Sun Inn*** (☎ 01539 625208, 🖳 suninndent.co.uk; 1D en suite, 1T/1D/1Tr share facilities; WI-FI), with rates from £27.50pp (or £32.50pp to £37.50 for the en suite room; sgl occ from £45). However, do note that there's a minimum stay of two nights over a weekend.

The other pub, ***The George and Dragon*** (☎ 01539 625256, 🖳 thegeorgeand dragondent.co.uk; **fb**; 1S/2T/4D/1Tr/ 1Qd, all en suite; ☕; 🐕; WI-FI; Ⓛ), is a friendly place and a great local boozer, though the rooms are looking a little tired. B&B rates are from £46pp (£50 sgl, £65 sgl occ).

Your final option is ***Stone Close Tearoom & B&B*** (☎ 01539 625231, 🖳 stoneclose.com; 1D or T en suite, 1D/1Tr with shared bathroom; ☕; 🐕; WI-FI; Ⓛ), a cosy snug where guests are allowed to use the tearoom in the evenings – a nice place to relax and play one of their board games. Evening meals (£25 for three courses) are available by prior arrangement. Rates are from £40pp (sgl occ £50) and £50pp (sgl occ £70) for the en suite.

## Where to eat and drink

There are three decent cafés in Dent. Busy ***Stone Close Tearoom & B&B*** (see Where to stay; WI-FI; 🐕; Apr-Dec Wed-Sun 10.30am-4pm, Jan-Mar weekends only 11am-3.30pm), on Main St, has a lovely old flagstone floor and fireplace. Dog and walker friendly, it can get a little cramped so you may be asked to leave your bags outside the toilet in the vestibule. Offering a fine array of teas, they are also rightly proud of their range and variety of cakes.

Down the road and the hill, after Main St has turned into The Laning, ***Meadowside Café & Bar*** (☎ 01539 625453, 🖳 meadow sidecafe.co.uk; **fb**; WI-FI; 🐕; Mon, Tue & Fri 10.30am-3.30pm, Sat & Sun 10am-4pm) does great sandwiches (from £5.95), toasties and burgers. It's a lovely place to hunker down by the wood-burning stove if it's bucketing down outside. Note they are always closed on Wednesdays and Thursdays. Still further down the hill is the ***café*** at **Dent Village Museum** (see column opposite; WI-FI; 🐕; daily 9am-4pm).

## ❑ THE DENT FAULT SYSTEM

Between Dent and Brackensgill you cross over an important geological boundary known as the Dent Fault (or, more correctly, the Dent Fault System). This fault in the Earth's crust defines the north-western limit of what is known as the **Askrigg Block** – a huge block of granite that lies deep underneath pretty much all of the Yorkshire Dales. Indeed, so deep underground is it that proof of its existence only arrived recently when bore samples from a deep-drilling rig near Semerwater were examined.

But though it lies deep underground, the Askrigg Block has important consequences for the land above it. As granite is a very hard rock, so the land that lies upon the Askrigg Block, which was mainly laid down during the Carboniferous period (around 350-300 million years ago), has enjoyed relative stability and has been subjected to less pressure to buckle, shift and crumple when compared to similarly aged rock elsewhere. As a result, the distinctive, horizontal limestone terraces and scars of the Dales (think of Loup Scar, outside Burnsall, which is a classic example) have been able to form and survive. Alight from the Askrigg Block, however, by, for example, crossing over the Dent Fault System (though there is no actual vertical jump on the path to suggest you are doing this), and you enter the Howgill Fells, their characteristic smooth-topped hills comprised of much older Silurian and Ordovician (anywhere from 485 million to 419 million years ago) slate and gritstones.

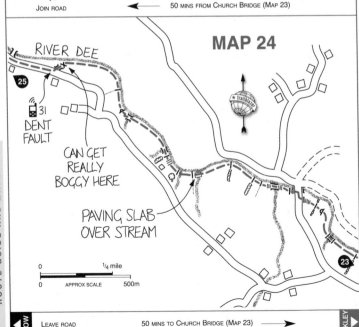

JOIN ROAD          ← 50 MINS FROM CHURCH BRIDGE (MAP 23)

RIVER DEE

**MAP 24**

25

31
DENT
FAULT

CAN GET
REALLY
BOGGY HERE

PAVING SLAB
OVER STREAM

23

0          ¼ mile
0    APPROX SCALE    500m

For evening meals, *The George and Dragon* (see Where to stay; summer daily noon-2pm & 6-8.30pm, winter variable) does the best food; tasty no-nonsense pub grub, including toad in the hole with mash & gravy (£13). They also serve local ales.

*Sun Inn* (see Where to stay; 🐾; food Tue-Thur 5.30-8.30pm, Fri-Sun noon-2pm & 6-8.30pm) also does standard pub grub to accompany their real ales and is slightly cheaper.

Back on the trail, much of the next three miles are as flat as the proverbial pancake and continue the riparian theme, shadowing the river wherever it meanders. So far, so familiar – but at the same time, things are subtly changing too. For near where you rejoin the road you cross the geological feature known as the **Dent Fault**. And though the geology described by the system is happening way below ground (see box opposite), there are subtle changes above ground too. The buildings are still made from the local stone, but that stone is now largely slate, rather than the limestone, sandstone and gritstone of the Dales. It is another minor yet significant sign that you are leaving the Dales behind and heading for the Lake District, which traditionally uses a lot of slate in its buildings.

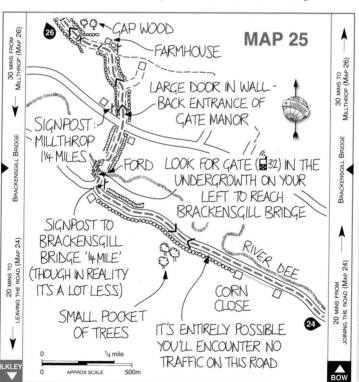

MAP 25

26

GAP WOOD

FARMHOUSE

LARGE DOOR IN WALL - BACK ENTRANCE OF GATE MANOR

SIGNPOST: MILLTHROP 1¼ MILES

FORD

LOOK FOR GATE (📱32) IN THE UNDERGROWTH ON YOUR LEFT TO REACH BRACKENSGILL BRIDGE

SIGNPOST TO BRACKENSGILL BRIDGE '¼ MILE' (THOUGH IN REALITY IT'S A LOT LESS)

SMALL POCKET OF TREES

RIVER DEE

CORN CLOSE

IT'S ENTIRELY POSSIBLE YOU'LL ENCOUNTER NO TRAFFIC ON THIS ROAD

24

30 MINS FROM MILLTHROP (MAP 26)

BRACKENSGILL BRIDGE

20 MINS TO LEAVING THE ROAD (MAP 24)

ILKLEY ▼

30 MINS TO MILLTHROP (MAP 26)

BRACKENSGILL BRIDGE

20 MINS FROM JOINING THE ROAD (MAP 24)

0    ¼ mile
0    APPROX SCALE    500m

ROUTE GUIDE AND MAPS

▲ BOW

There's more evidence that you are leaving the Dales in a couple of miles, but first you must cross the sturdy **Brackensgill Bridge** (Map 25) and leave the river to head up an old farm track, passing the lovely old wooden back door of **Gate Manor** on the way, to **Gap Wood**. It's a smashing stretch, this, with terrific views beyond the wood over the lush pastures of Dentdale. It's also your last chance to glimpse a 'proper' Dales landscape for it's not long before you're savouring the views across to Sedbergh while descending to photogenic **Millthrop** (Map 26), with the smooth undulations of the Howgills a spectacular backdrop. The trail itself heads off west after 18th-century Millthrop Bridge, though most people opt to take the 10-minute road walk into town.

## SEDBERGH          [see map p143]

Sedbergh is both dominated by and synonymous with the ancient and highly regarded school (see box below) that sits to the southwest of the town centre. Refreshingly, there seems to be little of the 'town-and-gown' friction that afflicts other major seats of learning in the UK – but then, as the school has been here since 1525, they have had a long time to get used to each other. Sedbergh's other claim to fame is that it describes itself as 'England's Book Town'; don't come expecting a northern version of Hay-on-Wye, though there are about half-a-dozen book stores on the main street.

The town, like so many others on the trail, doesn't actually lie on the path but 10 minutes from it. Furthermore, the road that you take is sometimes pavement-less and not particularly pleasant. But Sedbergh is the last town before Bowness within walking distance of the trail that offers a decent selection of amenities and it's a lovely place to while away an afternoon, resting your bunions, blisters, corns and callouses in one of the town's lovely cafés while watching the world go by.

For details about Sedbergh Music Festival and Sedbergh Sheep Fest, see box on p14.

### Services

Sedbergh's **tourist information centre** (🖳 sedbergh.org.uk; daily 10am-4pm), which also contains a good bookshop, is the last tourist info centre before the end of the trail. The town also has a **post office** (Mon-Fri 8.30am-12.30pm & 1.30-5.30pm, Sat 8.30am-12.30pm).

---

### 🖳 SEDBERGH SCHOOL

Sedbergh School (🖳 sedberghschool.org) is today a co-educational boarding school, comprising a junior school for pupils aged 4-13, which opened in 2002, and a senior school which has admitted girls since 2001. It was founded by Roger Lupton, who was born at nearby Cautley. In 1525 Lupton, then provost at Eton, provided for a chantry school close to his hometown. He also provided various scholarships to the brightest pupils to enable them to study at St John's College, Cambridge, and to this day the college appoints the school's headmasters.

Today there are over 500 pupils attending Sedbergh, paying the £8500 tuition fees (or £11,000-plus if boarding) per term. For that money your son or daughter gets to study at a school that is renowned not only for its academic achievements but its sporting ones too, particularly on the rugby field where past alumni have included ex-England captain, Will Carling, and World Cup winner, Will Greenwood. Thankfully, the school doesn't ignore the glories of its surroundings but celebrates them. Indeed, the school song, *Winder*, is named after the nearby fell that overlooks Sedbergh and tradition dictates that all pupils must climb it at least once during their school career.

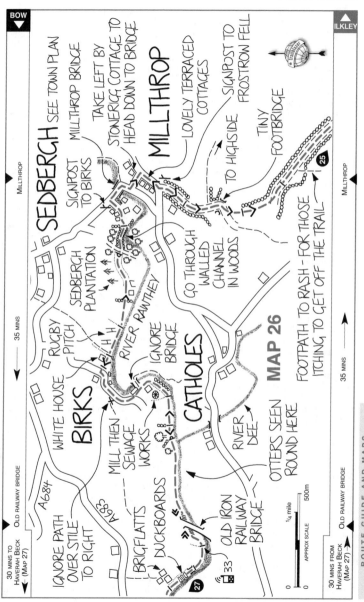

BOW ▼

ILKLEY ▲

▼ MILLTHROP

SEDBERGH SEE TOWN PLAN

SIGNPOST MILLTHROP BRIDGE

TAKE LEFT BY STONERIGG COTTAGE TO HEAD DOWN TO BRIDGE

MILLTHROP

LONELY TERRACED COTTAGES

SIGNPOST TO FROSTROW FELL

TINY FOOTBRIDGE

SIGNPOST TO BIRKS

TO HIGHSIDE

25

SEDBERGH PLANTATION

GO THROUGH WALLED CHANNEL IN WOODS

RIVER RAWTHEY

IGNORE BRIDGE

MILLTHROP ▼

MILLTHROP ▲

MAP 26

RUGBY PITCH

WHITE HOUSE

BIRKS

FOOTPATH TO RASH - FOR THOSE ITCHING TO GET OFF THE TRAIL

35 MINS

35 MINS

A684

MILL THEN SEWAGE WORKS

CATHOLES

RIVER DEE

OTTERS SEEN ROUND HERE

IGNORE PATH OVER STILE TO RIGHT

BRIGFLATTS

DUCKBOARDS

OLD IRON RAILWAY BRIDGE

33

27

¼ mile

500m

APPROX SCALE

0

0

30 MINS TO HAVERAH BECK (MAP 27) ◀

OLD RAILWAY BRIDGE

30 MINS FROM HAVERAH BECK (MAP 27) ▶

OLD RAILWAY BRIDGE

For **provisions** your best bet is the large Spar (daily 7am-10pm), built on the old cattle market to the west of town, though there is a smaller, independent grocery store called Powell's (Mon-Sat 7am-5pm), which is more central and likely to have all you'll need, food-wise.

The local independent **outdoor shop** is the curiously named Sleepy Elephant (Mon-Sat 10am-5pm, Sun 1-5pm), a boots specialist, which also has a small selection of trekking clothes and paraphernalia, including good hiking socks, alongside an array of books and maps. There's also a Boots the **chemist** (Mon-Fri 9am-5.30pm, Sat to 1pm) across the road.

For money there's an **ATM** on Main St, close to Powell's, and another outside the Spar.

### Transport

[See pp47-9] It may be one of the largest towns in the Howgills but don't expect Sedbergh to have a frequent **bus** service to anywhere else; the only options are the S1, S3, S4 & W1.

### Where to stay

There is **no campsite** within 2½ miles (4km) of Sedbergh and, frustratingly, the renovated barn at *Howgills Barn* (☎ 0800 832 1632, ▢ howgillsaccommodation.co .uk), 600m east of town on Castlehaw Farm, is for groups only. However, they provide **B&B** (2D/2T/2Qd bunk-bed rooms, all en suite; WI-FI) during the week (Mon-Fri) in the house. B&B costs from £170 for a bunk-bed room and £80pp (sgl occ £120) for the other rooms; the rate includes use of their hot tubs.

*Daleslea* (☎ 015396 21789, ▢ dales leabnb.co.uk; 2D/1Tr, all en suite; ✆; WI-FI), on the corner of Station Rd and Highfield Rd, is a very friendly option for B&B. It's a large Victorian semi-detached townhouse just a small stroll from the centre and has very spacious rooms, priced at £45-47.50pp (sgl occ from £70). An additional bed can be provided in one of the rooms for an extra £30 and there is a microwave and fridge in the most expensive room.

Nearby, up the hill on Highfield Rd at No 7, *Summerhill* (☎ 015396 20360, ▢ summerhillsedbergh.com; 1D en suite, 1D/1D or T private bathroom unless both rooms are booked by a group or family; ✆; ✖; WI-FI; ⓛ) is a very clean and efficiently run B&B as you'd expect, given that the owner is a trainer and coach – and previously organiser of the Everest marathon. It's a good little place with some nice touches, including a welcome slice of cake on arrival and organic, home-grown food, much of it locally sourced, for breakfast. Rates are £50-60pp (sgl occ £90-108) per night but there is a minimum two-night stay. Subject to prior arrangement and for a charge the owner will pick up/drop off from places such as Cowgill.

There are also two pubs with good-quality rooms: *The Dalesman Country Inn* (☎ 015396 21183, ▢ thedalesman.co.uk; 1S/3D or T/1D, all en suite; ✆; ⓛ; WI-FI), on Main St, is a smart, swanky affair with rates that reflect this (£54-88pp, sgl occ £83-136, sgl from £50). They also have a self-catering cottage, which can sleep up to six people; this costs £66pp for two sharing (sgl occ £102) plus £25 for each extra person. Breakfast is an additional £12.50pp.

Equally smart, if not more so, *Black Bull Inn* (☎ 015396 20264, ▢ theblackbull sedbergh.co.uk; 18D, all en suite; ✆; ✖; ⓛ ; WI-FI) has reopened again after flood-damage repairs and has beautifully decorated rooms, influenced by Japanese design. Some have balconies, some bathtubs and one its own Japanese-style tub. B&B rates range from £62.50pp to £99.50pp (sgl occ room rate). No single-night stays on Saturdays.

### Where to eat and drink

The best café for a sit-down meal is *Smatt's Duo* (☎ 015396 20552, ▢ smattsduo.co.uk; fb; summer Mon 9am-4pm, Wed-Sun to 6pm, Nov-Mar closed also on Wed; WI-FI; ✖); it does a good line in paninis (£6-7) as well as create-your-own-omelettes (£6.45) and has a variety of home-cooked lunches (£8-10). The cakes are top-notch as are the cream teas (£4.20).

*Three Hares* (☎ 015396 21058, ▢ threeharescafe.co.uk; daily 10am-4pm,

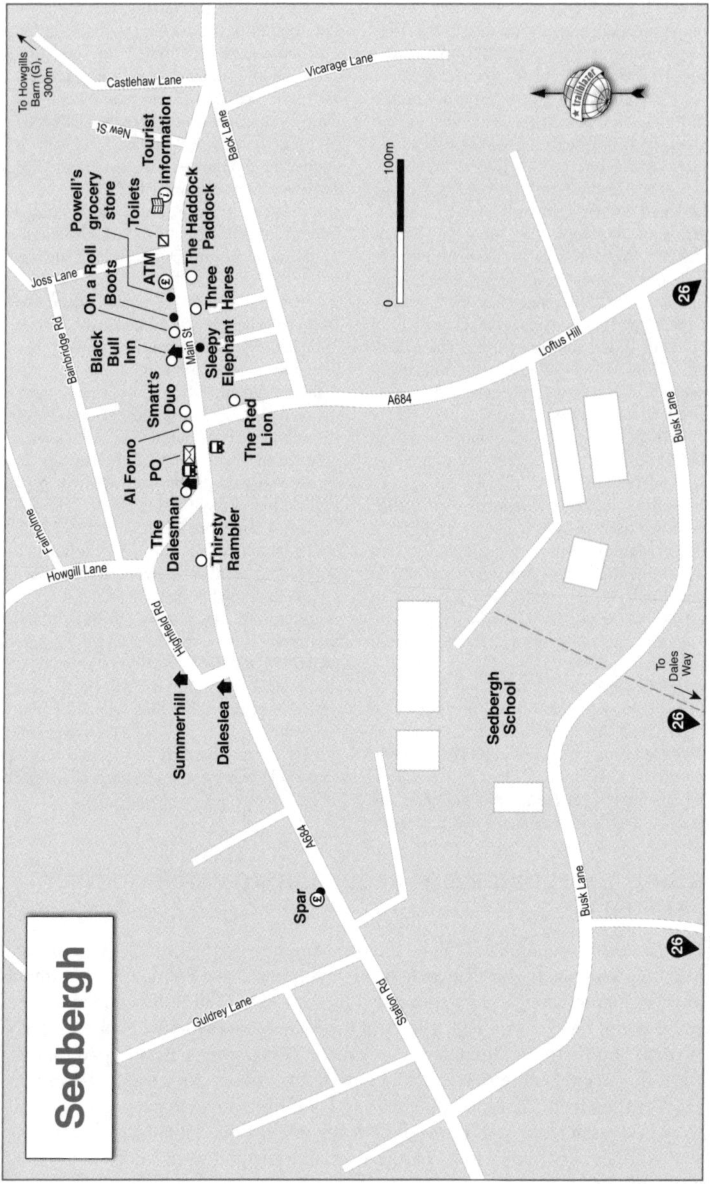
Sedbergh
To Howgills Barn (G), 300m
Castlehaw Lane
Vicarage Lane
New St
Tourist information
Powell's grocery store
Toilets
Back Lane
The Haddock Paddock
ATM
On a Roll
Boots
Joss Lane
Black Bull Inn
Main St
Three Hares
Sleepy Elephant
Bainbridge Rd
Smatt's Duo
Al Forno
PO
The Red Lion
A684
Loftus Hill
The Dalesman
Thirsty Rambler
Fairholme
Howgill Lane
Highfield Rd
Summerhill
Daleslea
0
100m
trailblazer
Sedbergh School
To Dales Way
26
Busk Lane
Spar
A684
26
Busk Lane
26
Guldrey Lane
Station Rd

winter Tue-Sat only; WI-FI) is also highly recommended, though it's more of a take-away place as there's hardly any seating room. They bake pretty much everything they sell themselves, so turn up in the morning and you'll be welcomed by the smell of freshly baked bread or cinnamon. Great coffee too.

The cheapest café in town is the one attached to the brilliantly named chippy, **Haddock Paddock** (fb; Mon & Thur 5-7.30pm, Wed, Fri & Sat 11.30am-1.30pm & 5-7.30pm), where you can get a bacon bap and a cup of tea for less than £3. As you'd expect, the fish & chips are excellent.

For quick food-on-the-go, *On a Roll* (fb; Mon-Sat 8am-2.30pm) is a takeaway sandwich place where each baguette is filled in front of you.

In the evenings, it's either one of the three pubs in town or the highly recommended Italian restaurant *Al Forno* (☎ 01539 634040, 🖳 alfornoitaliankitchen.co.uk; fb; summer daily 5-10pm, winter Tue-Sat 5-9pm). Mains cost £12-18 and include baked aubergine, tuna steak loin, all the pasta you can think of and more than 30 different types of pizza. There's also a separate vegan menu (mains £8-11) and a selection of Italian wines.

All three of the main pubs in town have a good reputation when it comes to food. Most down to earth, and cheapest, is *The Red Lion* (☎ 015396 20433; fb; WI-FI; 🐾; food daily noon-2.30pm & 5-8.30pm); the menu is pretty standard pub fare but considering how reasonable the prices are

(mains £11-13) the quality is very good. The food at the 16th-century coaching inn, *The Dalesman* (see Where to stay; food daily noon-2pm & 5-8pm) is excellent, with pub classics including an award-winning Cumberland sausage dish. The beef is sourced locally (from Birks Farm in Sedbergh) and most mains cost around £16. There's a fine selection of real ales, too, as you'd expect from a traditional Cumbrian freehouse, and they also stock Sedbergh's very own local gin. Dogs are only allowed in the garden.

The menu at the revamped *Black Bull Inn* (see Where to stay; food Wed-Sat noon-3pm & 6-9pm, Sun noon-3pm & 6-8pm) is particularly good for a pub, and has even garnered attention from food critics in the national press. It's inspired not only by the surrounding Dales but also by the Japanese heritage of head chef Nina Matsunaga. So you'll find wild halibut with shiso & apple (£20.95) sitting alongside Howgill Herdwick lamb loin shepherd's pie (£18.95), while desserts range from sticky toffee pudding to yuzu & matcha green tea cheesecake.

Walkers who just fancy an evening drink will be hard pushed not to stop in at the appropriately named *Thirsty Rambler* (☎ 07874 838816, 🖳 thethirstyrambler.co.uk; Thur & Sun 5-10pm, Fri & Sat 4-11pm; 🐾), a cosy micro bar that opened on Main St in the summer of 2021. They welcome muddy boots (and dirty paws), and serve a small selection of real ales as well as craft ciders, fine wines and plenty of gin.

## STAGE 5: MILLTHROP (FOR SEDBERGH) TO BURNESIDE (FOR KENDAL)
MAPS 26-32

On paper this looks like the most unpromising day on the trail. A quick glance at a map will show you that on this stage you leave one national park without covering quite enough ground to reach the next one. You'll also notice that en route you'll have to contend with both the M6 motorway and a couple of busy A roads. Furthermore, there are no towns or villages en route so opportunities for refreshments are few. It is also, by necessity, quite a long stage at **16 miles (25.7km; 6¾hrs)** – not forgetting the extra half mile/800m to get you to the trail from Sedbergh at the start of the day – with only the occasional B&B providing you with an opportunity to break the stage into two halves.

But if there's one lesson learnt about the Dales Way by now, it's that it does provide ample rewards in return for all the efforts it demands. And once again on this stage it's not the natural landscape that sticks in the mind so much as the mighty constructions that man has placed upon it. Less than two miles from Millthrop Bridge, for example, the trail takes you by an old and impressive iron railway bridge, while further on you'll find yourself shuffling open-mouthed in amazement beneath two huge old Victorian viaducts that served the same railway.

Throughout this stage there's plenty of good walking too, much of it through lush farmland via the little-visited valley of Lunesdale, on the edge of the impressive Howgill Fells, with good views aplenty looking west towards the jagged tops of the Lake District. And if 16 miles is too ambitious for a single day there's a few accommodation opportunities scattered along – or just off – the trail too.

## The route
For the initial part of this stage you'll be largely walking through grounds owned by Sedbergh School – which, considering the large amount of prime real-estate you go through, gives you some idea of how much money must be

---

### ❏ THE HOWGILLS
It can't be easy for a range of hills that soar almost 700 metres high to be overlooked. But that's exactly what has happened to the Howgills, a triangular area of fells bounded by the Lune and Rawthey rivers, with the towns of Sedbergh, Kirkby Stephen and Tebay the three corners (approximately) of that triangle.

But it's fair to say that most walkers, unless they live in the area, won't have heard of them. There aren't many guidebooks or other publications about them (Alfred Wainwright's *Walks on the Howgill Fells*, published way back in 1972, is probably the most famous). And, up until now, despite the Howgills' undoubted beauty, they've been largely ignored by the authorities too – though the recent extensions to Dales National Park has rectified this, and pretty much all the Howgills now fall within the boundaries of the enlarged park.

It really is curious how little-known and seldom visited the Howgills are, for their landscape and character seem so inviting to anyone who likes hiking in high places. For one thing, the paths are certainly very quiet, particularly when compared to the Lakes and the Dales which definitely receive the lion's share of walkers. As a result, you may well have the place to yourself, with only sheep and the occasional wild pony for company. The Howgills – the name, incidentally, comes from the old Norse words for hill ('haugr') and valley ('gil') – are renowned for having few walls and fences, too, so there are few stiles and gates to negotiate, thus enabling you to enjoy some great views across to the neighbouring Yorkshire Dales, Northern Pennines and the Eastern Lake District. Nor are the Howgills bereft of their own attractions, including **Cautley Spout**, at 180m one of England's highest (cascade) waterfalls.

Plus, of course, there are the Howgills' distinguishing, smooth summits; hilltops that over the years have been compared by various people to a herd of sleeping elephants (Alfred Wainwright's description), the backs of hippos, a basket of labrador puppies, and the smooth, unwrinkled bottoms of babies. The highest of these summits is **Calf** at 676m, with Calders only just behind at 674m and Great Dummacks a further 11m shorter at 663m.

sloshing around the top-tier educational establishments in this country! Eventually, however, you leave the outer reaches of the town to join the lane leading down to **Birks** (Map 26) and a ramble along the Rawthey. Soon you're scaling an embankment that leads to a 19th-century **iron railway bridge** – now closed to human traffic, though it carries a gas pipeline on part of its structure.

A little way further on, and hidden by a fence to the right of the trail, is **Brigflatts**, a place of monumental importance to the Quaker faith (see box p86).

It's not long before you're forsaking one river for another, as you bid farewell to Rawthey in favour of the Lune. Until 2016, the Lune marked the western boundary of Yorkshire Dales National Park in this region (it's now been extended to the M6), and once upon a time the river marked the county boundary between Yorkshire and the defunct county of Westmoreland.

The trail takes a more northerly course now, and for much of the next hour you adhere closely to the riverbank before climbing away from it after Lune Viaduct. If the urge to stay for the night beside The Lune is too much to resist, cross over it at the unusually narrow, 17th-century **Lincoln's Inn Bridge** to reach ***Lincoln's Inn Farm*** (Map 27; ☎ 015396 21320 or ☎ 07812 397872; 🐕 on lead), a simple, hiker-friendly **campsite** (£12 for one person in tent then £5 for additional people) with toilets and sinks already available, but showers apparently coming soon. They have a handy campers' hut, with a kettle, toaster and microwave, where, providing you have your own supplies, you can make hot drinks and snacks whilst sheltering from any inclement weather. And there's a lovely open-sided riverside shelter with tables and chairs where you can eat your camping-stove noodles, drink your flask of tea or just sit down and relax and contemplate your place in nature.

Back on trail, soon after Lincoln's Inn Bridge you reach the first of the great Victorian viaducts on this stage, **Lune** (or **Waterside) Viaduct** (see box pp122-3), which you walk underneath before climbing to **Low Branthwaite**. From here you can take the path to ***Ash Hining Farm*** (off Map 27; ☎ 07774 281767, 💻 ashhiningfarm.co.uk; 2D/2T, all en suite; ▼; WI-FI; Ⓛ), an award-winning B&B set on a 17th-century working farm, the guest lounge boasting exposed beams, an open fire and terrific views down Lune Valley and over the Howgills – and all very reasonable value from £40pp (£50 sgl occ). The farm is off Howgill Lane; take the lane to the junction and from there turn right – it's about half a mile from the path. For dinner they offer lifts (up to 9.45pm) to and from Sedbergh.

A little further on, and right on the path, is the excellent B&B and campsite at ***Bramaskew Farm*** (☎ 01539 621529, 💻 drawellcottage.co.uk; 1D/1D or T, both en suite; WI-FI; Ⓛ) a dairy and sheep farm which has received several very good reviews from fellow walkers. Rates are from £42.50pp (£45 sgl occ) in the B&B, with evening meals also available if arranged in advance. They also offer **camping** for £8pp in a field beside the farmhouse; the price includes use of a shower and toilet in a downstairs utility room.

With cattle studying your progress for much of the way, the path now eases back down to the river and the gorgeous late medieval **Crook of Lune Bridge** (Map 28), built perhaps as early as the 16th century. *(cont'd on p150)*

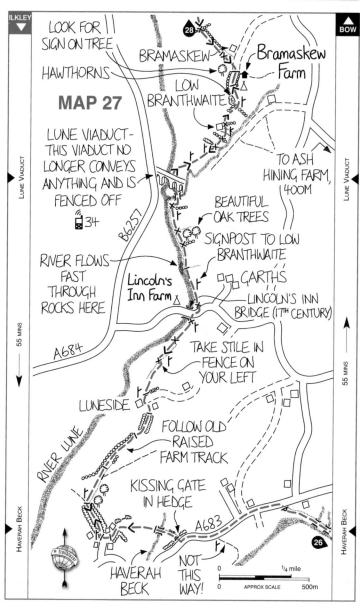

ILKLEY ▼

▲ BOW

LOOK FOR
SIGN ON TREE

HAWTHORNS

**MAP 27**

LUNE VIADUCT-
THIS VIADUCT NO
LONGER CONVEYS
ANYTHING AND IS
FENCED OFF
📱34

RIVER FLOWS
FAST
THROUGH
ROCKS HERE

B6257

A684

LUNESIDE

RIVER LUNE

28

BRAMASKEW

LOW
BRANTHWAITE

Bramaskew
Farm

TO ASH
HINING FARM,
400M

BEAUTIFUL
OAK TREES

SIGNPOST TO LOW
BRANTHWAITE

Lincoln's
Inn Farm

GARTHS

LINCOLN'S INN
BRIDGE (17TH CENTURY)

TAKE STILE IN
FENCE ON
YOUR LEFT

FOLLOW OLD
RAISED
FARM TRACK

KISSING GATE
IN HEDGE

A683

HAVERAH
BECK

NOT
THIS
WAY!

26

0        1/4 mile
APPROX SCALE
0        500m

★ trailblazer

LUNE VIADUCT

LUNE VIADUCT

55 MINS

55 MINS

HAVERAH BECK

HAVERAH BECK

ROUTE GUIDE AND MAPS

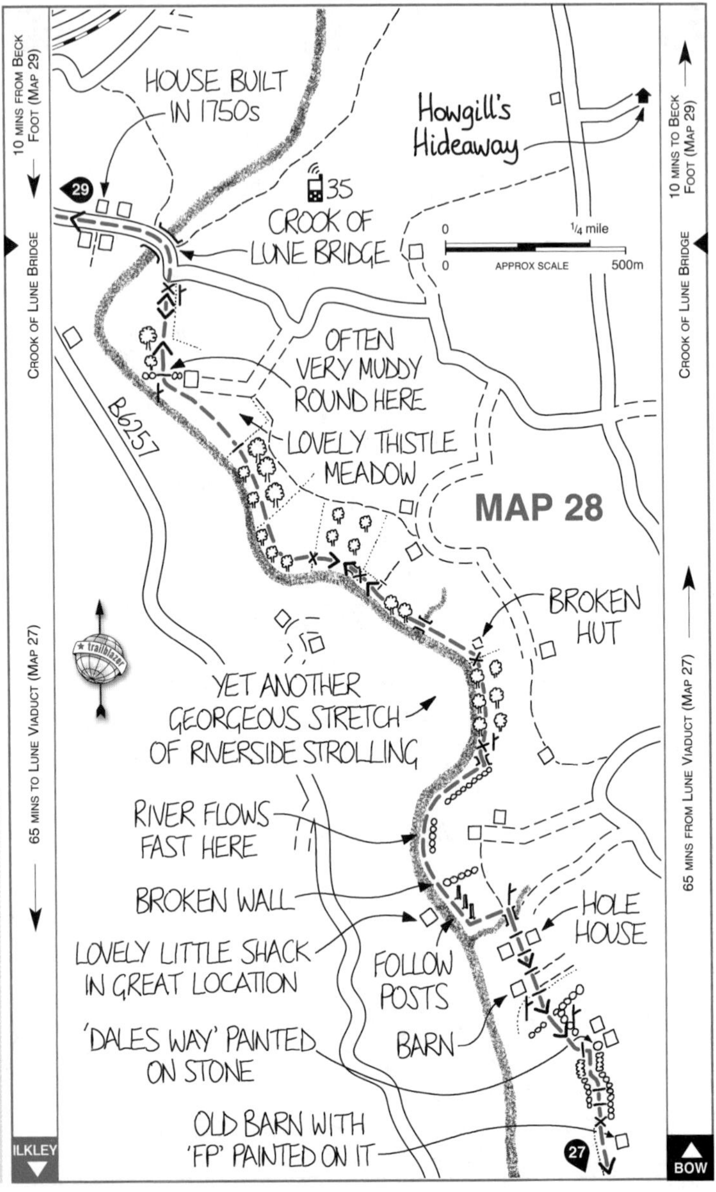

HOUSE BUILT
IN 1750s

Howgill's
Hideaway

29

📱35

CROOK OF
LUNE BRIDGE

0          ¼ mile
0          500m
APPROX SCALE

OFTEN
VERY MUDDY
ROUND HERE

LOVELY THISTLE
MEADOW

MAP 28

BROKEN
HUT

YET ANOTHER
GEORGEOUS STRETCH
OF RIVERSIDE STROLLING

RIVER FLOWS
FAST HERE

BROKEN WALL

LOVELY LITTLE SHACK
IN GREAT LOCATION

FOLLOW
POSTS

BARN

HOLE
HOUSE

'DALES WAY' PAINTED
ON STONE

OLD BARN WITH
'FP' PAINTED ON IT

27

B6257

★ trailblazer

10 MINS FROM BECK FOOT (MAP 29)

CROOK OF LUNE BRIDGE

65 MINS TO LUNE VIADUCT (MAP 27)

ILKLEY ▼

10 MINS TO BECK FOOT (MAP 29)

CROOK OF LUNE BRIDGE

65 MINS FROM LUNE VIADUCT (MAP 27)

BOW ▲

ROUTE GUIDE AND MAPS

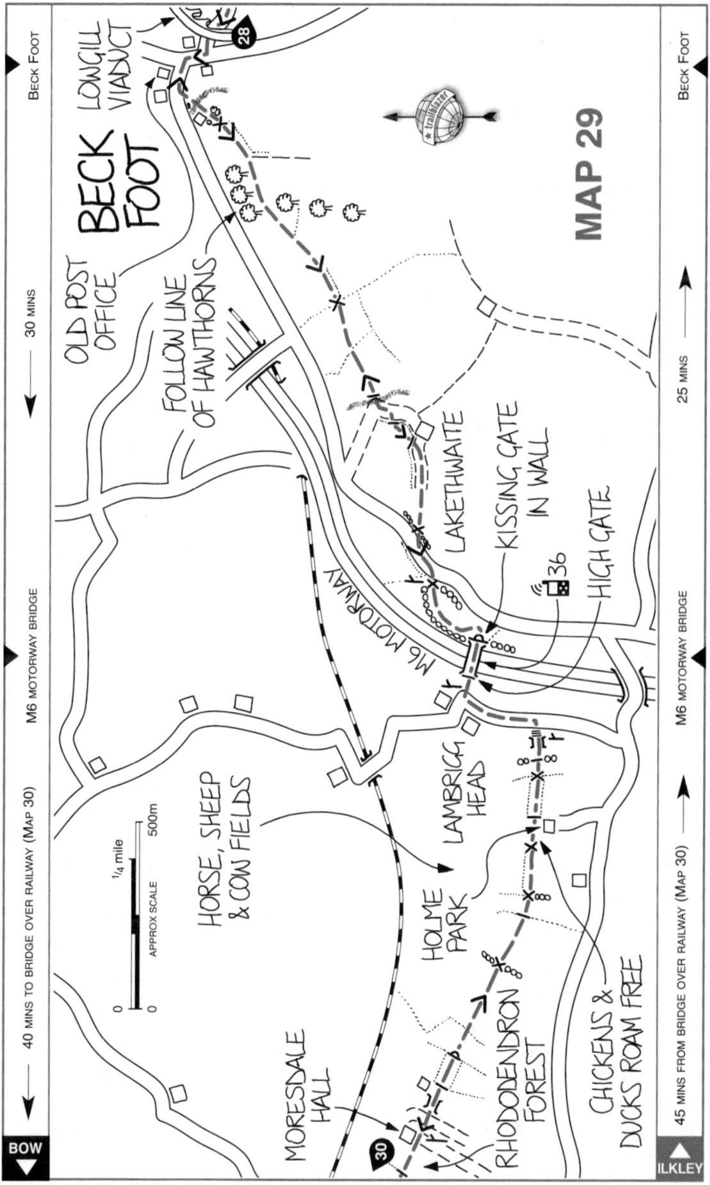
40 mins to bridge over railway (Map 30)
M6 motorway bridge
30 mins
Beck Foot
BOW
45 mins from bridge over railway (Map 30)
M6 motorway bridge
25 mins
Beck Foot
ILKLEY
BECK FOOT
LOWGILL VIADUCT
OLD POST OFFICE
FOLLOW LINE OF HAWTHORNS
M6 MOTORWAY
LAKETHWAITE
KISSING GATE IN WALL
HIGH GATE
36
LAMBRIGG HEAD
HORSE, SHEEP & COW FIELDS
HOLME PARK
RHODODENDRON FOREST
CHICKENS & DUCKS ROAM FREE
MORESDALE HALL
28
30
trailblazer
MAP 29
APPROX SCALE
0
1/4 mile
0
500m

*(cont'd from p146)* Those who have had enough for the day could make a detour off the path before the bridge and wind their way up to ***Howgills Hideaway*** (☎ 07866 448748, 🖳 howgillshideaway.co.uk; **fb**; 🍷; Ⓛ; 🐾) at Beck House, a family-run farm that offers **luxury camping accommodation** in four camping pods (up to two adults/two children; from £70), two static caravans (up to 6; from £80). The caravans and one of the pods are en suite; the rest share a clean shower-and-toilet block. Breakfast (£6pp) and packed lunches are available, as are BBQ packs (meat or vegetarian; £5-6pp) ready for you to cook on your own BBQ set (£5-10). There's also a small honesty shop selling a few basic provisions.

Back on the path, cross Crook of Lune Bridge to climb to the second magnificent viaduct, the 11-arch **Lowgill Viaduct** (Map 29) which soars 27m above the road.

The next stretch of the trail from here to Burneside is, in all honesty, one of the least appealing parts of the whole walk. This is partly to do with the fact that one must negotiate both the M6 (where you finally leave Yorkshire Dales National Park) and the A6, and while the traversing of neither is in any way difficult – there is a footbridge across the former, and the latter, while fast, is quiet enough to allow plenty of opportunities to cross safely – their noisy presence is an interruption to one's enjoyment of the scenery around here. It's also partly to do with the cattle which for some reason seem more aggressive here. Remember if you have a canine companion with you, give all cattle a wide berth and keep him or her on a short lead – unless the bellicose bovines behave aggressively towards you, in which case drop the lead, head to safety, and call your dog to you as quickly as you can.

The scenery, too, while pleasant enough, does lack the pizzazz of earlier stages; just as the scenery improved markedly once you entered the park near Bolton Abbey all those miles ago, so it deteriorates – slightly but noticeably – as you now leave it.

Pressing on through the fields and across the railway, you'll see **Grayrigg** in the distance, its church tower one of the major landmarks in this area. More fields need to be crossed and cattle dodged as you swerve your way through the pastoral landscape to the A685 via ***Grayrigg Foot Campsite*** (Map 30; ☎ 01539 824655; 🐾), a working farm that charges passing walkers (£7pp) to pitch a tent on their immaculate garden lawn. There's a simple wash house outside with a wash basin and a toilet but no shower. And, although the owners do welcome you with tea and biscuits, remember that you'll have to bring your own food for an evening meal or be prepared to catch a taxi to Kendal for about a tenner.

Across the road the path continues over the River Mint and up to a second campsite in a walled garden: ***Low Barn Campsite*** (☎ 07443 656855, 🖳 moon feather7@gmail.com; 🐾) charges £8pp to **camp**. They also have a very comfortable **bell tent** (£80 per night for up to four people), with a wood-burning stove and futon beds. Breakfasts (£6) and evening meals (£10) are also available if arranged in advance. It's a great place with very friendly owners but there is no shower – just a sink and toilet.

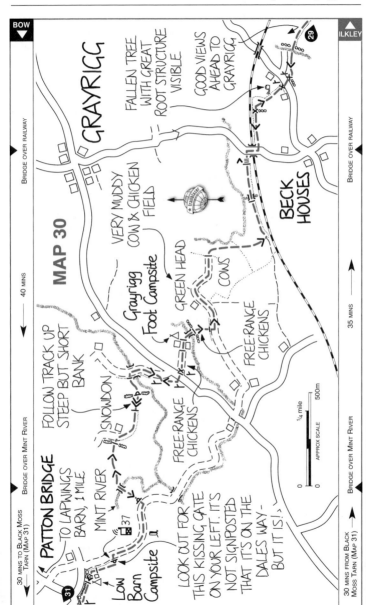

BOW ▼

▲ ILKLEY

29

GRAYRIGG

FALLEN TREE WITH GREAT ROOT STRUCTURE VISIBLE

GOOD VIEWS AHEAD TO GRAYRIGG

BRIDGE OVER RAILWAY

VERY MUDDY COW & CHICKEN FIELD

MAP 30

BECK HOUSES

40 MINS

Grayrigg Foot Campsite

GREEN HEAD

COWS

FREE-RANGE CHICKENS

BRIDGE OVER RAILWAY

PATTON BRIDGE

FOLLOW TRACK UP STEEP BUT SHORT BANK

SNOWDON

MINT RIVER

TO LAPWINGS BARN, 1 MILE

35 MINS

FREE-RANGE CHICKENS

37

Low Barn Campsite

31

LOOK OUT FOR THIS KISSING GATE ON YOUR LEFT. IT'S NOT SIGNPOSTED THAT IT'S ON THE DALES WAY – BUT IT IS!.

¼ mile

0    APPROX SCALE    500m

Just around the corner, you come to a quiet lane, with **Biglands Farm** (Map 31) opposite. One mile from the trail here, and a few hundred metres past Whinfell Tarn, is *Lapwings Barn* (off Map 30; ☎ 01539 824373, 🖳 lapwings barn.co.uk; 2D or T, both en suite; 🖛; Ⓛ; WI-FI) at Howestone Barn, which promises a warm welcome and two lovely rooms, one with its own lounge and balcony, the other with some outdoor seating on a gravel patio. **B&B** costs £45-60pp for the room with the lounge, and £40-50pp for the other room (sgl occ from £80). Evening meals are also available (three courses, £22). Note, no single-night stays on Fridays or Saturdays. To reach the barn, come off the trail opposite Biglands Farm, turning right down the hill to **Patton Bridge**. After the bridge, take the second left, go past Borrans Farm then take the left fork and keep going for about 600m. Subject to prior arrangement the owners offer to pick you up from and drop you back at the path.

Those sticking with the trail have the joys of **Black Moss Tarn** to look forward to, though it's really little more than an oversized pond with delusions of grandeur than an actual tarn; still, it's a smashing place to stop and recover for five minutes if you can find a dry patch of grass on which to sit. Thereafter, there's some pleasant enough rural rambling leading down to and beyond the A6, though the undulating terrain and sheer number of stiles will sap any last vestiges of energy and enthusiasm that you may have managed to save.

It's with some relief, therefore, that you finally hit the road leading into Burneside. Note that the old route here, along the sometimes-busy road over Sprint Bridge, has been replaced by a route that takes you past Sprint Mill and Tenement Farm; turn right to cross the little river bridge at Sprint Mill and walk between the buildings then follow the waymarked track through a garden and past Tenement Farm. Then turn left onto the quiet country lane that leads back to the main road where a quick right then left will bring you onto Hall Rd for **Burneside**.

## BURNESIDE            [Map 32, p155]

It may sound a bit harsh but the main attraction of Burneside for most Dales Way walkers is the chance it offers to leave it immediately and head to Kendal (see p154).

Burneside does have a **food store** (Premier Convenience Store; Mon-Sat 7am-8pm, Sun 7.30am-7.30pm) but not much else, whereas you'll find everything a walker could need in its bigger neighbour two miles (3km) to the south.

Northern Rail's Manchester Airport/ Oxenholme Lake District to Windermere **train** services call here; from Burneside it's four minutes to Kendal, or travelling in the other direction it's 6 minutes to Staveley and 12 to Windermere; for further details see box p45.

**Bus** No 45 (see pp47-9) stops at various places in the village.

There are two options for **camping** here. Firstly, just before you reach Burneside, there is *Sprint Mill* (☎ 01539 725168 or ☎ 07806 065602, 🖳 mail@ sprintmill.uk; **fb**; WI-FI; 🐕 on lead), an 1849 water mill set on a bend of the River Sprint and surrounded by wild-flower meadows. The historic 19th-century building now houses exhibits of artefacts such as tools and rural bygones. You can camp for £5pp, which includes use of a shower. A simple bunkhouse-type facility for shelter may be available. Simple DIY **refreshments** are always available in the mill; there is an honesty box for donations.

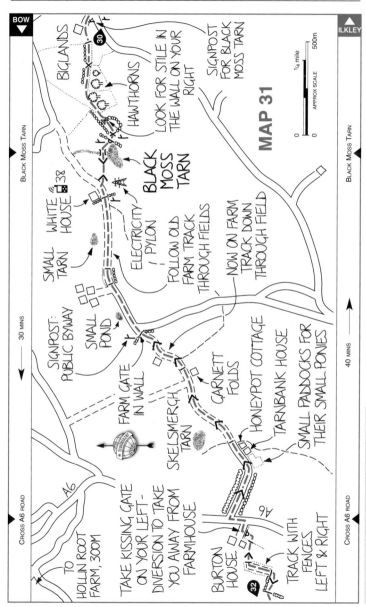

Secondly, there is the also lovely – if somewhat knackered – **Burnside Hall** (☎ 01539 722017; 🐾), a farmhouse on the way into the village that has been built beside an old 14th-century *pele* tower. (A pele or peel tower was a fortified watchtower built in the borderlands between England and Scotland; fires would be lit at the top of the tower at the first sign of any approaching danger to warn locals and summon defences.) Burnside Hall and its grounds was closed to the public during the Covid pandemic, but previously camping cost just £3pp, though there was no shower; just an outside toilet and a hot and cold tap.

The best option for **B&B** is the highly recommended **Lakeland Hills** (off Map 32; ☎ 01539 722054, 🖳 toneoldbone@gmail .com; 1T en suite; WI-FI), at 1 Churchill Court, run by a couple who are keen walkers themselves. B&B costs from £45pp (sgl occ £45) and if wanted includes a lift into Kendal for an evening meal.

There's also the local pub, *Jolly Anglers* (☎ 01539 732552, 🖳 jollyanglers inn.co.uk; **fb**; 1D/1T/2Tr, all en suite; 🐾; WI-FI in the bar), though it is a little rundown. B&B rates are from £37.50pp (sgl occ £55). **Food** (just standard pub grub with most mains costing less than a tenner) is served daily 6pm to 8pm.

The only other option for food is the small takeaway chippy near the church: *Jolly Fryer* (**fb**; Wed-Sat 11.30am-1.15pm, Wed & Sat 4.30-7pm, Thur 4.30-7.30pm, Fri 4.30-8pm).

North-east of Burnside, in **Garth Row**, and half a mile or so from the Way is *Hollin Root Farm B&B* (off Map 31; ☎ 01539 823638, 🖳 www.hollinrootbandb .co.uk; 1D/1D or T/1Tr, all en suite; WI-FI; Ⓛ); B&B costs £36.50-43pp (sgl occ 70-80) with either a continental or Cumbrian breakfast. Subject to prior arrangement they will pick you up from the Way. They serve tea/coffee and cake between 4-5pm.

## KENDAL [see map p157]

It comes as something of a surprise to find that the market town of Kendal, a town so inextricably identified with the Lake District, actually lies outside the border of the national park. In all other ways, however, this place is quintessentially Cumbrian, from its sombre limestone buildings (which give the town its nickname of 'Auld Grey'), its glowering nearby hills, its friendly, no-nonsense residents and its, errm, 'changeable' weather. But don't be misled into thinking that Kendal is a gloomy place – indeed, not so long ago *The Sunday Times* was voting it the second best place to live in the UK, thanks to its 'superlative shopping, bags of community spirit and an enviable location'. Though your stop here may be brief, Kendal is small enough (the population is only 26,000) that you should have the chance to sample each of these aspects.

See p14 for details of Kendal Mountain Festival.

### Services

Amongst the many services available in Kendal is the main **post office** (Mon-Fri 9am-5.30pm, Tue from 9.30am, Sat 9am-12.30pm) with a **phone box** outside; there are also **chemists** such as Boots (Mon-Fri 8.30am-6pm, Sat to 5.30pm, Sun 10.30am-4.30pm), at 66 Stricklandgate; and **trekking outlets** such as Mountain Warehouse (Mon-Sat 9am-5.30pm, Sun 10am-4pm), at 30-36 Stricklandgate, or Nevisport (Mon-Fri 9.30am-5.30pm, Sat 9am-5.30pm, Sun 10am-4pm) at 13-14 Finkle St. There are several **ATMs** around Stricklandgate, too.

For provisions there are two large **supermarkets** within the environs of the town centre: an M&S (Mon-Thur & Sat 8.30am-6.30pm, Fri 8am-7pm, Sun 10am-4pm) and a Booths (Mon-Sat 7am-9pm, Sun 10am-4pm), both a block west of Stricklandgate.

If your boots are struggling to last, The Key **Cobbler** (Mon-Sat 9am-5pm) is on the main square, Market Place. While if your dog's struggling, there's Highgate **Vets** (☎ 01539 721344, 🖳 highgatevets.com; Mon-Fri 8.30am-7.30pm, Sat 9am-12.30pm) at 173 Highgate.

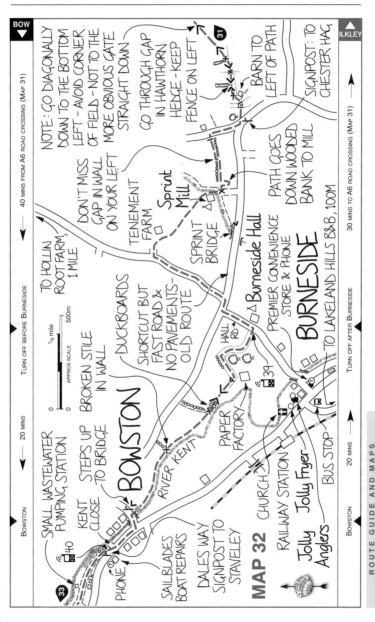

MAP 32

NOTE: GO DIAGONALLY DOWN TO THE BOTTOM LEFT - AVOID CORNER OF FIELD - NOT TO THE MORE OBVIOUS GATE STRAIGHT DOWN

GO THROUGH GAP IN HAWTHORN HEDGE - KEEP FENCE ON LEFT

BARN TO LEFT OF PATH

SIGNPOST: TO CHESTER HAG

DON'T MISS GAP IN WALL ON YOUR LEFT

Sprint Mill

TENEMENT FARM

SPRINT BRIDGE

Burneside Hall

PATH GOES DOWN WOODED BANK TO MILL

Premier convenience store & phone

BURNESIDE

TO LAKELAND HILLS B&B, 100M

HALL RD

PAPER FACTORY

TO HOLLIN ROOT FARM, 1 MILE

DUCKBOARDS

SHORTCUT BUT FAST ROAD & NO PAVEMENTS - OLD ROUTE

BROKEN STILE IN WALL

BOWSTON

RIVER KENT

CHURCH

RAILWAY STATION

Jolly Fryer

Jolly Anglers

BUS STOP

SMALL WASTEWATER PUMPING STATION

STEPS UP TO BRIDGE

KENT CLOSE

PHONE

SAILBLADES BOAT REPAIRS

DALES WAY SIGNPOST TO STAVELEY

0   ¼ mile
APPROX SCALE
0   500m

40 MINS FROM A6 ROAD CROSSING (MAP 31)

30 MINS TO A6 ROAD CROSSING (MAP 31)

TURN OFF BEFORE BURNESIDE

TURN OFF AFTER BURNESIDE

20 MINS

20 MINS

BOWSTON

BOWSTON

BOW

ILKLEY

31

33

39

40

ROUTE GUIDE AND MAPS

## Transport
Kendal is a stop on Northern's Manchester Airport to Windermere **train** service; see box p45. For **bus** services, the S1, W1, X6, 45, 555, 599 & 755 call here (see pp47-9); the 755 takes at least half an hour to reach Bowness.

The bus station is on Blackhall Rd.

## Where to stay
For **campers**, *Kendal Camping and Caravanning Club* (☎ 01539 741363, 🖥 campingandcaravanningclub.co.uk; WI-FI; 🐾; £8-12pp; Easter to end Oct) is on Shap Rd about 1½ miles (2.4km) north of the railway station. It's a lovely little campsite, if you don't mind the inconvenient location. They do get pretty busy, though, so it's one of the few campsites where it's recommended you book in advance (or at least call ahead).

There's a **hostel** in Kendal and it's a good one. The independent, family-run *Kendal Hostel* (☎ 01539 724066, ☎ 0779 519 8197, 🖥 kendalhostel.co.uk; 14 en suite rooms with 1-6 beds in each; WI-FI; 🐾) is at 118-120 Highgate – the interesting end of the main shopping street. It boasts a lounge with log burner and TV, a self-catering kitchen, a separate dining room and, crucially for Dales Way hikers, a drying room for wet gear. The hostel charges from £20 per bed, or £30 for single occupancy of a private twin room.

As for **B&Bs**, pretty close to the station at 65 Castle St is *Bridge House* (☎ 07813 679411, 🖥 bridgehouse-kendal.co.uk; 1D/1T, both en suite; ☛; WI-FI; Ⓛ), a smart, listed building with a lovely garden, a drying room and a warm welcome to walkers and cyclists; they are happy to suggest places to eat. Rates are £55-60pp (sgl occ £60-70). Convenient for the centre is the award-winning *Sonata Guest House* (🖥 sonata guesthouse.co.uk; 2D/1D or T/1T, all en suite; ☛; WI-FI), another mid 19th-century property, situated at 19 Burneside Rd. However, at the time of research they hadn't decided whether they would re-open so check their website.

Most central of all, *Premier Inn Kendal* (central reservations ☎ 0333 003

1745, 🖥 premierinn.com; 42D/50D or T, all en suite; ☛; WI-FI) is pretty much identical to all the other establishments in this chain. The tariff varies greatly depending on all sorts of factors. They advertise rooms from as little as £29(!) but you're more likely to pay around £90 for a standard room in peak season if you book and pay well in advance; in the low season about £52. Breakfast is an extra £9.50pp.

Moving away from the centre, and coming with great recommendations, *Balcony House* (☎ 07528 360339 or ☎ 01539 731402, 🖥 balconyhouse.co.uk; 1D or T/1T both en suite, 1D or T private bathroom; ☛; WI-FI) is a lovely, super-smart B&B though it is 600m north of the railway station (and thus a long way from town). The tariff is from £42.50pp (sgl occ £60, room rate in the summer). However, at the time of research they were only accepting stays of a minimum of two nights.

The highly recommended *Stonecross Manor Hotel* (☎ 01539 733559, 🖥 stone crossmanor.co.uk; 32D or T, all en suite; ☛; WI-FI), on Milnthorpe Rd, is a smart place housed in a former orphanage. Facilities include a heated indoor swimming pool and spa. B&B rates start at around £75pp (sgl occ from £110). Food is available daily noon-9pm. Unfortunately, it's over 1¼ miles (2km) from Kendal station, lying across town on the southern side, so treat yourself to a taxi from Oxenholme railway station (which is actually slightly closer).

## Where to eat and drink
For those early starts there's dog-friendly *Caffe Nero* (🐾; Mon-Sat 7.30am-6pm, Sun 8am-5.30pm), or dog-unfriendly *Costa* (Mon-Fri 8am-6pm, Sat to 5pm, Sun 9am-5pm).

Considerably more memorable is the UK's oldest coffee roaster, *Farrer's* (☎ 01539 731707, 🖥 farrers.co.uk/visit; **fb**; WI-FI; 🐾; Mon-Sat 9am-4.30pm), which has been serving up a fantastic array of the finest teas and coffees from the same location since 1819. The shop itself is very handsome, all wood panelled and polished brass. They also serve tasty **café** food –

Kendal

sandwiches, scones etc – but it's the coffee here that truly stands out.

Farrer's is just one of several cafés with a bit of history to them, including *1657 Chocolate House* (☎ 01539-740702, 🖥 chocolatehouse1657.co.uk; **fb**; Mon-Sat 10am-4pm), though in this case the history is largely about the 17th-century building rather than the shop itself, which has been in residence for only the past 30 years or so. Nevertheless for chocoholics it's an essential visit, with an array of luxury chocolates that can be boxed up for your walk. At the time of research the café part was closed but they were still offering five types of hot chocolate (from £3) to take away – pretty much the perfect warming pick-me-up on a soggy Kendal day.

There's also *Master's House Tearoom* (☎ 01539-720723; **fb**; 🐾; Tue-Sat 10am-3pm), at 80b Highgate; it's a tiny and traditional dog-friendly place housed in one of the oldest buildings in Kendal, and the ideal place for afternoon tea.

The **vegetarian** café-bistro *Waterside* (☎ 01539 729743; Mon-Sat 9.30am-4pm; WI-FI; 🐾), with tables overlooking the River Kent, has one of the best vegetarian menus you'll find; home-made cakes, vegan breakfasts, stuffed mushrooms, peanut-butter noodles... and the detox smoothies are superb.

The artisan sandwich shop, **Relish**, has moved from the other side of Market Place and renamed itself *Relish No 37* (☎ 01539 727279, 🖥 relish37.com; WI-FI; 🐾; **fb**; Mon-Sat 9am-5pm). It now has a more extensive menu including all-day breakfasts (from £8.95), ciabatta-roll sandwiches, hot paninis, salads, soups (£4.50) and home-made cakes (from £2.50) available for eat-in or takeaway. It is also now licensed.

Other cheap-eats in Kendal include the long-established café-restaurant *Finkle's* (☎ 01539 727325; **fb**; WI-FI; 🐾; summer Mon-Sat 9am-4pm, winter closed on Tue) where you can get the local take on shepherd's pie, Cumbrian shearman's pie (£7). It has some outdoor roadside seating, too.

Also good value, and open all day long, *Miles Thompson* (☎ 01539 815710, 🖥 jdwetherspoon.com; WI-FI; food daily 8am-11pm), on Allhallows Lane, is owned by the dog-unfriendly Wetherspoon's pub chain, which serves standard pub grub pretty much all the time they're open. The building used to be the local baths, which were designed by the eponymous Mr Thompson.

Across the road is the cheerful *Farmhouse Kitchen* (☎ 01539 728722; 🖥 fhk-kendal.co.uk; **fb**; WI-FI; 🐾; daily Mon-Thur 9am-4.30pm, Fri-Sun 8.30am-5pm), great for a wholesome breakfast or lunch, with chorizo hash (£9.50), beetroot wraps (£8.75) and Cumbrian ham & eggs (£9.75) all featuring on an eclectic menu.

For the evenings, *The Globe Inn* (food noon-9pm), is a traditional pub serving real ales and no-nonsense pub grub; particularly dog-friendly, too.

Nearby, also on Market Place, is the good-value Japanese-Filipino café *Teayempo* (☎ 01539 726757; Tue-Sat noon-9pm, Sun 5-9pm), where you can tuck into delights such as *donburi* (rice-bowl dishes; £9-10), *sushi* (£3-5 for four pieces) and udon noodles (£6-7).

For Thai food, try *Jintana* (☎ 01539 723123, 🖥 jintanathaicuisine.com/kendal; Mon-Thur 5-10pm, Fri & Sat to 10.30pm), a stylish restaurant with helpful staff and a friendly ambience.

On Highgate *The Moon* (☎ 01539 729254, 🖥 themoonhighgate.com; Thur-Sat 5-10pm, Sun noon-6pm) serves beautifully presented 'modern British food' such as roast halibut with English asparagus, cockles & capers (£19.10), and slow-cooked ox cheek (£18.80).

At the other end of the main shopping thoroughfare, at 128 Stricklandgate, award-winning *Pedro's Casa* (☎ 01539 722332; **fb**; Thur & Fri & Sun-Tue 5-9pm, Sat to 10pm), is a very popular tapas place (dishes £3-8) that offers much bigger portions than your average tapas. Mexican food also features heavily on the menu – and they do a mean cocktail too.

The best place for fish & chips is *Fish Express* (Mon-Thur 11.30am-8pm, Fri & Sat to 8.30pm), an eat-in restaurant and takeaway that doesn't disappoint. Fish & chips cost £6.50.

Other takeaways include: *Teayempo*; Thai restaurant *Jintana* (see opposite for both); the pizzeria *Geno's Pizzeria* (🖥 genospizzeria.co.uk; daily 5pm-midnight), on Allhallows Lane; the kebab house

*Marmaris* (☎ 01539-734443; daily 4pm-midnight), on Kent St; and *Silver Mountain* (☎ 01539 729911; Tue-Thur & Sun 5-11.30pm, Fri & Sat to midnight) for Chinese food.

## STAGE 6: BURNESIDE TO BOWNESS-ON-WINDERMERE
### MAPS 32-36

And so you come to the final stage on the walk, an undaunting **9½-miler (15.4km; 3½hrs)** with glorious views back to the rolling Howgills and ahead to the sharper crags of the Lake District. This can, of course, be done in a busy morning but it seems a shame to hurry through to the end, so it's worth taking a short diversion for lunch into Staveley, where there's a good choice of eateries for such a small place.

The perceptive walker will notice how this ultimate stage seems somehow out of character with much of what's gone before. The landscape is now craggier and more 'pointed', particularly when juxtaposed with the smooth-topped Howgills. When one compares the landscape and buildings now with the beginning of the walk, when you were atop the Askrigg Block (see box p138), the change is startling: even the grass is different here, the soil more acid meaning the rougher, browner lakeland pasture thrives. It's a sign that the end is near and your time on the Dales Way is almost over. So don't be in too much of a hurry to get this last leg completed; wherever you may be heading to afterwards, it's unlikely to be more dramatic, or more beautiful!

### The route

For some people, the day will begin with a train back from Kendal to Burneside and a walk through the village back to the Dales Way. Once on the trail the going is easy as you stroll through fields of livestock by the River Kent, a waterway you follow via **Bowston** and the residential development at **Cowan Head**, across the boundary of the **Lake District National Park** and on to **Staveley** (Map 33).

### STAVELEY          [see map p160]

Staveley is another one of those places – like Buckden, Dent, Sedbergh et al – that the Dales Way doesn't *quite* visit (it merely brushes against it as much as anything) but which is nevertheless very much part of the trail. It's a shame to miss the place, if only because it has several good eateries and as such is an ideal spot for lunch before the final amble to Bowness.

There are a few amenities here that you may want to take advantage of too. You can pick up **provisions** in The Beehive (☎ 01539 821253; Mon-Fri 10am-2pm), which also houses the village **post office**, or opposite in

the Spar (Mon-Sat 8am-7pm, Sun from 9.30am) which has much longer opening hours. Just up the street is a **pharmacy** (Mon-Fri 9am-6pm, Sat to 12.30pm).

Northern's (Manchester Airport to Windermere) **train** services (see box p45) call at the railway station. For **buses**, the 555 (Keswick to Lancaster) stops on Abbey Square; for details see pp47-9.

For **accommodation**, the most central place is *Meadow View B&B* (☎ 07799 860113, 🖥 sarah@classicadventure.co.uk; 2T/1Tr, all en suite, WI-FI; 🐾; Ⓛ), which is run by outdoor enthusiasts so they welcome walkers and cyclists. The rooms are smallish but comfortable with invigorating showers. They offer a healthy breakfast of porridge, fruit and home-made bread, jams and yoghurt. Minimum stay two nights; from £45pp (sgl occ £40pp) per night. Their '**tool shed**' (shared family shower room and toilet) sleeps up to four; sleeping bag needed but camp bed and pillow provided. The room costs £20 per night plus £5pp.

Half a mile out of the village, the 400-year-old farmhouse known as *Li'le Hullets* (off Map 33; ☎ 01539 821148, 🖳 anne gardner173@btinternet.com; 1D/1T both en suite, 1D in attic with private bathroom; 🛏; WI-FI; Ⓛ) is a great choice. The restoration of the property has been sympathetic, so that many of the original features that make this place so charming are still present, including the oak-beamed lounge, oak staircases and even a bread oven. The name, incidentally, means 'little owl' in the old Westmoreland dialect. The rates are exceptional given the charm of this place, with the tariff including breakfast from £40pp (£60 sgl occ), or £35pp (£50 sgl occ) in the smaller double room in the attic. However, they don't accept bookings for less than two nights now. To reach it, walk west on Windermere Rd, which in turn becomes Danes Rd. Seed Howe is on your right, with Li'le Hullets at No 3.

Much nearer to the path, and with a reputation for good pub grub, is the curiously named *Eagle and Child* (☎ 01539 821320, 🖳 eaglechildinn.co.uk; 3D/1T/ 1Tr, all en suite; 🛏; WI-FI; Ⓛ; B&B from £47.50-55pp, sgl occ room rate) with smart, tastefully decorated rooms and lovely countryside views. The name, incidentally, comes from an old tale about a local aristocrat, Sir Thomas Latham, who fathered a longed-for son by a servant girl (his wife having given him only daughters). To introduce the boy into the family, Sir Thomas deposited the child beneath a tree where an eagle was nesting. His wife, strolling past the tree, discovered the boy and, assuming the eagle had dropped the child, took him back home and adopted him as her own, much as Sir Thomas had planned. To this day the Latham family crest has an eagle and a child on it.

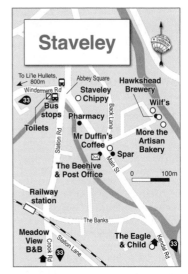

## Where to eat and drink

While your feet may not thank you for forcing them to walk the extra few minutes into Staveley, your stomach certainly will as there is a surprising range of good places to eat and drink.

Coffee lovers will find it almost impossible to resist following their noses to *Mr Duffin's Coffee* (☎ 01539 822192; **fb**; Mon-Sat 10am-5pm), a local roasters who do what is arguably the best coffee on the whole trail. They also serve speciality teas, plus freshly filled rolls (from £4.25), artisan chocolate, luxury ice cream and home-made flapjacks. It's tiny, with only two or three bar stools to sit at, so most people take away.

The other options lie on a small commercial estate off Main St. The main draw is *Hawkshead Brewery & Beer Hall* (☎ 01539 825260, 🖳 hawksheadbrewery.co.uk; **fb**; food Mon-Thur noon-8pm, Fri & Sat to 11pm, Sun 11am-8pm), a modern glass affair with a large menu (gourmet burgers, BBQ ribs etc), much of it designed to accompany their excellent range of beers. Off to one side of the brewery is *Wilf's Café* (☎ 01539 822329, 🖳

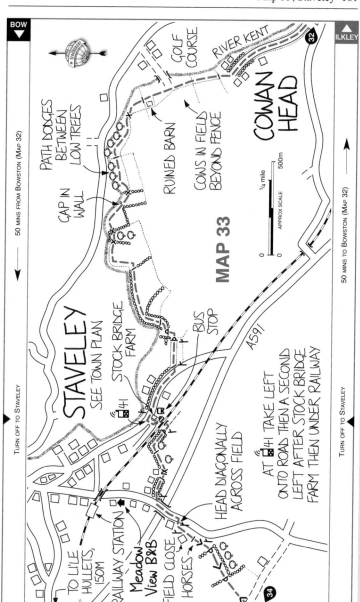

BOW ▼

ILKLEY ▲

← 50 MINS FROM BOWSTON (MAP 32) →

PATH DODGES BETWEEN LOW TREES

GOLF COURSE

RIVER KENT

32

COWAN HEAD

RUINED BARN

COWS IN FIELD BEYOND FENCE

GAP IN WALL

¼ mile

0          500m

APPROX SCALE

0

MAP 33

STAVELEY
SEE TOWN PLAN

STOCK BRIDGE FARM

BUS STOP

A591

← TURN OFF TO STAVELEY

50 MINS TO BOWSTON (MAP 32) →

TURN OFF TO STAVELEY ►

AT A591 TAKE LEFT ONTO ROAD THEN A SECOND LEFT AFTER STOCK BRIDGE FARM THEN UNDER RAILWAY

RAILWAY STATION

Meadow View B&B

FIELD CLOSE HORSES

TO L'ILE HULLETS, 150M

HEAD DIAGONALLY ACROSS FIELD

34

wilfs-cafe.co.uk; **fb**; WI-FI; 🐾; daily 9am-4pm) a friendlier, more down-to-earth place, that's more suited to passing walkers. There's outdoor seating out front and also at the back beside the river; the menu is good value and includes all-day breakfasts (from £8.25), sandwiches, salads (from £6.95), baps and jacket potatoes (£6.50).

On the other side of the brewery is a swish bakery called **More the Artisan Bakery** (☎ 01539 825110, 🖥 moreartisan .co.uk; Mon & Thur 8am-3pm, Fri-Sun to 4pm) that does pastries, sandwiches and, on Friday and Saturday evenings (4-8pm), stone-baked pizza (**More Dough**).

The main option for evening meals, though, is the excellent pub grub at **Eagle and Child** (see Where to stay; Tue bar from 4pm, food Wed-Thur 5-8pm, Fri noon-2pm & 5-8pm, Sat & Sun food noon-8pm), including home-made short-crust pastry pies (£12-14), Moroccan lamb with couscous (£14.50) and spicy lentil, bean & spinach chilli (£12). They're a CAMRA pub, too, so have a great choice of real ales.

For takeaway, near the centre of the village is **Staveley Chippy** (☎ 01539 821457; **fb**; Wed & Sat 5-8pm, Thur & Fri 11.45am-1.15pm & 5-8pm).

With Staveley visited and the A591 safely crossed, things start to get a little more interesting, particularly beyond **New Hall** (Map 34) where the path climbs steeply to afford some great views south-east to the Howgill Fells and the western edge of the Dales, as well as Cross Fell on the northern Pennines (at 893m, the highest point in England outside of the Lakes), and, of course, to your left, the Lakeland Fells. More great views follow after the next climb as you finally leave the tarmac to enter a series of wild fields, the air heavy with the coconut-scent of the gorse bushes that grow thickly here. The farmhouses of **Crag House**, **Outrun Nook** and **Hag End** help you to count off the yards. The end feels close now and the view from the minor hill of **Grandsire** (Map 35) confirms this – a vista that on a good day encompasses many of the *grand-dames* of the Lakes, with Crinkle Crags, Bowfell, Langdale Pikes, School Knott and even the grandest of them all, Scafell Pike, appearing through the haze. From here it's a bit of a messy end, with plenty of small fields to march through and even a bit of road walking before the final drop to the finish.

The end – just like the beginning all those miles ago – is marked by a simple stone bench where you can sit, congratulate your companions, reflect on your expedition – and steel yourself for the hurly-burly below.

## BOWNESS-ON-WINDERMERE
### [Map 36, p165]

No matter how much you think you've missed civilisation the reality, when you finally reach it again at the very end of your trek, is a bit of a shock – and not, for most walkers, a particularly pleasant one. For the majority of Dales Way walkers find Bowness just a bit too noisy, crowded and 'touristy'. And isn't it strange, and not a little depressing, to be back in a place where people don't bid you a 'good morning' as you walk by?

What brings the masses here are Bowness's historic connections with Beatrix Potter (including the town's number one attraction, the large **World of Beatrix Potter** (☎ 015394 88444, 🖥 hop-skip-jump.com; Apr-Oct daily 10am-5.30pm, rest of year 4.30pm; adult/child £8.20/4.20). The town also has associations with the Romantic poets of the 18th and 19th centuries (though some may say you won't find a less romantic spot on the entire walk than Bowness). The wonders of

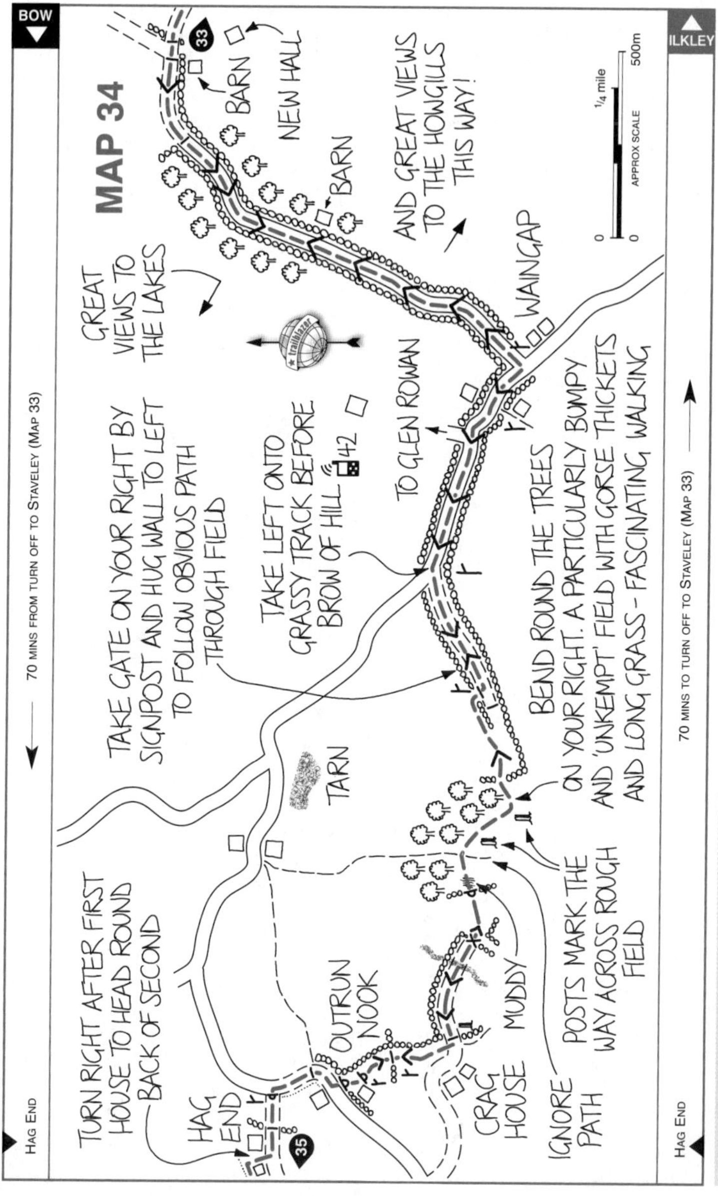

ILKLEY ▲

MAP 34

33

BARN

NEW HALL

BARN

AND GREAT VIEWS
TO THE HOWGILLS
THIS WAY!

WAINGAP

500m

0

0          1/4 mile

APPROX SCALE

GREAT VIEWS TO
THE LAKES

← 70 MINS FROM TURN OFF TO STAVELEY (MAP 33)

TAKE GATE ON YOUR RIGHT BY
SIGNPOST AND HUG WALL TO LEFT
TO FOLLOW OBVIOUS PATH
THROUGH FIELD

TAKE LEFT ONTO
GRASSY TRACK BEFORE
BROW OF HILL 📷 42

TO GLEN ROWAN

BEND ROUND THE TREES
ON YOUR RIGHT. A PARTICULARLY BUMPY
AND 'UNKEMPT' FIELD WITH GORSE THICKETS
AND LONG GRASS — FASCINATING WALKING.

70 MINS TO TURN OFF TO STAVELEY (MAP 33) →

TARN

TURN RIGHT AFTER FIRST
HOUSE TO HEAD ROUND
BACK OF SECOND

HAG END

HAG END

35

OUTRUN
NOOK

CRAG
HOUSE       MUDDY

IGNORE
PATH

POSTS MARK THE
WAY ACROSS ROUGH
FIELD

HAG END

Wharfedale, pretty little Dent and charming Sedbergh all seem light years away now. Perhaps that's why Colin Speakman, who created the Dales Way, chose to end the walk *above* the town rather than in it, so you can still enjoy Bowness's main appeal – the views it offers of gorgeous Lake Windermere – without actually having to throw yourself into the maelstrom below.

Having said that, Bowness does offer pretty much everything a walker could want, including restaurants and cafés galore, over 200 B&Bs, hotels and other accommodation, a large and helpful information centre – plus, most importantly for those who wish to head home after their long hike, good transport connections.

So all that remains is to perform whatever ritual you find necessary to mark the end of your odyssey: dip one foot in the lake, maybe?.. collect your Dales Way certificate from the outdoor outfitters Hawkshead?.. or perhaps just get roaringly drunk in the Hole in t'Wall (see Where to eat)? Oh, and congratulations on finishing the Dales Way – wasn't that a beautiful journey!

See box on p14 for details of Bowness's Summer of Fun festival.

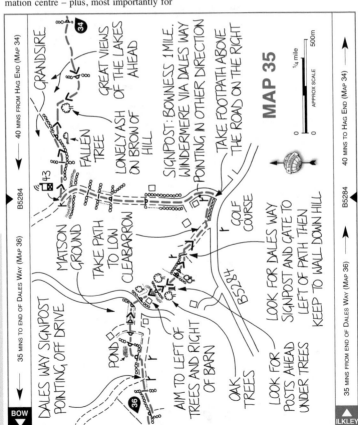

MAP 35

40 MINS FROM HAG END (MAP 34)

GRANDSIRE

GREAT VIEWS OF THE LAKES AHEAD

FALLEN TREE

LONELY ASH ON BROW OF HILL

SIGNPOST: BOWNESS 1 MILE. WINDERMERE VIA DALES WAY POINTING IN OTHER DIRECTION

TAKE FOOTPATH ABOVE THE ROAD ON THE RIGHT

GOLF COURSE

MATSON GROUND

TAKE PATH TO LOW CLEABARROW

LOOK FOR DALES WAY SIGNPOST AND GATE TO LEFT OF PATH THEN KEEP TO WALL DOWN HILL

DALES WAY SIGNPOST POINTING OFF DRIVE

POND

AIM TO LEFT OF TREES AND RIGHT OF BARN

OAK TREES

LOOK FOR POSTS AHEAD UNDER TREES

0   1/4 mile
0   500m
APPROX SCALE

35 MINS TO END OF DALES WAY (MAP 36)

B5284

40 MINS TO HAG END (MAP 34)

35 MINS FROM END OF DALES WAY (MAP 36)

BOW

ILKLEY

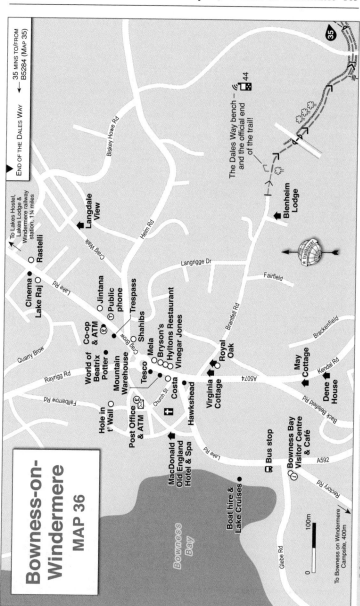

# Bowness-on-Windermere
## MAP 36

Bowness Bay

To Bowness on Windermere Campsite, 400m

0    100m

Boat hire & Lake Cruises

Glebe Rd

MacDonald Old England Hotel & Spa

Hawkshead

Lake Rd

Rectory Rd

A592

Bowness Bay Visitor Centre & Café

Bus stop

Post Office & ATM

Hole in t' Wall

Fallbarrow Rd

Rayrigg Rd

Church St

Costa

Tesco

Mountain Warehouse

World of Beatrix Potter

Co-op & ATM

Quarry Brow

Craig Brow

Virginia Cottage

Vinegar Jones

Hyltons Restaurant

Bryson's

Mela

Shahibs

Trespass

Public phone

Jintana

Cinema
Lake Raj

Lake Rd

Rastelli

To Lakes Hostel, Lakes Lodge & Windermere railway station, 1¼ miles

END OF THE DALES WAY

35 MINS TO/FROM B5284 (MAP 35)

Biskey Howe Rd

Langdale View

Craig Walk

Helm Rd

Langrigge Dr

Fairfield

Royal Oak

A5074

Brantfell Rd

Back Belsfield Rd

May Cottage

Dene House

Kendal Rd

Brackenfield

Blenheim Lodge

The Dales Way bench – and the official end of the trail!

35

## Services

Down by the lake, **Bowness Bay Visitor Centre** (Apr-Oct daily 9.30am-5.30pm, Nov-Mar daily 10am-4.30pm; WI-FI) sells maps, books and souvenirs and has a *café*.

Up the hill on St Martin's Parade, a little back street, is the **post office** (Mon-Fri 9am-5.30pm, Sat 9am-1pm). On the main drag there are a couple of **supermarkets**: Co-op (daily 7am-10pm) and, back down the hill, Tesco Express (daily 7am-11pm). There's an **ATM** outside the post office and at the Co-op which also has a **payphone** opposite.

If you're starting your trek in Bowness or planning on doing some further walking in the Lake District, there are a few **trekking outfitters** including Mountain Warehouse (Mon-Sat 9am-5.30pm, Sun 9am-5pm), Trespass (Mon-Sat 9am-5.30pm, Sun 10am-5pm) and Hawkshead (Mon-Sat 9am-5.30pm, Sun 10am-5pm). From Hawkshead you can also pick up a **Dales Way Certificate**.

## Transport

The main **bus** stop is on the lakeshore, just before the visitor centre. The 6, 508, 599 & 755 service links Bowness with its Siamese twin, Windermere (which, ironically, isn't actually on the lake but a mile and more up the hill); see pp47-9 for details. Windermere **railway station** is the last stop on Northern Rail's service from Manchester Airport (see box p45).

**Windermere Lake Cruises** (see p46) offer cruises on the lake with 'steamers' heading to Brockhole, Lakeside and Waterhead (for Ambleside), but also a Cross Lakes Shuttle (May-Oct approx 10/day; single/return £3.30/5.60; 🐾 free) from Bowness to Ferry House. Mountain Goat provides a bus connection from Ferry House to Hawkshead; see box p45.

**Taxi** firms include Lakeside Taxis (☎ 015394 88888, 🖥 lakesidetaxis.co.uk), who have an 8-seater vehicle and claim to be the cheapest in the area.

## Where to stay

The nearest **campsite**, situated on the eastern shore of Lake Windermere, is *Bowness on Windermere* (off Map 36; ☎ 015394 42177, 🖥 campingandcaravanningclub.co .uk; 🐾 must be kept on leads). It was closed for renovations during 2021, but should be open again by the time you read this. As with all Camping and Caravanning Club sites, there is a complicated pricing structure but walkers tended to be charged around £10pp. Walk down Rectory Rd, turn left at the end and it's on the right.

The closest **hostel** to the end of the walk is the newly refurbished and re-branded *Lakes Hostel* (off Map 36; ☎ 015394 46374, 🖥 lakeshostel.co.uk; 5 rooms, 19 beds in 1- to 5-bed rooms; WI-FI). It's a mile up the hill in Windermere on the High St, close to the railway station (plenty of buses ply the route). There's a self-catering kitchen, a lounge, a laundry room, and each bed has a charging point and reading light. At the time of research the proprietor wasn't sure whether they would stay with exclusive hire between April and October or return to accepting individual bookings as it did pre-Covid (Nov-Mar it is open for either). For individual bookings rates would be £35-45pp (sgl/sgl occ rates on request).

Opposite the hostel, at No 1 High St, you'll find *Lakes Lodge* (☎ 015394 42751, 🖥 lakes-lodge.co.uk; 2S/1T/1D/2D or T/2Tr/1Qd all en suite, 1S shower in room but private toilet; WI-FI), a cheap hotel which, unusually for this area, is generally happy to allow single-night stays. They also have some single rooms – again unusual. Rates start at £35pp (sgl from £40, sgl occ £35). Breakfast is an extra £5.

If these two options seem a bit out of the way, do bear in mind that they are both only a minute's walk from the railway station (which you'll probably be using at some stage) and are in amongst a great choice of cafés, pubs, restaurants and shops that line the main road leading down from the station.

Back near the lake, in Bowness, you'll find dozens and dozens of **hotels and B&Bs**. As such, the following is just a tiny selection, largely made up of the accommodation most popular with Dales Way walkers. Note that, **at virtually all the accom-**

modation in Bowness, there is a two-night minimum stay at weekends.

*Blenheim Lodge* (☎ 015394 43440, ⌨ blenheim-lodge.com; 3S/6D/1Tr all en suite, 1D private bathroom; ✆; WI-FI weather dependent) is on a cul de sac off Brantfell Rd about a minute's walk from the end of Dales Way. Most of the rooms have views of Lake Windermere and there is a lounge for guests but at the time of research it was closed due to Covid. B&B costs £49-73pp (sgl from £77, sgl occ room rate).

Just a short way down the hill from the end of the trail, *Royal Oak* (☎ 015394 43970, ⌨ royaloak-windermere.co.uk; 8D all en suite/2D with shared bathroom; ✆; WI-FI) proudly proclaims itself as 'the official finishing pub for the Dalesway (sic)' thanks to an endorsement by a writer of an old guidebook; and with a location at the bottom of Brantfell Rd it's hard to argue with that. B&B costs from £50pp (sgl occ £70).

There's a whole string of B&Bs stretching south from the centre of town along the A5074, aka Kendal Rd, the lofty vantage point allowing views of the lake from any of them. One such is *Dene House* (☎ 015394 48236, ⌨ denehouse-guest house.co.uk; 2D or T/4D all en suite; ✆; WI-FI); it is one of the few B&Bs in the area with a single room (and the single is the only room that has access to a bath); rates are from £57.50pp (sgl from £75, sgl occ room rate) and a vegetarian option is available at breakfast.

Heading north back into the centre, *May Cottage* (☎ 015394 46478, ⌨ may cottagebowness.co.uk; 1D/2D or T, all en suite; ✆; WI-FI) is also recommended. Rates are from £45pp (sgl occ £50).

Further north, homely *Virginia Cottage* (☎ 015394 44891, ⌨ vir ginia-cottage.co.uk; 11D, all en suite; ✆; WI-FI; 🐾) is one of the few places to stay in the town centre that **allows (small) dogs**. It's a long-established place, the building (originally two cottages) having been here for over 150 years and the business running for over 45 years. Rates start at £42.50pp (sgl occ £76.50).

Regularly receiving rave reviews, *Langdale View* (☎ 015394 44076, ⌨ lang daleview.co.uk; 4D/1D or T, all en suite; WI-FI) is one of the older properties in Bowness, having been built in the mid 19th century on Craig Walk, about 500m from the lakeshore. Rates are from £55pp (sgl occ from £90).

Finally, *MacDonald Old England Hotel & Spa* (☎ 0344 879 9144, ⌨ mac donaldhotels.co.uk; 106 rooms; ✆; WI-FI) with its smart rooms overlooking the lakeshore and uniformed staff bustling around the lobby, is perhaps the most up-market place in town. The tariff, of course, reflects this, with B&B starting at £114pp (sgl occ from £211).

## Where to eat and drink

There are a lot of mouths to feed in the high season in Bowness and as a consequence a lot of cafés and restaurants to cater for them. The following, therefore, is but the briefest of overviews. If you want something familiar, there's a large *Costa* (daily 9am-5pm) right in the centre of the action. Opposite, is a more traditional option: *Bryson's* (☎ 015394 88726, ⌨ brysons ofkeswick.co.uk; daily 9.30am-5pm), a tea-room and bakery that started up in Keswick 70 years ago, but which now has these premises in Bowness, too. Expect standout baked goods, light lunches and cracking cream teas.

**Pubs** that do food include *Royal Oak* (see Where to Stay; food daily 11am-8.30pm), with its popular front terrace overlooking the street below; mains cost from £13 including steak & ale pie, foot-long sausage & chips and traditional chicken pub curry.

There's also the hugely atmospheric *Hole in t'Wall* (☎ 015394 43488, ⌨ holeintwall.co.uk; WI-FI; food Mon & Thur-Sat noon-8pm, Sun to 3pm), tucked away on a quiet side street and with a history going back 400 years. Good-value mains cost £11-13 and include Cumberland sausage and fish pie. There are also sandwiches and jacket potatoes (both from £5.95), as well as a great selection of real ales.

In a similar vein, food-wise, though not a pub, *Hyltons Restaurant* (☎ 015394 43060, 🖥 hyltonsbowness.co.uk; **fb**; WI-FI; daily noon-9pm) does mains such as beef & ale pie (£14.90) and spaghetti bolognese (£12) and is popular with families, as is *Rastelli* (☎ 015394 44227, 🖥 rastelli.co.uk; Sun, Mon & Wed-Fri 5-9pm, Sat to 9.30pm), an Italian pizzeria up by the cinema.

**Takeaways** include the chippy *Vinegar Jones* (☎ 015394 44846, 🖥 vinegarjones.co.uk; **fb**; Thur-Mon noon-4pm &

4.45-8pm), and *Jintana* (☎ 015394 45002, 🖥 jintanathaicuisine.com/bowness; daily noon-10pm), sister branch of the one in Kendal. There are also several good Indian restaurants (for takeaway or eating in) including *Shahib's* (☎ 015394 43944, 🖥 shahibs.co.uk; daily 12.15-2.15pm & 5.15-11.15pm, Sat to 12.15am), *Mela* (☎ 015394 45777; daily 5-11pm), and *Lake Raj* (☎ 015394 45900, 🖥 lakeraj.com; daily noon-2pm & 5-11pm).

## Map key

| | | | |
|---|---|---|---|
| ♠ | Where to stay (G) = groups only | ℹ | Tourist Information |
| O | Where to eat and drink | 📖 | Library/bookstore |
| Λ | Campsite | @ | Internet |
| ⊠ | Post Office | 🏛 | Museum/gallery |
| ⓕ | Bank/ATM | ✚ | Church/cathedral |
| | | ☎ | Telephone |
| | | ⌀ | Public toilet |

□ Building • Other CP Car park 🚌 Bus station/stop Rail line & station Park GPS waypoint 082

Dales Way — Gate — Stone Wall — Other path — Stile — Water — 4 x 4 track — Kissing gate — Trees/woodland — Tarmac road — River and bridge — Bench, table — Steps — Hedge — Signpost — Slope/Steep slope — Fence — 21 Map continuation

ROUTE GUIDE AND MAPS

# APPENDIX A: GPS WAYPOINTS*

| MAP | REF | GPS WAYPOINTS | DESCRIPTION |
|-----|-----|---------------|-------------|
| 1 | 01 | 30 U 576772 5976258 | Old Bridge at Ilkley, start of trail |
| 2 | 02 | 30 U 573871 5977822 | Gate to road in Addingham after church |
| 3 | 03 | 30 U 573101 5979864 | Gate near Quaker Farfield Meeting House |
| 3 | 04 | 30 U 573010 5982227 | Footbridge by Bolton Abbey |
| 4 | 05 | 30 U 573256 5983390 | Cavendish Pavilion |
| 5 | 06 | 30 U 571889 5984476 | The Strid |
| 5 | 07 | 30 U 571166 5984895 | Barden Bridge |
| 6 | 08 | 30 U 570110 5988074 | Footpath to Appletreewick |
| 7 | 09 | 30 U 568611 5989207 | Burnsall Bridge |
| 7 | 10 | 30 U 567891 5990358 | Hebden Suspension Bridge |
| 8 | 11 | 30 U 565481 5991344 | Bridge with views of weir |
| 9 | 12 | 30 U 564783 5995246 | Limekiln |
| 10 | 13 | 30 U 564135 5996639 | Gated stile by Conistone Pie |
| 11 | 14 | 30 U 562686 5999438 | Turn off road thro' gate by K'well ⅝ mile sign |
| 11 | 15 | 30 U 562246 6000216 | Kettlewell maypole |
| 12 | 16 | 30 U 560302 6002386 | Dales Way signpost |
| 13 | 17 | 30 U 559112 6005225 | Buckden Bridge |
| 14 | 18 | 30 U 557825 6006096 | Hubberholme Church |
| 15 | 19 | 30 U 554364 6007554 | Bridge at Deepdale |
| 16 | 20 | 30 U 552491 6008022 | Bridge at Beckermonds |
| 16 | 21 | 30 U 551264 6009956 | Nethergill Farm |
| 17 | 22 | 30 U 549817 6010256 | Swarthghyll Farm |
| 18 | 23 | 30 U 547534 6009914 | Cam Houses |
| 18a | 23a | 30 U 547738 6011031 | Cold Keld Gate |
| 18a | 23b | 30 U 546390 6010913 | Gavel Gap |
| 18b | 23c | 30 U 544569 6011240 | Onto road at Newby Head |
| 18c | 23d | 30 U 544251 6013823 | Galloway Gate; junction at Arten Gill |
| 18 | 24 | 30 U 546423 6009422 | Join Cam High Road/high point of Way |
| 19 | 25 | 30 U 543446 6007900 | Far Gearstones |
| 20 | 26 | 30 U 542806 6012063 | Dent Head Viaduct |
| 21 | 27 | 30 U 542122 6013562 | Stone House |
| 21 | 28 | 30 U 541405 6014335 | Leave road by bridge at Lea Yeat |
| 22 | 29 | 30 U 538242 6013787 | Nelly Bridge |
| 23 | 30 | 30 U 535748 6014725 | Church Bridge/turn-off to Dent |
| 24 | 31 | 30 U 533141 6016084 | Join road near Dent Fault! |
| 25 | 32 | 30 U 531681 6016860 | Gate before Brackensgill Bridge |
| 26 | 33 | 30 U 529263 6018405 | Gate – view of old railway bridge |
| 27 | 34 | 30 U 528030 6020490 | Lune Viaduct |
| 28 | 35 | 30 U 526932 6023678 | Onto road before Crook of Lune Bridge |
| 29 | 36 | 30 U 524861 6023233 | Across M6 motorway |
| 30 | 37 | 30 U 520737 6024355 | Kissing gate off track |
| 31 | 38 | 30 U 519533 6024522 | White house after pylon |
| 32 | 39 | 30 U 515727 6023210 | Turn-off before reaching Burneside |
| 32 | 40 | 30 U 514598 6023997 | Turn off road at Bowston |
| 33 | 41 | 30 U 512216 6025039 | Turn-off before reaching Staveley |
| 34 | 42 | 30 U 509773 6023777 | Turn off road onto grassy farm track |
| 35 | 43 | 30 U 507093 6024249 | Sharp left turn by signpost |
| 36 | 44 | 30 U 505618 6023844 | Finish! |

# APPENDIX B: WALKING WITH A DOG

## THE DALES WAY WITH A DOG

Many are the rewards that await those prepared to make the extra effort required to bring their best friend along the trail. You shouldn't underestimate the amount of work involved, though. Indeed, just about every decision you make will be influenced by the fact that you've got a dog: how you plan to travel to the start of the trail, where you're going to stay, how far you're going to walk each day, where you're going to rest and where you're going to eat in the evening etc.

If you're sure your dog can cope with (and will enjoy) walking 12 miles or more a day for several days in a row, you need to start preparing accordingly. Extra thought also needs to go into your itinerary. The best starting point is to study the town and village facilities table on p32 (and the advice below), and plan where to stop and where to buy food.

### Looking after your dog

To begin with, you need to make sure that your own dog is fully **inoculated** against the usual doggy illnesses, and also up to date with regard to **worm pills** (eg Drontal) and **flea preventatives** such as Frontline – they are, after all, following in the pawprints of many a dog before them, some of whom may well have left fleas or other parasites on the trail that now lie in wait for their next meal to arrive.

**Pet insurance** is also a very good idea; if you've already got insurance, do check that it will cover a trip such as this.

On the subject of looking after your dog's health, perhaps the most important implement you can take with you is the **plastic tick remover**, available from vets for a couple of quid. These removers, while fiddly, help you to remove the tick safely (ie without leaving its head behind buried under the dog's skin).

Being in unfamiliar territory also makes it more likely that you and your dog could become separated. For this reason, make sure your dog has a **tag with your contact details on it** (a mobile phone number would be best if you are carrying one with you); the fact that now all dogs in the UK have to be **microchipped** provides further security.

### When to keep your dog on a lead

● **When crossing farmland**, particularly in the **lambing season** (around May) when your dog can scare the sheep, causing them to lose their young. Farmers are allowed by law to shoot at and kill any dogs that they consider are worrying their sheep. During lambing, most farmers would prefer it if you didn't bring your dog at all.

The exception to the dogs on leads rule is if your dog is being attacked by cows. Some years ago there were three deaths in the UK caused by walkers being trampled as they tried to rescue their dogs from the attentions of cattle. The advice in this instance is to let go of the lead, head speedily to a position of safety (usually the other side of the field gate or stile) and call your dog to you.

● **Around ground-nesting birds** It's important to keep your dog under control when crossing an area where certain species of birds nest on the ground. Most dogs love foraging around in the woods but make sure you have permission to do so; some woods are used as 'nurseries' for game birds and dogs are only allowed through them if they are on a lead.

● **On mountain tops** It's a sad fact that, every year, a few dogs lose their lives falling over the edge of steep slopes.

### What to pack

You've probably already got a good idea of what to bring to keep your dog alive and happy, but the following is a checklist:

- **Food/water bowl** Foldable cloth bowls are popular with walkers, being light and taking up little room in the rucksack. You can get also get a water-bottle-and-bowl combination, where the bottle folds into a 'trough' from which the dog can drink.
- **Lead and collar** An extendable one is probably preferable for this sort of trip. Make sure both lead and collar are in good condition – you don't want either to snap on the trail, or you may end up carrying your dog through sheep fields until a replacement can be found.
- **Medication** You'll know if you need to bring any lotions or potions.
- **Bedding** A simple blanket may suffice, or you can opt for something more elaborate if you aren't carrying your own luggage.
- **Poo bags** Essential.
- **Hygiene wipes** For cleaning your dog after it's rolled in stuff.
- **A favourite toy** Helps prevent your dog from pining for the entire walk.
- **Food/water** Remember to bring treats as well as regular food to keep up the mutt's morale. That said, if your dog is anything like mine the chances are they'll spend most of the walk dining on rabbit droppings and sheep poo anyway.
- **Corkscrew stake** Available from camping or pet shops, this will help you to keep your dog secure in one place while you set up camp/doze.
- **Tick remover** See opposite.
- **Raingear** It can rain!
- **Old towels** For drying your dog.

When it comes to packing, I always leave an exterior pocket of my rucksack empty so I can put used poo bags in there (for deposit at the first bin). I always like to keep all the dog's kit together and separate from the other luggage (usually inside a plastic bag inside my rucksack). I have also seen several dogs sporting their own 'doggy rucksack', so they can carry their own food, water, poo etc – which certainly reduces the burden on their owner.

### Cleaning up after your dog
It is extremely important that dog owners behave in a responsible way when walking the path. Dog excrement should be cleaned up. In towns, villages and fields where animals graze or which will be cut for silage, hay etc, you need to pick up and bag the excrement.

### Staying with your dog
In this guide you will see the symbol 🐾 to denote where a **hotel, pub, or B&B** welcomes dogs. However, this always needs to be arranged in advance – many places have only one or two rooms suitable for people with dogs. In some cases dogs need to sleep in a separate building. Some places make an additional charge (usually per night but occasionally per stay) while others may require a deposit which is refundable if the dog doesn't make a mess.

**Hostels** (both YHA and independent) do not permit them unless they are an assistance (guide) dog.

Smaller **campsites** tend to accept dogs, but some of the larger holiday parks do not; look for the 🐾 symbol in the text.

When it comes to **eating**, most landlords allow dogs in at least a section of their pubs; the same applies for cafés though few restaurants do. Make sure you always ask first and ensure your dog doesn't run around the pub but is secured to your table or a radiator.

**Henry Stedman**

# INDEX

Page references in red type refer to maps

# TRAILBLAZER TITLE LIST
## see also overleaf for our British Walking Guides

Adventure Cycle-Touring Handbook
Adventure Motorcycling Handbook
Australia by Rail
Cleveland Way (British Walking Guide)
Coast to Coast (British Walking Guide)
Cornwall Coast Path (British Walking Guide)
Cotswold Way (British Walking Guide)
The Cyclist's Anthology
Dales Way (British Walking Guide)
Dorset & Sth Devon Coast Path (British Walking Gde)
Exmoor & Nth Devon Coast Path (British Walking Gde)
Glyndŵr's Way (British Walking Guide)
Great Glen Way (British Walking Guide)
Hadrian's Wall Path (British Walking Guide)
Himalaya by Bike – a route and planning guide
Iceland Hiking – with Reykjavik City Guide
Inca Trail, Cusco & Machu Picchu
Japan by Rail
Kilimanjaro – the trekking guide (includes Mt Meru)
London Loop (British Walking Guide)
London to Walsingham Camino
Madeira Walks – 37 selected day walks
Moroccan Atlas – The Trekking Guide
Morocco Overland (4x4/motorcycle/mountainbike)
Nepal Trekking & The Great Himalaya Trail
Norfolk Coast Path & Peddars Way (British Walking Gde)
North Downs Way (British Walking Guide)
Offa's Dyke Path (British Walking Guide)
Overlanders' Handbook – worldwide driving guide
Pembrokeshire Coast Path (British Walking Guide)
Pennine Way (British Walking Guide)
Peru's Cordilleras Blanca & Huayhuash – Hiking/Biking
Pilgrim Pathways: 1-2 day walks on Britain's sacred ways
The Railway Anthology
The Ridgeway (British Walking Guide)
Scottish Highlands – Hillwalking Guide
Siberian BAM Guide – rail, rivers & road
The Silk Roads – a route and planning guide
Sinai – the trekking guide
South Downs Way (British Walking Guide)
Thames Path (British Walking Guide)
Tour du Mont Blanc
Trans-Canada Rail Guide
Trans-Siberian Handbook
Trekking in the Everest Region
The Walker's Anthology
The Walker's Anthology – further tales
West Highland Way (British Walking Guide)

## www.trailblazer-guides.com

# TRAILBLAZER'S BRITISH WALKING GUIDES

We've applied to destinations which are closer to home Trailblazer's proven formula for publishing definitive practical route guides for adventurous travellers. Britain's network of long-distance trails enables the walker to explore some of the finest landscapes in the country's best walking areas. These are guides that are user-friendly, practical, informative and environmentally sensitive.

*'The same attention to detail that distinguishes its other guides has been brought to bear here'.*

THE
SUNDAY TIMES

● **Unique mapping features** In many walking guidebooks the reader has to read a route description then try to relate it to the map. Our guides are much easier to use because walking directions, tricky junctions, places to stay and eat, points of interest and walking times are all written onto the maps themselves in the places to which they apply. With their uncluttered clarity, these are not general-purpose maps but fully edited maps drawn by walkers for walkers.

● **Largest-scale walking maps** At a scale of just under 1:20,000 (8cm or 3¹/₈ inches to one mile) the maps in these guides are bigger than even the most detailed British walking maps currently available in the shops.

● **Not just a trail guide – includes where to stay, where to eat and public transport** Our guidebooks cover the complete walking experience, not just the route. Accommodation options for all budgets are provided (pubs, hotels, B&Bs, campsites, bunkhouses, hostels) as well as places to eat. Detailed public transport information for all access points to each trail means that there are itineraries for all walkers, for hiking the entire route as well as for day or weekend walks.

**Cleveland Way** *Henry Stedman*, 1st edn, ISBN 978-1-905864-91-1, 240pp, 98 maps

**Coast to Coast** *Henry Stedman*, 9th edn, ISBN 978-1-912716-11-1, 268pp, 109 maps

**Cornwall Coast Path (SW Coast Path Pt 2)** *Stedman & Newton*, 7th edn, ISBN 978-1-912716-26-5, 352pp, 142 maps

**Cotswold Way** *Tricia & Bob Hayne*, 4th edn, ISBN 978-1-912716-04-3, 204pp, 53 maps

**Dales Way** *Henry Stedman,* 1st edn, ISBN 978-1-905864-78-2, 192pp, 50 maps

**Dorset & South Devon (SW Coast Path Pt 3)** *Stedman & Newton*, 2nd edn, ISBN 978-1-905864-94-2, 340pp, 97 maps

**Exmoor & North Devon (SW Coast Path Pt I)** *Stedman & Newton*, 3rd edn, ISBN 978-1-9912716-24-1, 224pp, 68 maps

**Glyndŵr's Way** *Chris Scott*, 1st edn, ISBN 978-1-912716-32-6, 220pp, 70 maps

**Great Glen Way** *Jim Manthorpe*, 2nd edn, ISBN 978-1-912716-10-4, 184pp, 50 maps

**Hadrian's Wall Path** *Henry Stedman*, 6th edn, ISBN 978-1-912716-12-8, 250pp, 60 maps

**London LOOP** *Henry Stedman*, 1st edn, ISBN 978-1-912716-21-0, 236pp, 60 maps

**Norfolk Coast Path & Peddars Way** *Alexander Stewart*, 1st edn, ISBN 978-1-905864-98-0, 224pp, 75 maps

**North Downs Way** *Henry Stedman*, 2nd edn, ISBN 978-1-905864-90-4, 240pp, 98 maps

**Offa's Dyke Path** *Keith Carter*, 5th edn, ISBN 978-1-912716-03-6, 268pp, 98 maps

**Pembrokeshire Coast Path** *Jim Manthorpe*, 6th edn, 978-1-912716-13-5, 236pp, 96 maps

**Pennine Way** *Stuart Greig*, 5th edn, ISBN 978-1-912716-02-9, 272pp, 138 maps

**The Ridgeway** *Nick Hill*, 5th edn, ISBN 978-1-912716-20-3, 208pp, 53 maps

**South Downs Way** *Jim Manthorpe*, 7th edn, ISBN 978-1-912716-23-4, 204pp, 60 maps

**Thames Path** *Joel Newton*, 3rd edn, ISBN 978-1-912716-27-2, 256pp, 99 maps

**West Highland Way** *Charlie Loram*, 7th edn, ISBN 978-1-912716-01-2, 218pp, 60 maps

*'The Trailblazer series stands head, shoulders, waist and ankles above the rest.*
*They are particularly strong on mapping ...'*
THE SUNDAY TIMES

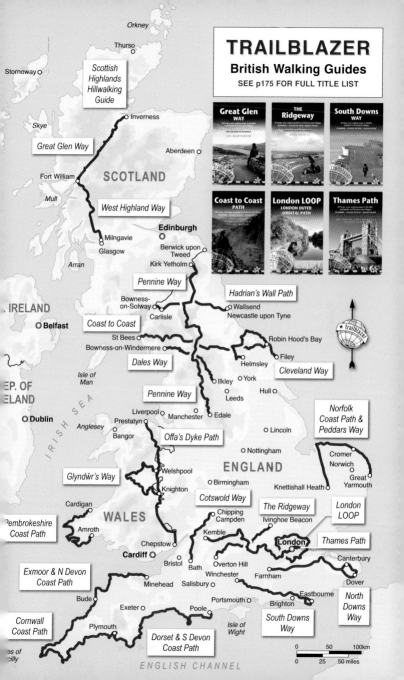

# TRAILBLAZER
## British Walking Guides
### SEE p175 FOR FULL TITLE LIST

Great Glen Way

THE Ridgeway

South Downs WAY

Coast to Coast PATH

London LOOP LONDON OUTER ORBITAL PATH

Thames Path

*Orkney*

*Thurso*

Stornoway ○

*Skye*

○ Inverness

*Scottish Highlands Hillwalking Guide*

*Great Glen Way*

Fort William ○

Aberdeen ○

SCOTLAND

*Mull*

*West Highland Way*

○ Milngavie
Glasgow ○

**Edinburgh** ○

*Arran*

Berwick upon Tweed
Kirk Yetholm ○

*Pennine Way*

*Hadrian's Wall Path*

IRELAND

○ Belfast

Bowness-on-Solway ○
Carlisle ○

○ Wallsend
Newcastle upon Tyne

*Coast to Coast*

St Bees ○
Bowness-on-Windermere ○

Robin Hood's Bay ○
○ Filey

*Dales Way*

○ Helmsley
○ York

*Cleveland Way*

EP. OF
ELAND

*Isle of Man*

○ Ilkley

○ Dublin

*Pennine Way*

Leeds ○

Hull ○

○ Liverpool  ○ Manchester
Prestatyn ○
Bangor ○

*Anglesey*

○ Edale

Lincoln ○

*Offa's Dyke Path*

ENGLAND

○ Nottingham

*Norfolk Coast Path & Peddars Way*

Cromer ○
Norwich ○

Great
Yarmouth

*Glyndŵr's Way*

○ Welshpool

○ Birmingham

Knettishall Heath ○

Knighton ○

WALES

Cardigan ○

*Cotswold Way*

Chipping
Campden ○

*The Ridgeway*

*London LOOP*

Pembrokeshire
Coast Path

Amroth ○

Kemble ○

Ivinghoe Beacon ○

**London** ○

*Thames Path*

Chepstow ○

**Cardiff** ○

Bristol ○  Bath ○

Overton Hill ○
Winchester ○

Farnham ○

Canterbury ○

*Exmoor & N Devon Coast Path*

Minehead ○

Salisbury ○

Dover ○

Bude ○

Exeter ○

Poole ○

Portsmouth ○

Brighton ○

Eastbourne ○

*North Downs Way*

*Cornwall Coast Path*

Plymouth ○

*Isle of Wight*

*South Downs Way*

*es of
illy*

*Dorset & S Devon Coast Path*

ENGLISH CHANNEL

IRISH SEA

| 0 | 50 | 100km |
| 0 | 25 | 50 miles |

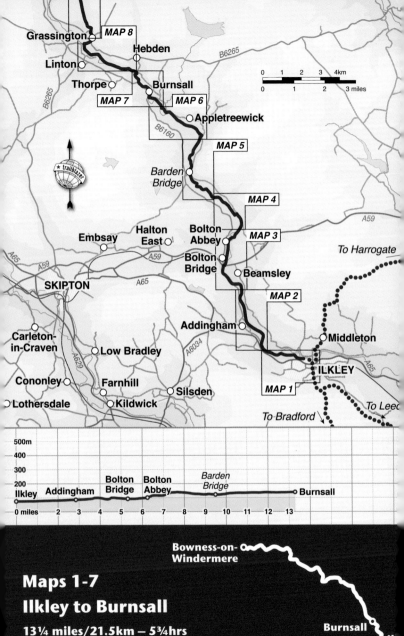

MAP 8
MAP 7
MAP 6
MAP 5
MAP 4
MAP 3
MAP 2
MAP 1

Grassington
Hebden
Linton
Thorpe
Burnsall
Appletreewick
B6160
B6265
B6265
B6265

Barden
Bridge

Embsay
Halton
East
Bolton
Abbey
Bolton
Bridge
Beamsley
A59

To Harrogate

SKIPTON
A65
A59

Carleton-
in-Craven
Addingham
Middleton
ILKLEY
A65

Cononley
Low Bradley
Farnhill
Silsden
Lothersdale
Kildwick

To Bradford
To Leeds

0   1   2   3   4km
0      1        2      3 miles

500m
400
300
200
100
Ilkley   Addingham   Bolton   Bolton   *Barden*   Burnsall
                      Bridge   Abbey    *Bridge*
0 miles   2   3   4   5   6   7   8   9   10   11   12   13

Bowness-on-
Windermere

Burnsall

# Maps 1-7
# Ilkley to Burnsall

**13¼ miles/21.5km – 5¾hrs**

**NOTE: Add 20-30% to these times to allow for stops**

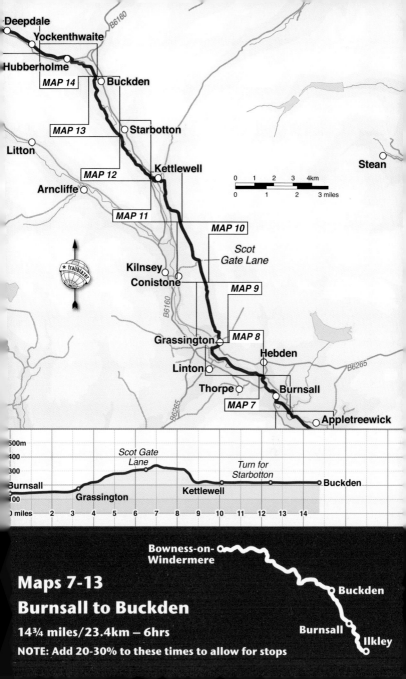

# Maps 7-13
## Burnsall to Buckden

**14¾ miles/23.4km – 6hrs**

**NOTE: Add 20-30% to these times to allow for stops**

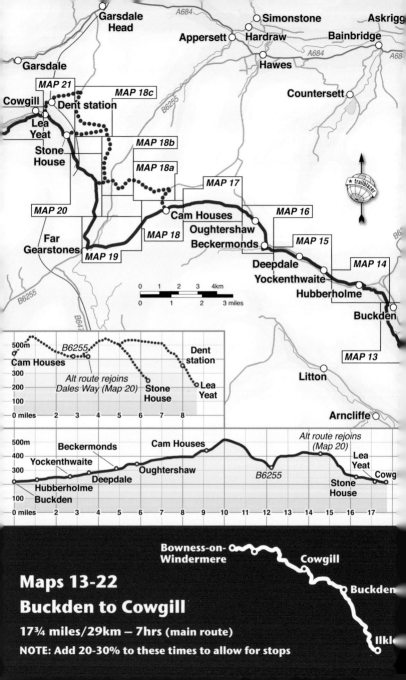

Garsdale Head

Simonstone

Askrigg

Appersett   Hardraw   Bainbridge

Garsdale

A684

Hawes

A68

MAP 21

Cowgill

Dent station

MAP 18c

Countersett

B6255

Lea Yeat

Stone House

MAP 18b

MAP 18a

MAP 20

MAP 17

Cam Houses

Far Gearstones

MAP 18

Oughtershaw

MAP 16

Beckermonds

MAP 15

MAP 19

Deepdale

Yockenthwaite

MAP 14

B6647

Hubberholme

B6

0   1   2   3   4km

0   1   2   3 miles

Buckden

MAP 13

500m

B6255

Dent station

Cam Houses

Litton

300

Alt route rejoins
Dales Way (Map 20)

Stone House

Lea Yeat

200

100

0 miles   2   3   4   5   6   7   8

Arncliffe

500m

Beckermonds

Cam Houses

Alt route rejoins
(Map 20)

400

Yockenthwaite

Oughtershaw

Lea Yeat

300

Deepdale

B6255

Stone House

Cowg

Hubberholme

100

Buckden

0 miles   2   3   4   5   6   7   8   9   10   11   12   13   14   15   16   17

Bowness-on-
Windermere

Cowgill

# Maps 13-22
# Buckden to Cowgill

Buckden

**17¾ miles/29km – 7hrs (main route)**

Ilkl

NOTE: Add 20-30% to these times to allow for stops

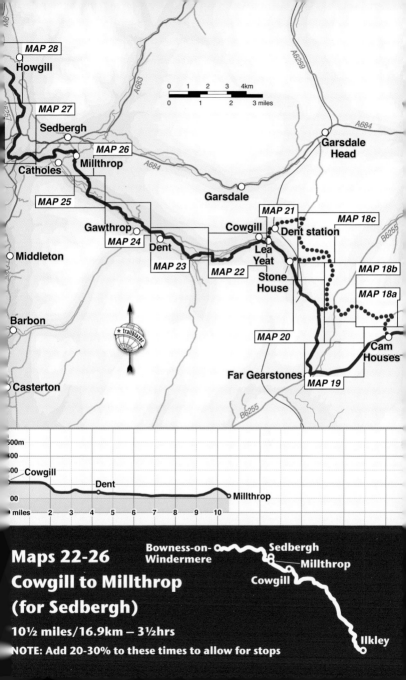

MAP 28
Howgill

MAP 27
Sedbergh

MAP 26
Millthrop

Catholes

MAP 25

Gawthrop          MAP 24          Cowgill          MAP 21
Middleton              Dent                    Dent station          MAP 18c

MAP 23          Lea          MAP 18b
Yeat
MAP 22          Stone          MAP 18a
House

Barbon          MAP 20          Cam
Houses

Casterton          Far Gearstones          MAP 19

Garsdale
Head          A684

Garsdale

0  1  2  3  4km
0    1    2    3 miles

★ trailblazer

500m
400
300  Cowgill
Dent
200                                            Millthrop
miles   2   3   4   5   6   7   8   9   10

# Maps 22-26
# Cowgill to Millthrop
# (for Sedbergh)

Bowness-on-Windermere · · · Sedbergh
Millthrop
Cowgill
Ilkley

**10½ miles/16.9km – 3½hrs**

**NOTE: Add 20-30% to these times to allow for stops**

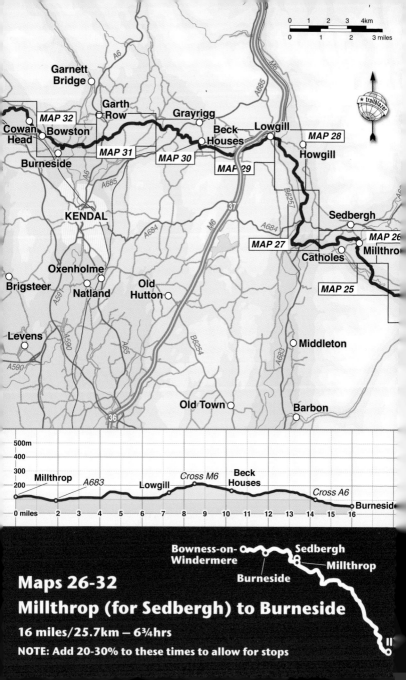

# Maps 26-32
## Millthrop (for Sedbergh) to Burneside

16 miles/25.7km — 6¾hrs

NOTE: Add 20-30% to these times to allow for stops